YOUR CHINESE
HOROSCOPE 1999

———◆◆◆———

ABOUT THE AUTHOR

Neil Somerville is one of the leading writers in the West on Chinese horoscopes. He has been interested in Eastern forms of divination for many years and believes that much can be learned from the ancient wisdom of the East. His annual book on Chinese horoscopes has built up an international following and he is also the author of *Chinese Love Signs* (Thorsons, 1995).

Neil Somerville was born in the year of the Water Snake. His wife was born under the sign of the Monkey, his son is an Ox and daughter a Horse.

YOUR CHINESE HOROSCOPE 1999

NEIL SOMERVILLE

———◆———

What the Year of the Rabbit holds in store for you

Thorsons
An Imprint of HarperCollinsPublishers

TO ROS, RICHARD AND EMILY

Thorsons
An Imprint of HarperCollins*Publishers*
77–85 Fulham Palace Road
Hammersmith, London W6 8JB

Published by Thorsons 1998
10 9 8 7 6 5 4 3 2 1

© Neil Somerville 1998

Neil Somerville asserts the moral right to
be identified as the author of this work

A catalogue record for this book
is available from the British Library

ISBN 0 7225 3569 4

Printed and bound in Great Britain by
Caledonian International Book Manufacturing Ltd, Glasgow, G64

CONTENTS

———◆———

ACKNOWLEDGEMENTS

In writing *Your Chinese Horoscope 1999* I am grateful for the assistance and support that those around me have given. I wish to acknowledge Theodora Lau's *The Handbook of Chinese Horoscopes* (Harper & Row, 1979; Arrow, 1981), which was particularly useful to me in my research.

In addition to Ms Lau's work, I commend the following books to those who wish to find out more about Chinese horoscopes: Kristyna Arcarti, *Chinese Horoscopes for Beginners* (Headway, 1995); Catherine Aubier, *Chinese Zodiac Signs* (Arrow, 1984), series of 12 books; Paula Delsol, *Chinese Horoscopes* (Pan, 1973); E. A. Crawford and Teresa Kennedy, *Chinese Elemental Astrology* (Piatkus, 1992); Barry Fantoni, *Barry Fantoni's Chinese Horoscopes* (Warner, 1994); Bridget Giles and the Diagram Group, *Chinese Astrology* (Collins Gem, HarperCollins*Publishers*, 1996); Jean-Michel Huon de Kermadec, *The Way to Chinese Astrology* (Unwin, 1983); Kwok Man-Ho, *Authentic Chinese Horoscopes* (Arrow, 1987), series of 12 books; Lori Reid, *The Complete Book of Chinese Horoscopes* (Element Books, 1997); Paul Rigby and Harvey Bean, *Chinese Astrologics* (Publications Division, South China Morning Post Ltd, 1981); Derek Walters, *Ming Shu* (Pagoda Books, 1987) and *The Chinese*

ACKNOWLEDGEMENTS

Astrology Workbook (The Aquarian Press, 1988); Suzanne White, *Suzanne White's Book of Chinese Chance* (Fontana/Collins, 1978) and *The New Astrology* (Pan, 1987) and *The New Chinese Astrology* (Pan, 1994).

INTRODUCTION

The origins of Chinese horoscopes have been lost in the mists of time. It is known that Oriental astrologers practised their art many thousands of years ago and, even today, Chinese astrology continues to fascinate and intrigue.

In Chinese astrology there are 12 signs named after 12 different animals. No one quite knows how the signs acquired their names, but there is one legend that offers an explanation.

According to this legend, one Chinese New Year the Buddha invited all the animals in his kingdom to come before him. Unfortunately – for reasons best known to the animals – only 12 turned up. The first to arrive was the Rat, followed by the Ox, Tiger, Rabbit, Dragon, Snake, Horse, Goat, Monkey, Rooster, Dog and finally Pig.

In gratitude, the Buddha decided to name a year after each of the animals and those born during that year would inherit some of the personality of that animal. Therefore those born in the year of the Ox would be hard-working, resolute and stubborn – just like the Ox – while those born in the year of the Dog would be loyal and faithful – just like the Dog.

While not everyone can possibly share all the characteristics of a sign, it is incredible what similarities do occur and this is partly where the fascination of Chinese horoscopes lie.

In addition to the 12 signs of the Chinese zodiac there are also five elements and these have a strengthening or moderating influence upon the sign. Details about the effects of the elements are given in each of the chapters on the 12 signs.

To find out which sign you were born under, refer to the tables on pages x–xiii. As the Chinese year is based on the lunar year and does not start until late January or early February, it is particularly important for anyone born in those two months to check carefully the dates of the Chinese year in which they were born.

Also included, in the Appendix, are two charts showing the compatibility between the signs for both personal and business relationships, and details about the signs ruling the different hours of the day. From this it is possible to locate your ascendant and, as in Western astrology, this has a significant influence on your personality.

In writing this book, I have taken the unusual step of combining the intriguing nature of Chinese horoscopes with the Western desire to know what the future holds and have based my interpretations upon various factors relating to each of the signs. This is the twelfth year in which *Your Chinese Horoscope* has been published and I am pleased that so many have found the sections on the forthcoming year of interest and hope that the horoscope has been constructive and of help. Remember, though, that at all times you are the master of your own destiny. I sincerely hope that *Your Chinese Horoscope 1999* will prove interesting and helpful for the year ahead.

THE CHINESE YEARS

———◆———

Rat	18 February	1912	to	5 February	1913
Ox	6 February	1913	to	25 January	1914
Tiger	26 January	1914	to	13 February	1915
Rabbit	14 February	1915	to	2 February	1916
Dragon	3 February	1916	to	22 January	1917
Snake	23 January	1917	to	10 February	1918
Horse	11 February	1918	to	31 January	1919
Goat	1 February	1919	to	19 February	1920
Monkey	20 February	1920	to	7 February	1921
Rooster	8 February	1921	to	27 January	1922
Dog	28 January	1922	to	15 February	1923
Pig	16 February	1923	to	4 February	1924
Rat	5 February	1924	to	23 January	1925
Ox	24 January	1925	to	12 February	1926
Tiger	13 February	1926	to	1 February	1927
Rabbit	2 February	1927	to	22 January	1928
Dragon	23 January	1928	to	9 February	1929
Snake	10 February	1929	to	29 January	1930
Horse	30 January	1930	to	16 February	1931
Goat	17 February	1931	to	5 February	1932
Monkey	6 February	1932	to	25 January	1933
Rooster	26 January	1933	to	13 February	1934
Dog	14 February	1934	to	3 February	1935
Pig	4 February	1935	to	23 January	1936

Rat	24 January	1936	to	10 February	1937
Ox	11 February	1937	to	30 January	1938
Tiger	31 January	1938	to	18 February	1939
Rabbit	19 February	1939	to	7 February	1940
Dragon	8 February	1940	to	26 January	1941
Snake	27 January	1941	to	14 February	1942
Horse	15 February	1942	to	4 February	1943
Goat	5 February	1943	to	24 January	1944
Monkey	25 January	1944	to	12 February	1945
Rooster	13 February	1945	to	1 February	1946
Dog	2 February	1946	to	21 January	1947
Pig	22 January	1947	to	9 February	1948
Rat	10 February	1948	to	28 January	1949
Ox	29 January	1949	to	16 February	1950
Tiger	17 February	1950	to	5 February	1951
Rabbit	6 February	1951	to	26 January	1952
Dragon	27 January	1952	to	13 February	1953
Snake	14 February	1953	to	2 February	1954
Horse	3 February	1954	to	23 January	1955
Goat	24 January	1955	to	11 February	1956
Monkey	12 February	1956	to	30 January	1957
Rooster	31 January	1957	to	17 February	1958
Dog	18 February	1958	to	7 February	1959
Pig	8 February	1959	to	27 January	1960
Rat	28 January	1960	to	14 February	1961
Ox	15 February	1961	to	4 February	1962
Tiger	5 February	1962	to	24 January	1963
Rabbit	25 January	1963	to	12 February	1964
Dragon	13 February	1964	to	1 February	1965
Snake	2 February	1965	to	20 January	1966
Horse	21 January	1966	to	8 February	1967

Goat	9 February	1967	to	29 January	1968
Monkey	30 January	1968	to	16 February	1969
Rooster	17 February	1969	to	5 February	1970
Dog	6 February	1970	to	26 January	1971
Pig	27 January	1971	to	14 February	1972
Rat	15 February	1972	to	2 February	1973
Ox	3 February	1973	to	22 January	1974
Tiger	23 January	1974	to	10 February	1975
Rabbit	11 February	1975	to	30 January	1976
Dragon	31 January	1976	to	17 February	1977
Snake	18 February	1977	to	6 February	1978
Horse	7 February	1978	to	27 January	1979
Goat	28 January	1979	to	15 February	1980
Monkey	16 February	1980	to	4 February	1981
Rooster	5 February	1981	to	24 January	1982
Dog	25 January	1982	to	12 February	1983
Pig	13 February	1983	to	1 February	1984
Rat	2 February	1984	to	19 February	1985
Ox	20 February	1985	to	8 February	1986
Tiger	9 February	1986	to	28 January	1987
Rabbit	29 January	1987	to	16 February	1988
Dragon	17 February	1988	to	5 February	1989
Snake	6 February	1989	to	26 January	1990
Horse	27 January	1990	to	14 February	1991
Goat	15 February	1991	to	3 February	1992
Monkey	4 February	1992	to	22 January	1993
Rooster	23 January	1993	to	9 February	1994
Dog	10 February	1994	to	30 January	1995
Pig	31 January	1995	to	18 February	1996
Rat	19 February	1996	to	6 February	1997
Ox	7 February	1997	to	27 January	1998

| Tiger | 28 January | 1998 | to | 15 February | 1999 |
| Rabbit | 16 February | 1999 | to | 4 February | 2000 |

Note: The names of the signs in the Chinese zodiac occasionally differ in the various books on Chinese astrology, although the characteristics of the signs remain the same. In some books the Ox is referred to as the Buffalo or Bull, the Rabbit as the Hare or Cat, the Goat as the Sheep and the Pig as the Boar.

For the sake of convenience, the male gender is used throughout this book. Unless otherwise stated, the characteristics of the signs apply to both sexes.

Each year is like a trail containing many tracks.
And as a traveller, it is for us to decide which tracks to take.
Some are familiar, offering a sense of security.
Some are unknown and lead to nowhere special.
But there are also other tracks that lead us on,
tracks that are worthy of exploring.
And as a traveller, it is for us to decide which tracks to take.

Neil Somerville

WELCOME TO
THE YEAR OF THE RABBIT

Unaware of my presence, the rabbits played contentedly in the glade. They hopped over brambles and fallen twigs, nibbled at the grass and occasionally sought refuge under the bushes. On their own, and with no apparent threat to disturb them, they seemed secure in their groups and at one with their surroundings.

These gentle creatures will cast an agreeable influence over their own year, a year that will bring opportunity, pleasure and new hope to the lives of many. The Year of the Rabbit will be a generally pleasant year with numerous benefits arising.

One notable feature of the year will be the readiness of politicians to meet and address some of the world's problems. It was in a previous Rabbit year that the hot line between Moscow and Washington was established and other Rabbit years have seen meetings which have often culminated in major undertakings. It was, for example, in the last Rabbit year that the historic INF treaty between America and the Soviet Union was signed, a treaty which paved the way for the destruction of all land-based medium and short range nuclear missiles. This pattern of discussion and agreement will continue and the year could again see major summits and conferences which will have long-lasting and beneficial results.

There will be particular emphasis on humane and environmental issues during the year and some far-reaching decisions will be made and implemented. Attention, too, will focus on the preservation of certain threatened areas of the world and on assisting countries experiencing drought and hardship. The help given will not only aim to alleviate immediate suffering but will also include an examination of long-term solutions to recurring problems. In this, progress will be made.

There will also be a continuing emphasis on the openness of government, with greater accountability and in some countries the foundation of new local authorities and assemblies. One example of this was in the Rabbit year of 1987 when Mikhail Gorbachev proceeded with his policy of *glasnost*, or openness, introducing the stream of social and economic reforms which so transformed life in the former Soviet Union. In addition, this year there will be efforts in many countries to cut bureaucracy, with the streamlining of certain procedures and services and the elimination of unnecessary red tape.

This will be a generally positive year for economic matters, with unemployment levels stabilizing and falling. Again government initiatives will be concentrated in this area, with some headway being made. It will also be a relatively good year for investors, with many economies buoyant. However, the investor may recall that Black Monday occurred in the last Rabbit year and 1999 too could see several corrections and bouts of profit taking which will lead to sharp fluctuations in the stock market.

Another recurring feature of Rabbit years has been the major breakthroughs made by the medical profession. Past successes have included the invention of the iron lung, which has helped so many with respiratory problems. Further headway in this area will again be made over 1999.

Education matters too will receive much prominence, with many governments increasing the funding for teacher training, schools and other places of learning, or encouraging contributions from commercial sectors. There will be new initiatives to make training courses more available, particularly for those seeking work. The Rabbit year very much favours personal development and many will make a conscious effort to improve themselves during 1999 – perhaps as a part of a personal quest or resolution for the millennium. This could be by taking up new interests or courses of study or embarking on a personal campaign of, say, more exercise and getting into trim. Over the year cultural, sporting and recreational pursuits will be favoured and the entertainment industry too will serve us many delights to enjoy, with further strides being made in home and computer entertainment.

Although the Year of the Rabbit will be a time of considerable achievement, sometimes the previous year, the Year of the Tiger, leaves such a powerful legacy that events gather their own fearful momentum and culminate in violence and war, as was the case in 1939. The year too could see some confrontations between certain nations stemming from continuing disputes but, unlike previous Rabbit years, international pressure will be so great that such outbreaks will be short lived. It should be noted, however, that for all its positive qualities, the Rabbit year is still not free from isolated acts of violence and terrorism. The assassination of President Kennedy is one such example.

However, for the most part, this is a year many will enjoy. It will have an upbeat and positive air and, with the millennium celebrations falling during the year, will be a time of much rejoicing and jubilation. Indeed, the celebrations at the end of 1999 will be an event that will live on in the memories of millions and the year will be assured of some good and high-spirited occasions.

The Rabbit year is a time which offers us the chance to develop and improve ourselves, and it is those who take advantage of these opportunities who will fare the best. As George Eliot, born under the sign of the Rabbit, wrote, 'It's them that take advantage that get advantage i' this world.'

I sincerely hope that you will be one of those who prosper and shine under the kindly and encouraging influence of the year and may good luck and good fortune go with you.

31 JANUARY 1900 ～ 18 FEBRUARY 1901	*Metal Rat*
18 FEBRUARY 1912 ～ 5 FEBRUARY 1913	*Water Rat*
5 FEBRUARY 1924 ～ 23 JANUARY 1925	*Wood Rat*
24 JANUARY 1936 ～ 10 FEBRUARY 1937	*Fire Rat*
10 FEBRUARY 1948 ～ 28 JANUARY 1949	*Earth Rat*
28 JANUARY 1960 ～ 14 FEBRUARY 1961	*Metal Rat*
15 FEBRUARY 1972 ～ 2 FEBRUARY 1973	*Water Rat*
2 FEBRUARY 1984 ～ 19 FEBRUARY 1985	*Wood Rat*
19 FEBRUARY 1996 ～ 6 FEBRUARY 1997	*Fire Rat*

THE
RAT

THE PERSONALITY OF THE RAT

Life is a great big canvas, and you should throw all the
paint you can on it.

— *Danny Kaye: a Rat*

The Rat is born under the sign of charm. He is intelligent,
popular and loves attending parties and large social gatherings. He is able to establish friendships with remarkable ease
and people generally feel relaxed in his company. He is a
very social creature and is genuinely interested in the welfare
and activities of others. He has a good understanding of
human nature and his advice and opinions are often sought.

The Rat is a hard and diligent worker. He is also very
imaginative and is never short of ideas. However, he does
sometimes lack the confidence to promote his ideas as
much as he should and this can often prevent him from
securing the recognition and credit he so often deserves.

The Rat is very observant and many Rats have made
excellent writers and journalists. The Rat also excels at
personnel and PR work and any job which brings him into
contact with people and the media. His skills are particularly appreciated in times of crisis, for the Rat has an
incredibly strong sense of self-preservation. When it comes
to finding a way out of an awkward situation, he is certain
to be the one who comes up with a solution.

The Rat loves to be where there is a lot of action, but
should he ever find himself in a very bureaucratic or
restrictive environment he can become a stickler for discipline and routine.

He is also something of an opportunist and is constantly on the look-out for ways in which he can improve his wealth and lifestyle. He rarely lets an opportunity go by and can become involved in so many plans and schemes that he sometimes squanders his energies and achieves very little as a result. He is also rather gullible and can be taken in by those less scrupulous than himself.

Another characteristic of the Rat is his attitude to money. He is very thrifty and to some he may appear a little mean. The reason for this is purely that he likes to keep his money within his family. He can be most generous to his partner, his children and close friends and relatives. He can also be generous to himself, for he often finds it impossible to deprive himself of any luxury or object he fancies. The Rat is also very acquisitive and can be a notorious hoarder. He hates waste and is rarely prepared to throw anything away. He can also be rather greedy and will rarely refuse an invitation for a free meal or a complimentary ticket to some lavish function.

The Rat is a good conversationalist, although he can occasionally be a little indiscreet. He can be highly critical of others – for an honest and unbiased opinion, the Rat is a superb critic – and sometimes will use confidential information to his own advantage. However, as the Rat has such a bright and irresistible nature, most are prepared to forgive him for his slight indiscretions.

Throughout his long and eventful life, the Rat will make many friends and will find that he is especially well suited to those born under his own sign and those of the Ox, Dragon and Monkey. He can also get on well with those born under the signs of the Tiger, Snake, Rooster, Dog and

Pig, but the rather sensitive Rabbit and Goat will find the Rat a little too critical and blunt for their liking. The Horse and Rat will also find it difficult to get on with each other – the Rat craves security and will find the Horse's changeable moods and rather independent nature a little unsettling.

The Rat is very family orientated and will do anything to please his nearest and dearest. He is exceptionally loyal to his parents and can himself be a very caring and loving parent. He will take an interest in all his children's activities and will see that they want for nothing. The Rat usually has a large family.

The female Rat has a kindly, outgoing nature and involves herself in a multitude of different activities. She has a wide circle of friends, enjoys entertaining and is an attentive hostess. She is also conscientious about the upkeep of her home and has superb taste in home furnishings. She is most supportive to the other members of her family and, due to her resourceful, friendly and persevering nature, can do well in practically any career she enters.

Although the Rat is essentially outgoing and something of an extrovert, he is also a very private individual. He tends to keep his feelings to himself and, while he is not averse to learning what other people are doing, he resents anyone prying too closely into his own affairs. He also does not like solitude and if he is alone for any length of time he can easily get depressed.

The Rat is undoubtedly very talented, but more often than not he fails to capitalize on his many abilities. He has a tendency to become involved in too many schemes and chase after too many opportunities all at one time. If he were to slow down and concentrate on one thing at a time he could become very successful. If not, success and wealth could elude him. But the Rat, with his tremendous ability to charm, will rarely, if ever, be without friends.

THE FIVE DIFFERENT TYPES OF RAT

In addition to the 12 signs of the Chinese zodiac, there are five elements and these have a strengthening or moderating influence on the sign. The effects of the five elements on the Rat are described below, together with the years in which the elements were exercising their influence. Therefore all Rats born in 1900 and 1960 are Metal Rats, those born in 1912 and 1972 are Water Rats, and so on.

Metal Rat: 1900, 1960

This Rat has excellent taste and certainly knows how to appreciate the finer things in life. His home is comfortable and nicely decorated and he is forever entertaining or mixing in fashionable circles. He has considerable financial acumen and invests his money well. On the surface the Metal Rat appears cheerful and confident, but deep down he can be troubled by worries that are quite often of his own making. He is exceptionally loyal to his family and friends.

Water Rat: 1912, 1972

The Water Rat is intelligent and very astute. He is a deep thinker and can express his thoughts clearly and persuasively. He is always eager to learn and is talented in many different areas. The Water Rat is usually very popular, but his fear of loneliness can sometimes lead him into mixing with the wrong sort of company. He is a particularly skilful writer, but he can get side-tracked very easily and should try to concentrate on just one thing at a time.

Wood Rat: 1924, 1984

The Wood Rat has a friendly, outgoing personality and is most popular with his colleagues and friends. He has a quick, agile brain and likes to turn his hand to anything he thinks may be useful. His one fear is insecurity, but given his intelligence and capabilities, this fear is usually unfounded. He has a good sense of humour, enjoys travel and, due to his highly imaginative nature, can be a gifted writer or artist.

Fire Rat: 1936, 1996

The Fire Rat is rarely still and seems to have a never-ending supply of energy and enthusiasm. He loves being involved in the action – be it travel, following up new ideas or campaigning for a cause in which he fervently believes. He is an original thinker and hates being bound by petty restrictions or the dictates of others. He can be forthright in his views, but can sometimes get carried away in the excitement of the moment and commit himself to various undertakings without checking what all the implications might be. Yet he has a resilient nature and, with the right support, can often go far in life.

Earth Rat: 1948

This Rat is astute and very level-headed. He rarely takes unnecessary chances and, while he is constantly trying to improve his financial status, he is prepared to proceed slowly and leave nothing to chance. The Earth Rat is probably not as adventurous as the other types of Rat and prefers to remain in familiar areas rather than rush headlong into something he knows little about. He is talented, conscientious and caring towards his loved ones, but at the same time can be self-conscious and worry a little too much about the image he is trying to project.

PROSPECTS FOR THE RAT IN 1999

The Chinese New Year starts on 16 February 1999. Until then, the old year, the Year of the Tiger, is still making its presence felt.

The Year of the Tiger (28 January 1998 to 15 February 1999) will have been a variable one for the Rat. Although he will have made some progress this will not have been without considerable effort on his part and some of his plans may not have gone as well as he would have liked. However, although the Tiger year will have contained its challenges, the Rat is resourceful and will often have been able to turn the situations in which he has found himself to his advantage. In addition, the trials and tribulations of the year will have brought some benefit to the Rat. He will not only have gained useful experience, but will also have learnt much from any reversals he may have had or mistakes he may have made and this knowledge will serve him well in the future. As the Chinese proverb reminds us, 'The gem cannot be polished without friction – nor the man perfected without trials.'

For what remains of the Tiger year, the Rat should continue to set about his activities with care. This is not a time when he can afford to take undue risks or be too independent in his actions. In his work he should keep a close watch on all that is going on around him but at the same time look for opportunities to progress and ways of adding to his skills. In particular, if he is able to learn about new aspects of his work or display an interest in taking on other responsibilities he will do much to enhance his prospects. For those Rats seeking work or looking for a change from their current position, some interesting openings could arise in October and November.

The Rat will also need to exercise care in financial matters during the closing stages of the Tiger year. This will prove expensive for him and he would do well to take his time over any major purchase he is considering as well as check any obligations he might be placed under. Although the Rat is usually diligent when dealing with finance, the Tiger year is one which does call for increased vigilance.

The Rat can, however, look forward to some meaningful times with both his family and friends and in the closing months of the year will find himself much in demand. Some parties, functions and get-togethers he attends will prove particularly pleasurable, with late November and December being a favoured and active time. Another well aspected area is travel and many Rats will make some interesting and sometimes unexpected journeys towards the end of the year. If the Rat gets the chance, he should also try to visit relations or friends he has not seen for some time. Such a meeting will prove especially pleasurable.

Although the Tiger year may not have been the smoothest of years for the Rat, it will still have contained some happy and agreeable occasions and the Rat will have gained much of value from the events of the last 12 months.

The Year of the Rabbit starts on 16 February and will be a reasonable one for the Rat. Again, his progress may not be as straightforward as he would like but he will continue to build on his experience and, with determination, will make creditable progress. Furthermore, what he accomplishes in the Rabbit year will do much to lay the foundation for the excellent advances he will make in 2000 and the years beyond. In addition, the Rabbit year will contain many satisfying and fulfilling times for the Rat, particularly where his hobbies, interests and recreational pursuits are concerned.

In his work the Rat will need to be his resourceful self, making the most of the new and changing situations that arise. Admittedly he may have misgivings about some of what takes place and some of the tasks he is given, but by rising to the challenges that occur and giving of his best, he can accomplish much as well as greatly impress others. While some signs may weaken their resolve when faced with daunting tasks, not so the Rat. Instead a challenge often gives him an added incentive to try even harder and make the most of what is happening; this will be the case in 1999. Throughout, the Rat's resourcefulness, perceptiveness and enterprising nature will serve him well and help him to advance his position. Also, if he is able to go on any training courses or add to his qualifications, this too will be to his advantage. Indeed, the Rat will find that what he accomplishes over the year will help to prepare the way for the significant progress he can look forward to making next year.

Many of those Rats seeking work will also succeed in obtaining a position in 1999, although this may always not be in the sphere they were originally hoping for. However, in many cases, this position will enable the Rat to learn new skills and in some cases lead him to find his future forte. Often the Rabbit year will see the start of things which have far-reaching significance.

However, while the Rat will make progress in his work during the year, he must take care in his relations with his colleagues. Although usually masterful in handling relations with others, he does need to deal with any difference of opinion or disagreement that occurs with care and, as far as possible, defuse it as quickly and as amicably as he can. If not, there is a danger that it could escalate and undermine some of the good work that he has done. Rats, do take note!

In matters of finance the Rat will need to proceed with a certain caution. While he can be thrifty, he can also all too easily yield to temptation, and too many indulgences and spending sprees could leave him regretting the amount he has spent and even result in him having to make economies later. Throughout 1999 he should watch his level of spending and make allowances for major purchases. He should also be wary of any dubious or speculative schemes that he may come across. Although the Rat is always keen to improve his lot, in 1999 he must not let his desires blind him to the often considerable risks and costs involved.

More positively, however, the Rat will obtain much satisfaction from his hobbies and interests over the year. These will not only provide him with a valuable break from his usual daytime activities, but could also develop in a pleasing manner. For those Rats who enjoy creative pursuits, such as writing, painting, music, photography or the performing arts, it would certainly be worth furthering their interests and bringing their talents to the attention of others this year. By doing so, many will find their efforts well rewarded and will be encouraged and inspired to do more. Also, those Rats who have long-term creative aspirations should listen closely to any advice they are given from those who speak with experience. There will be much wisdom in what they are told and, as with so many aspects of the Rat's life in 1999, what he learns, accomplishes and sets in motion now could prove instrumental to the success he will enjoy in later years.

Any Rats who do not have a particular hobby at the moment really would find it in their interests to take one up, perhaps something they have been thinking about but never yet had the chance to do. By taking action they could find their new interest will lead to many fulfilling and absorbing times as well as allow them to develop another outlet for their talents. With personal interests so well aspected over the year this is an area no Rat should ignore or neglect.

With his warm and companionable nature, the Rat always places great store on his family and social life; indeed, he truly values the love and companionship of those around him and 1999 will be no exception to this. The Rat's personal life will certainly be active, with various family and household matters calling for his time and attention. Some of these, such as the progress and success of close relations, will be a source of much joy, but there could be other matters which give him concern. These could result from a difference of opinion, a misunderstanding or tetchiness, often caused by pressure or tiredness. In all cases, the Rat should do his utmost to defuse any tense or awkward situation that he finds himself in rather than allow it to linger unchecked. Sometimes he will find a spirit of openness will do much to clear the air.

Also, again to prevent possible tension, the Rat should not always expect others to accept his plans or suggestions without demur. Sometimes, he can let his enthusiasm and zest get the better of him and there will be occasions during the year when those around him will have their misgivings about his plans. The Rat will have to accept this and in 1999 he does need to remain mindful of the views of others. Fortunately, though, the Rat is usually adept in handling personal relations and his skill in this area will do much to minimize and avert the sometimes awkward situations that could arise.

On a social level the Rat can, however, look forward to spending many pleasant hours in the company of his friends and over the year will attend some interesting and sometimes unusual parties, functions and events. For the unattached, or those Rats seeking additional friends, there will be many opportunities to meet others, especially in the spring and late summer. However, while there will be opportunities for romance, the Rat should be wary of building high expectations after just a brief time. He will almost certainly find it better to let any new friendship develop gradually, enabling each side to get to know the other better, rather than rush into an all too hasty commitment. Overall, the Rat's social life will go well, but again he does need to remain respectful of the views of those around him.

Although the Year of the Rabbit will contain some testing moments for the Rat, for the most part these will not detract from the fulfilling times the year will bring or from his preparation for the considerably better times that await in 2000. In the meantime, this is a year which calls for care, discretion and the avoidance of risks. However, come November, the aspects will start to swing very much in the Rat's favour and these will gather pace as the millennium approaches. The prospects for the Rat are truly glittering and this year is, in many respects, one in which to consolidate his present position and to plan and set in motion activities and projects that will lead to the major advances he is soon to make.

As far as the different types of Rat are concerned, 1999 will be an interesting year for the *Metal Rat*. During the course of it he will make several important decisions that will have a considerable bearing over the next few years. Many

Metal Rats will decide to take a close look at their current work situation, their immediate prospects and what it is they hope to achieve in the future. By doing this, they will gain a clearer idea of the direction in which they are heading and which opportunities to go after and will, as a result, find they are setting about their activities in a more purposeful way. The Metal Rat knows he has it within him to achieve much and in 1999 he will decide that the time has come to make more of himself and realize his potential. In this he will also find it instructive to discuss his thoughts with those close to him and those with relevant experience. This way he will be given much useful advice as well as learn of openings and possibilities that he may not have considered before. In 1999 the Metal Rat can make good headway and set in motion significant plans, but it does rest with him to take the initiative. Those Metal Rats seeking employment should also remain determined in their quest and again would do well to approach those in a position to give advice or to make direct contact with companies they may like to work for. Throughout the year, they would do well to remember the proverb 'Nothing ventured, nothing gained' and will find a positive, persistent and enterprising approach will be rewarded. In addition, if any Metal Rat feels that he needs additional skills to further his aspirations, he should use this year to obtain them. Work-wise, what the Metal Rat decides, learns or achieves will be instrumental in preparing the way for the considerable advances he will make in 2000 and beyond. However, while there will be significant developments in the Metal Rat's work and future prospects, he does need to exercise care this year when dealing with finance. This is not a time for taking undue risks, entering into speculative ventures or stretching his resources without regard to his current situation. Fortunately the Metal Rat is usually adept when dealing with money matters, but he must not allow his usual vigilance to lapse or be lulled into a false sense of complacency. In particular, before entering into any large transaction, he would be advised to check all the terms involved as well as make sure he is aware of any obligations he may be placed under. Care and time spent checking the details and small print could prevent problems later. The Metal Rat's home life will, however, contain some truly pleasurable moments, including some personal and family celebrations, but mixed in with this could be occasions of worry and frustration. There could be matters on which others do not agree or the Metal Rat may feel that someone close to him is being difficult over a certain issue. If possible, he should use his considerable skills to defuse the situation rather than allow it to continue or should simply accept that a difference of viewpoint does exist. Fortunately, though, many of the difficulties or disagreements that surface are likely to be short-lived and, when handled with tact, are unlikely to mar the rewarding and gratifying times the Metal Rat will enjoy with those around him. On a personal level, the summer months hold much promise and a holiday or break taken then could do the Metal Rat and his companions considerable good as well as be something that all will greatly enjoy. The Metal Rat should also make sure he devotes time to his interests over the year; these too will bring him much benefit, especially as they will give him the opportunity to unwind and will help to take his mind off his everyday concerns. In addition, some Metal Rats could gain particular satisfaction from taking up an entirely new interest over the year. They will find the novelty and challenge this brings will lead to many absorbing and fulfilling hours. Generally, although the year may bring some vexations and a few niggling concerns, these will not detract from the many pleasurable occasions the Metal Rat will enjoy, nor from the longer term value and significance of the year.

The *Water Rat* has many commendable assets. He has a sharp mind, a clear idea of where his strengths lie and a warm and friendly personality. He has much in his favour and the future holds considerable promise for him. In 1999 he will do much to lay the foundations for that future. During the Rabbit year, however, he should consolidate any recent gains he may have made as well as pursue any openings that he feels would help him towards his objectives. If he obtains a new position, or has recently been given different responsibilities, he should concentrate on familiarizing himself with his new duties and learning about the different aspects of his work. By making the effort he will not only impress others but will also usefully add to his skills and knowledge; both will be to his longer term advantage. Also, if the Water Rat has the opportunity to discuss his future with those with experience and influence, he should do so. The advice he is given could prove significant and helpful. Those Water Rats seeking work or wishing to change their present position should also remain active in their quest. Admittedly this will require perseverance on their part, but their determination will be rewarded and, in many cases, in a most fortuitous and unexpected way. These Water Rats could also find that one position they attain, even though this may not be with the exact duties they were hoping for, will lead to other and better opportunities in a comparatively short space of time. Overall, as far as work matters are concerned, this will be a constructive year and what the Water Rat achieves and learns will contribute much to his longer term success. One point that he should bear in mind, though, is that he should remain willing to adapt in the face of change or to take advantage of the opportunities that arise, even if they don't quite fit in with his existing plans and ideas. It is better for him to get experience now and see how openings develop rather than not progress at all. Also, if he finds himself in any tense or difficult situation at work, he should aim to be his discreet, tactful self; 1999 is not a year in which to 'rock the boat'. The Water Rat also needs to exercise care in financial matters. He should keep a close watch over his level of spending and at times of large expense, particularly when dealing with household outgo-ings, travel or holidays, he should make sure he makes due allowance in his budget. This is not a year for complacency or for spending without regard to his current financial situation. His domestic life will, however, be both active and fulfilling and he will derive much pleasure from following and encouraging the activities of those around him. He will also have good reason to value the support and advice he receives and should pay particular attention to the words of a more senior relation. This person speaks with the Water Rat's best interests at heart and there will be much wisdom in what he is told. However, with the pressures of daily life, there will be occasions when the Water Rat will feel tired and anxious, and at these times he should make every effort not to take out any tension or feelings of irritability on others. Instead, he would find it helpful (even therapeutic) to talk openly about his feelings and concerns. Also, at demanding times, rather than drive himself relentlessly, he should make sure he gives himself the chance to relax and unwind. If he does not get much exercise during the day, he would do well to consider walking more or engaging in activities such as cycling or swimming or starting a suitable exercise course. He will find this will do much to help his well-being. Generally, the Water Rat can fare well over the Rabbit year. On a personal level the year will contain many pleasurable and meaningful occasions and he will get much useful support from those around him. There will also be interesting developments in his work, some of which will do much to help his long term prospects.

This will be a satisfying year for the *Wood Rat*. He will be well supported in his activities and when decisions have to be taken or he has any matters giving him concern, he should not hesitate to seek the views of others. Those around him do have his best interests at heart and over the year will do much to advise and encourage as well as to reassure. This particularly applies to those Wood Rats in education. While they will make good progress over the year, there will be times when they will be troubled over what is being asked of them, particularly with new subjects they do not yet fully understand. At these times it is important that the Wood Rats discuss their worries with others, especially with those in a position to give additional instruction. This way many of their anxieties will be allayed and they will find they will learn more by asking than by struggling on unaided. Similarly, there will be matters that arise that will give those Wood Rats born in 1924 moments of concern. These are most likely to involve accommodation and matters of finance. Again, when in doubt over any important action or decision they have to take, these Rats should seek advice and, if appropriate, further clarification. At no time should they allow themselves to be pressurized into taking action against their better judgement or be hurried and hassled into making a decision. Time is on the Wood Rat's side and he will often find that difficult matters have a habit of working themselves out – and many times in his favour. Although, as with any year, problems and concerns will arise, properly handled and with the support of others, these will not mar what will be a generally pleasant year. In particular the Wood Rat's home life will bring him much contentment. He will get considerable satisfaction from following and helping with the activities of others and will also get pleasure from carrying out projects in his home and garden, especially where decor is concerned. He does, however, need to take extra care when lifting or moving heavy items. A strain could cause him some unnecessary discomfort. Wood Rats, take note! However, the Wood Rat's social life will bring him much happiness and he can look forward to attending several interesting social events over the year, with the months from May to August being especially active. There will be the opportunity to build some new friendships at this time and for any Wood Rat who may be feeling lonely or who has had some adversity to overcome, it really would be in his interest to go out more and get in contact with others, perhaps by joining a special interest group or society. By doing so he will get to meet others with similar tastes and will be able to build up a new and pleasant social life. The Wood Rat will also benefit from any breaks and holidays he is able to take over the year, and hobbies of a creative nature will also bring him much personal satisfaction. Provided the Wood Rat sets about his activities at a sensible pace, seeks advice when he has concerns and uses his time wisely, he will fare well during the Rabbit year. The summer months in particular hold much promise for him.

This can be a pleasant and constructive year for the *Fire Rat*, but to make the most of it he needs to decide upon his priorities and have some idea of what he would like to accomplish over the next 12 months. This can include projects at work, at home, in the garden, personal interests or some other sphere, but by planning his activities and setting himself some objectives, the Fire Rat will find he is making better use of his time than if he were to go through the year without any goal in mind. In his work the Fire Rat can make pleasing progress, although he needs to be mindful of the views of his colleagues and if at any time he finds himself at variance with others, he should exercise tact and discretion. This is not a year in which he can afford to be too independent in his attitude or step out of line. If he does, he could find it could undermine some of the good work he has done of late. Work-wise, this is a year for care and watchfulness, with results coming from persistent and determined effort. Some Fire Rats will decide to retire during the year and those who do would do well to consider how to fill the extra time they have. They will get particular satisfaction from their hobbies over the year and it would be worth them developing these further, perhaps by learning about a different aspect or getting in contact with fellow enthusiasts. If the Fire Rat's interest is of a creative nature, he would also do well to show his work to others. This way he could be inspired to do more, possibly of an even more ambitious nature. Also, if there is an interest that the Fire Rat has been considering taking up but has not yet had the time for, he should hold back no longer but make the time and effort to start it now. As far as recreational interests are concerned, this will be a splendid year. The Fire Rat will also receive much useful encouragement from his family and friends and would do well to involve them in his activities as well as be forthcoming with his ideas and aspirations. Over the year he will have good reason to value the advice and encouragement he is given and he should heed the words of his loved ones. There will also be several family events which will be a source of much personal joy for the Fire Rat, with the summer being an active and pleasing time. For unattached Fire Rats or those seeking new friends, the months from May to August will be excellent for meeting others. The Fire Rat should also take advantage of any opportunity to travel over the year; his journeys will go well, with his chosen destination often surpassing expectations. As with all Rats, though, the Fire Rat should keep a close watch over his level of spending this year. Without care and some restraint, this could so easily creep up and become far greater than he thought or had budgeted for. This need not be an adverse year for money matters, but financial control and planning would certainly not come amiss. Overall, there will be much that the Fire Rat will enjoy during the year. However, early on in 1999, he does need to decide what he wishes to do over the year and direct his plans and energies accordingly. But with care and effective use of his time, this can be a positive and fulfilling year for him.

The Rabbit year will suit the *Earth Rat*. With his keen and determined nature and liking for order, he will be able to set about his activities in his usual efficient way and will, as a result, accomplish much. As well as consolidating any recent gains he has made, if he takes on a new position or is given different duties, he will be able to familiarize himself with his new role, and if he has set himself some goal in his work, he should be able to pursue this with determination. In 1999 the Earth Rat can make pleasing headway and should aim to make the most of his experience and of the opportunities that the year will bring. This also applies to those Earth Rats keen to change their present position or those seeking work – by going after any openings that they see and exploring the possibilities open to them they will make good progress. The early months of the year in particular will see some positive developments. As with all Rats, though, the Earth Rat does need to remain mindful of the views of his colleagues, and should he find himself in a difficult or fraught situation, he should remain his discreet and tactful self. Work-wise, this can be a positive year, but relations with colleagues do need that extra care. The Earth Rat will also need to keep a watchful eye over his financial situation. This is not a time when he should be tempted to take risks or be too lavish in his spending. To prevent problems occurring, he could find it helpful to check his financial situation regularly and maintain records of his income and outgoings. Care taken in managing his finances could do much to avert problems and even allow him to make additional savings. Domestically, this will be an eventful year for the Earth Rat, with much activity in his home life. This includes prospects of a major celebration, such as the engagement or marriage of a close relation, the birth of a grandchild or the success of a family member. Also, many Earth Rats will decide to carry out some projects on their home and garden over the year. Although these are likely to take up more time than they thought, they will be well pleased with what they are able to accomplish. The Earth Rat would do well, however, to involve others in any major household project, rather than tackle it single handed. This will not only make the task easier, but by pooling individual talents will lead to better results as well as be satisfying for all concerned. The Earth Rat will also enjoy any interests and hobbies that he can share with family members, and generally will find family activities are well favoured. His social life, too, will bring much pleasure, with there being some convivial times in the company of his friends, as well as a variety of interesting functions for him to attend. The summer will be an especially active time. Overall, the Rabbit year holds much promise for the Earth Rat and by setting about his activities in a purposeful manner he can make useful headway. The main areas of caution concern finance and his relations with colleagues, but given his generally careful nature, the Earth Rat should be able to avoid or conveniently side-step any difficulties that do arise. He will also notice a subtle change in his fortunes from late October and this will gather pace as the Rabbit year ends, bringing further opportunities for him and heralding in the favourably aspected Year of the Dragon. Great times await!

FAMOUS RATS

Alan Alda, Dave Allen, Ursula Andress, Louis Armstrong, Charles Aznavour, Lauren Bacall, Shirley Bassey, Jeremy Beadle, Irving Berlin, Kenneth Branagh, Marlon Brando, Charlotte Brontë, Chris de Burgh, George Bush, Lord Callaghan, Glen Campbell, Jimmy Carter, Maurice Chevalier, Linford Christie, Lloyd Cole, Barbara Dickson, Benjamin Disraeli, David Duchovny, Noël Edmonds, T. S. Eliot, Albert Finney, Clark Gable, Liam Gallagher, Al Gore, Hugh Grant, Thomas Hardy, Prince Harry, Vaclav Havel, Haydn, Charlton Heston, Damon Hill, Ian Hislop, Buddy Holly, Mick Hucknall, Englebert Humperdink, Henrik Ibsen, Jeremy Irons, Glenda Jackson, Jean-Michel Jarre, Gene Kelly, Kris Kristofferson, Lawrence of Arabia, Gary Lineker, Sir Andrew Lloyd Webber, Claude Monet, Richard Nixon, Sean Penn, Terry Pratchett, the Queen Mother, Patrick Rafter, Vanessa Redgrave, Burt Reynolds, Rossini, William Shakespeare, Yves St Laurent, Tommy Steele, Donna Summer, James Taylor, Leo Tolstoy, Henri Toulouse-Lautrec, Spencer Tracey, Anthea Turner, the Prince of Wales, George Washington, Dennis Weaver, Roger Whittaker, Richard Wilson, the Duke of York, Emile Zola.

19 FEBRUARY 1901 ～ 7 FEBRUARY 1902   *Metal Ox*

6 FEBRUARY 1913 ～ 25 JANUARY 1914   *Water Ox*

24 JANUARY 1925 ～ 12 FEBRUARY 1926   *Wood Ox*

11 FEBRUARY 1937 ～ 30 JANUARY 1938   *Fire Ox*

29 JANUARY 1949 ～ 16 FEBRUARY 1950   *Earth Ox*

15 FEBRUARY 1961 ～ 4 FEBRUARY 1962   *Metal Ox*

3 FEBRUARY 1973 ～ 22 JANUARY 1974   *Water Ox*

20 FEBRUARY 1985 ～ 8 FEBRUARY 1986   *Wood Ox*

7 FEBRUARY 1997 ～ 27 JANUARY 1998   *Fire Ox*

THE

OX

THE PERSONALITY OF THE OX

I am in earnest – I will not equivocate – I will not excuse –
I will not retreat a single inch; and I will be heard!.
– *William Lloyd Garrison: an Ox*

The Ox is born under the signs of equilibrium and tenacity. He is a hard and conscientious worker and sets about everything he does in a resolute, methodical and determined manner. He has considerable leadership qualities and is often admired for his tough and uncompromising nature. He knows what he wants to achieve in life and, as far as possible, will not be deflected from his ultimate objective.

The Ox takes his responsibilities and duties very seriously. He is decisive and quick to take advantage of any opportunity that comes his way. He is also sincere and places a great deal of trust in his friends and colleagues. He is, nevertheless, something of a loner. He is a quiet and private individual and often keeps his thoughts to himself. He also cherishes his independence and prefers to set about things in his own way rather than be bound by the dictates of others or be influenced by outside pressures.

The Ox tends to have a calm and tranquil nature, but if something angers him or he feels that someone has let him down, he can have a fearsome temper. He can also be stubborn and obstinate and this can lead him into conflict with others. Usually the Ox will succeed in getting his own way, but should things go against him, he is a poor loser and will take any defeat or setback extremely badly.

The Ox is often a deep thinker and rather studious. He is not particularly renowned for his sense of humour and does not take kindly to new gimmicks or anything too innovative. The Ox is too solid and traditional for that and he prefers to stick to the more conventional norm.

His home is very important to him and in some respects he treats it as a private sanctuary. His family tends to be closely knit and the Ox will make sure that each member does their fair share around the house. The Ox tends to be a hoarder, but he is always well organized and neat. He also places great importance on punctuality and there is nothing that infuriates him more than to be kept waiting – particularly if it is due to someone's inefficiency. The Ox can be a hard taskmaster!

Once settled in a job or house the Ox will quite happily remain there for many years. He does not like change and he is also not particularly keen on travel. He does, however, enjoy gardening and other outdoor pursuits and he will often spend much of his spare time out of doors. The Ox is usually an excellent gardener and whenever possible he will always make sure he has a large area of ground to maintain. He usually prefers to live in the country than the town.

Due to his dedicated and dependable nature, the Ox will usually do well in his chosen career, providing he is given enough freedom to act on his own initiative. He invariably does well in politics, agriculture and in careers which need specialized training. The Ox is also very gifted in the arts and many Oxen have enjoyed considerable success as musicians or composers.

The Ox is not as outgoing as some and it often takes him a long time to establish friendships and feel relaxed in another person's company. His courtships are likely to be long, but once he is settled he will remain devoted and loyal to his partner. The Ox is particularly well suited to those born under the signs of the Rat, Rabbit, Snake and Rooster. He can also establish a good relationship with the Monkey, Dog, Pig and another Ox, but he will find that he has little in common with the whimsical and sensitive Goat. He will also find it difficult to get on with the Horse, Dragon and Tiger – the Ox prefers a quiet and peaceful existence and those born under these three signs tend to be a little too lively and impulsive for his liking.

The female Ox has a kind and caring nature, and her home and family are very much her pride and joy. She always tries to do her best for her partner and can be a most conscientious and loving parent. She is an excellent organizer and also a very determined person who will often succeed in getting what she wants in life. She usually has a deep interest in the arts and is often a talented artist or musician.

The Ox is a very down-to-earth character. He is sincere, loyal and unpretentious. He can, however, be rather reserved and to some he may appear distant and aloof. He has a quiet nature, but underneath he is very strong-willed and ambitious. He has the courage of his convictions and is often prepared to stand up for what he believes is right, regardless of the consequences. He inspires confidence and trust and throughout his life he will rarely be short of people who are ready to support him or who admire his strong and resolute manner.

THE FIVE DIFFERENT TYPES OF OX

In addition to the 12 signs of the Chinese zodiac, there are five elements and these have a strengthening or moderating influence on the sign. The effects of the five elements on the Ox are described below, together with the years in which the elements were exercising their influence. Therefore all Oxen born in 1901 and 1961 are Metal Oxen, those born in 1913 and 1973 are Water Oxen, and so on.

Metal Ox: 1901, 1961
This Ox is confident and very strong-willed. He can be blunt and forthright in his views and is not afraid of speaking his mind. He sets about his objectives with a dogged determination, but he can become so wrapped up in his various activities that he is oblivious to the thoughts and feelings of those around him, and this can sometimes be to his detriment. He is honest and dependable and will never promise more than he can deliver. He has a good appreciation of the arts and usually has a small circle of very good and loyal friends.

Water Ox: 1913, 1973
This Ox has a sharp and penetrating mind. He is a good organizer and sets about his work in a methodical manner. He is not as narrow-minded as some of the other types of Oxen and is more willing to involve others in his plans and aspirations. He usually has very high moral standards and is often attracted to careers in public service. He is a good

judge of character and has such a friendly and persuasive manner that he usually experiences little difficulty in securing his objectives. He is popular and has an excellent way with children.

Wood Ox: 1925, 1985

The Wood Ox conducts himself with an air of dignity and authority and will often take a leading role in any enterprise in which he gets involved. He is very self-confident and is direct in his dealings with others. He does, however, have a quick temper and has no hesitation in speaking his mind. He has tremendous drive and will-power and has an extremely good memory. The Wood Ox is particularly loyal and devoted to the members of his family and has a most caring nature.

Fire Ox: 1937, 1997

The Fire Ox has a powerful and assertive personality and is a hard and conscientious worker. He holds strong views and has very little patience when things do not go his own way. He can also get carried away in the excitement of the moment and does not always take into account the views of those around him. He nevertheless has many leadership qualities and will often reach positions of power, eminence and wealth. He usually has a small group of loyal and close friends and is very devoted to his family.

Earth Ox: 1949

This Ox sets about everything he does in a sensible and level-headed manner. He is ambitious, but also realistic in his aims and is often prepared to work long hours in order to secure his objectives. He is shrewd in financial and business matters and is a very good judge of character. He has a quiet nature and is greatly admired for his sincerity and integrity. He is also very loyal to his family and friends and his views and opinions are often sought by others.

PROSPECTS FOR THE OX IN 1999

The Chinese New Year starts on 16 February 1999. Until then, the old year, the Year of the Tiger, is still making its presence felt.

The Year of the Tiger (28 January 1998 to 15 February 1999) will not have been the best of years for the Ox. The Tiger year is one which brings activity and change, and the Ox, who so likes to plan and set about his activities at a measured pace, will have felt ill at ease with some of the sudden events. As a result, his progress may not have been as good as he would have liked and he may have experienced some unwelcome pressures and anxieties.

However, disquieting though some aspects of the Tiger year might have been, there is still much of value that the Ox can gain from it. Ideally he should look on the Tiger year as a time to take stock of his present position and consider what he would like to achieve in the future. If this requires learning new skills or getting fresh experience, now would be a good time to obtain these. Anything constructive the Ox can do to help his prospects would certainly be to his advantage. He should also remain alert for opportunities to pursue towards the end of the year. The start of the Rabbit year could see a great deal of activity as far as his work prospects are concerned and some of this could arise from opportunities followed up or plans started late in the Tiger year.

Although the Ox is usually careful in money matters, the Tiger year does call for increased vigilance, so he should be wary of taking undue risks with his money at this time or of entering into any new agreement without checking the finer details. Also, with the latter part of the year being a traditionally expensive time, the Ox would do well to keep a watchful eye over his level of spending. If, in the months and weeks leading up to Christmas, he is able to set some money aside for the holiday season or is able to buy some presents in advance, he would find this helpful.

One of the more positive areas of the Ox's life in the Tiger year, however, is his domestic and social life, and he can look forward to many agreeable times with those around him, particularly in late November and December. The Ox will take much satisfaction from the activities and occasions in which he is involved. The end of year holidays will also give him an excellent chance to unwind and take his mind off some of his concerns and by January he will find himself considerably refreshed and determined to make the most of the forthcoming year.

The Year of the Rabbit begins on 16 February and will be an improved year for the Ox. He will find progress easier and will be able to conduct his activities in a more organized and efficient manner.

In his work the Ox will be able to make considerable progress and obtain the results that have recently proved so elusive. Indeed, almost as soon as the Rabbit year begins, the Ox will start to set about his activities with renewed vigour, determined to make more of himself and improve his current situation. His drive, will-power and sheer tenaciousness will lead to some very positive results.

Throughout the year the Ox should actively follow up any openings that he sees and if he is seeking promotion or is thinking of switching to a different type of work he should remain alert for opportunities to pursue. If none appear, he should make enquiries and see if he can find or even create some. An innovative and enterprising approach could yield some useful results, but as the Ox himself knows, to get the results he wants requires effort on his part. Most Oxen will be happy to make this.

Many of those Oxen seeking work will also find their quest for a position rewarded, with both the early and later months of year bringing some interesting opportunities. In addition to following up any suitable vacancies, the Ox could also find it to his advantage to make direct contact with companies and organizations he would like to work for, setting out his skills and experience and asking about possible openings. Again, some enterprising action on his part could produce useful results and information. Indeed, the Ox may well be advised of possibilities he had not considered before. In addition, some words with those currently engaged in the type of work he is seeking could bring some valuable tips and advice which again he will be able to profit from.

In 1999 almost all Oxen will be able to improve their position and very often this will be as a direct result of enterprising action on their part. The Ox knows he has it within him to accomplish much and during the year his efforts and faith in his abilities will be justified and rewarded.

In addition to the progress he will make in his work, the Ox would do well to promote any ideas he has and if there is a plan or scheme he has been considering, this would be a good year in which to take those all-important initial steps. As the Ox will find, much of what he accomplishes and sets in motion during the Rabbit year will go well for him as well as have a favourable bearing over the next few years.

As far as financial matters are concerned, this will be a reasonable year for the Ox and any problems or difficulties he may have been experiencing will gradually ease as the year progresses. He will also make some notable and useful purchases during the year. These could include a range of new clothes for himself (some Oxen will make a concerted effort to smarten up or change their present style), as well as some items and equipment connected with his hobbies and interests. With the Ox's keen ear for music, this could be a new audio system or, for the Ox musician, a new instrument. In addition, the Ox will spend much on his home, with many of his purchases enhancing the decor and comfort of his accommodation. However, when making sizeable purchases, he would do well to take his time, considering his options, the ranges available and the terms offered by retailers. By looking around he can make some fine acquisitions, often at keen prices.

Although the year will involve considerable outlay on his part, if the Ox does have any money he does not immediately need, he would do well to set some aside for travel and holidays, and to save or invest the remainder. By managing his finances he will be able to attain more than if he were to just let surplus funds 'burn a hole in his pocket'.

The Ox attaches great importance to his family life and, although busy, it will be a source of much contentment over the year. Those close to the Ox will provide much useful support and he will often be heartened by their faith in him and by the obvious affection in which he is held. Also, he will find that interests he shares with those around him will prove especially fulfilling. Generally, joint activities and hobbies should be encouraged over the year.

However, while there will be many pleasurable occasions in the Ox's domestic life, there will also be times of considerable activity. This could be caused by the commitments of family members or by projects the Ox himself is trying to complete, as well as the usual chores. At busy times the Ox will undoubtedly be helped by his ability to prioritize and simply get on with the tasks in question. Also, although he does like to do a lot himself, and without interference, at demanding times he should not hesitate to enlist the assistance of others. Those around are often keen and willing to lend a hand, but, knowing the Ox as they do, are not keen to interfere unless he says so. In 1999 it would be to everyone's advantage for him to say so more often!

Also, when tackling household projects the Ox needs to be realistic in his expectations. Although anxious to get tasks completed, he would do well to remember that Rome was not built in a day and some of his projects can't be either! With practical undertakings he should allow plenty of time.

In addition to the pleasure joint interests will bring, at particularly busy times the Ox could find it helpful to suggest activities all could enjoy, such as a meal out or a visit to some place of entertainment or local interest. Such pleasurable activities could do much to relieve some of the pressures (and any strains) that might have built up. The Ox will also greatly enjoy any family holidays and breaks that he takes and all Oxen should make sure they go away at least once during 1999. The break will prove most beneficial for all concerned.

The Ox can also look forward to leading a satisfying social life over the year and to some pleasant time spent in the company of his friends. In addition he will enjoy the various social events that he attends and while sometimes he may feel he has to cut back on his social life because of other commitments, he should try not to let this happen. His social life not only provides him with the chance to relax and unwind but he will also get much benefit from meeting and conversing with others. Although the Ox can sometimes be a loner, to keep himself too much himself over the year would be very much to his disadvantage and would deny him some meaningful and happy occasions.

One notable feature of the Ox is that he always chooses his friends with care and in 1999 many Oxen will strike up a new acquaintance which will become important in future years. For those Oxen who may feel they would like some additional company, the year will contain some wonderful opportunities for meeting others, with the late spring and summer being well aspected. For the unattached, romance is favourably aspected, with a new friendship blossoming over the year.

Generally, 1999 is a year which offers the Ox considerable potential. He can look forward to many pleasurable times with his family and friends and, as far as his work is concerned, there will be some excellent opportunities to develop and improve his position. With his fortitude, considerable skills and the favourable aspects that prevail, he will indeed do well and will also sow the seeds for further advancement in years to come.

As far as the different types of Ox are concerned, this will be a pleasing year for the *Metal Ox*. In recent times the Metal Ox will have gained much useful experience as well as overcome some testing problems. He will have learnt a lot, both from the successes he has enjoyed and also from any mistakes he may have made. In 1999 he will be able to build on what he has achieved and set forth with a renewed determination. This is a year for looking forward, for progress – and one that holds considerably brighter prospects. To help make the most of the year, however, early on in 1999 the Metal Ox would do well to consider his current aspirations and decide what he would most like to accomplish. Then, with some objectives in mind, he should pursue them in his usual resolute way. If he is seeking work, looking for promotion or hoping to transfer to a different type of work, he should remain alert for any opportunities to pursue as well as make enquiries about possible openings and vacancies. The first quarter of the year holds particular promise for him and his determined approach and sense of purpose will lead to significant developments. The Year of the Rabbit will also have several surprises for the Metal Ox and he could find that one position or task he is given is just a short stepping-stone to considerably greater responsibilities, such are the interesting and positive trends that prevail. The Metal Ox will also enjoy an upturn in his financial situation. However, with this improvement he should aim to manage his money well, perhaps saving some and putting other parts towards specific purposes. These could include items he may wish to buy for himself, travel, holidays and also any new furnishing and equipment he may want for his accommodation. Over the year his fine taste and eye for a keen buy will serve him well! As far as the Metal Ox's domestic life is concerned, this will be a busy year with numerous calls upon his time. He may often despair of all he has to do and all that is being asked of him but, despite the pressures, these will still be meaningful times. The Metal Ox will gain much personal satisfaction in guiding and encouraging someone younger than himself and will also be heartened by the support he is given for his own activities. However, at particularly active times, he should not hesitate to ask for assistance rather than try to do too much single handed. Also, if he does have any problems or matters concerning him, it really would be in his interests to talk these over with those close to him. He will feel much better for doing so as well as benefit from the advice and support he is given. A more senior relation will prove especially helpful, particularly as they speak from experience and with the Metal Ox's interests so much at heart.

The Metal Ox will also get much value from his personal interests over the year and will find that one of these will develop in a surprising and encouraging manner. If he can promote or display any work he has done or feels able to write about one of his interests, perhaps passing on his knowledge and experience, he could find this will bring a pleasing response and will lead to another outlet for his talents. In addition to the pleasure his interests will bring, outdoor activities too will prove satisfying and for those Metal Oxen who enjoy travel, being out in the country-side, or following or taking part in sport, the year will hold some special moments. Generally, this will be a favourable year for the Metal Ox. Much is possible and by setting about his objectives and activities in a purposeful manner, he can achieve some pleasing and worthwhile results.

This is a year which holds considerable promise for the *Water Ox*. With his personable nature and keen, deter-mined attitude he has much in his favour and during the year he will be given the chance to develop and use his skills. In addition, his personal life will contain some rich and rewarding times, including a personal celebration. This could be an engagement, marriage or birth in the family. The Water Ox will also take particular pleasure in following and encouraging the progress and interests of those around him, with their achievements being a source of considerable pride. He will be well supported by his loved ones and throughout the year should not hesitate to seek their opinions or assistance, especially if he feels under pressure. The advice he is given will prove helpful and reassuring, and he should particularly heed the words of a more senior relation. There will be much wise and shrewd advice in what he is told. The Water Ox will also lead a pleasant social life, with some interesting parties and events to attend. Those who have recently moved and are living in a new area will find it in their interests to join in with more group-oriented activities. By making the effort they will soon get to meet others, with one or two new friendships becoming important over the next few years. As far as his work is concerned, the Water Ox will be able to draw on his skills and past experience and make further headway. With his enthusiasm and commitment he will greatly impress over the year and this will lead him to being given greater responsibilities or transferring to another and more varied position. He should also pursue any openings that he feels would help his longer term aspirations as well as advance any ideas he has. In 1999 the Water Ox can make good progress and it rests with him to take full advantage of the encouraging trends that prevail. Similarly for those seeking work, the prospects are favourable. Again, these Water Oxen should remain active in following up any opportunities that they see. In some cases their quest will be rewarded in quite an unusual manner and that one position they attain, even though it might be different from what they were originally hoping for, will enable them to learn and develop new skills as well as open up some interesting possibilities for the future. As far as financial matters are concerned, the Water Ox will enjoy a modest improvement in his financial situation. However, while this will enable him to spend some extra on his accommodation as well as enjoy some well-deserved treats, he should still keep a watchful eye over his outgoings. Without that extra vigilance, these could easily creep up and turn out to be far greater than he anticipated or had allowed for. It would also be in his interest to make sure he goes away for a break or holiday over the year, perhaps visiting an area he has wanted to see for some time. He will find a change of scene and the break this gives him most beneficial. Generally travel is well aspected over the year. Also, if the Water Ox does not get much exercise during the day, he could find it helpful to his well-being to consider walking more or taking up activities such as cycling, swimming or something similar. By doing so, he could feel better in himself and have more zest and energy to carry out the things he would like to do. Generally, the Water Ox will fare well in 1999. He will make pleasing headway in his work and what he achieves will do much to advance his longer term prospects. His domestic and social life too will contain some special and memorable times, making this a rewarding and enjoyable year.

After some of the vexations of the last 12 months, this will be a much improved year for the *Wood Ox*. He will find his level of achievements are that much greater and his undertakings more satisfying. However, to benefit from these more favourable trends the Wood Ox would do well to consider what he wants to accomplish over the next year. These plans can concern almost any area of his life, from projects on his home or garden to travel, extending his hobbies, or learning a new subject or skill. But by setting himself some objectives he will find he is making more effective use of his time than if he were just to drift without anything particular in mind. He will also be encouraged by the supportive nature of those around him and, where appropriate, would do well to involve others in

his activities as well as regularly seek their views and opinions. Domestically, this will be a pleasing year and the
Wood Ox can look forward to many pleasurable occasions
with those around him, especially in pursuing and developing mutual interests. He will also delight in following
the activities of a much younger relation and while he may
not wish to appear interfering, if he feels he has some
advice he can pass on or assistance to offer, he will find his
efforts well received and appreciated. Others do regard his
advice and caring nature highly, as will be shown by their
response during the year. The Wood Ox's social life too is
favourably aspected, with there being some interesting
functions and events for him to attend. If he is involved in
a club or society he could find himself making an important contribution over the year, with his efforts bringing
him much satisfaction and some well-deserved praise. For
any Wood Ox who may have had some adversity over the
last few years or who may be feeling low, it really would be
in his interests to focus his attention on the present, rather
than dwell too much on what has gone before, and set
himself some positive goals and challenges as well as take
up some new activities. He could, perhaps, find it helpful to
get in contact with those who share similar interests or to
enrol on a course that would teach him another skill, but
whatever he decides, positive effort on his part will bring
satisfying results. The Wood Ox will also enjoy any travelling that he undertakes and some trips or breaks – particularly those arranged at short notice and as something of a
surprise – will prove especially pleasurable. As far as financial matters are concerned, the Wood Ox should not experience any undue problems. However, if he does find

himself involved in any great outlay, he should proceed with care and make sure he is conversant with any obligations he might be placed under. In 1999 matters concerning large transactions, legal agreements and important paperwork cannot be rushed. Those Wood Oxen born in 1985 will make good headway in their education over the year. However, at some time they could have to decide which subjects they would like to study in more detail. In this they should consider their options carefully. Although still at a young age, their choices could have an ultimate bearing on their future and they should not take any decision lightly. These Wood Oxen could find it particularly helpful to talk their choices over with those in a position to advise as well as be forthcoming about their own preferences. Also, if at any time they are worried about some aspect of their schoolwork, feel under too much pressure or have some work which they do not fully understand, they should seek advice rather than keep their worries to themselves or struggle on unaided. Those around are keen for the young Wood Oxen to succeed and they should make use of their willingness to help. Overall, this will be a satisfying year for the Wood Ox. By using his time well and setting about his activities in his usual purposeful way he can accomplish a considerable amount as well as enjoy the time spent with family and friends and in pursuing and developing his interests. Overall, this will be a satisfying year for him.

Much will have happened in the *Fire Ox*'s life in recent years. Some Fire Oxen will have moved, some seen changes in their family and many will have retired or taken on different responsibilities in their work. Some of these events will have brought moments of pressure and hard decision-making and the Fire Ox may not always have had the time to carry out all the activities he would have liked. However, with the influence of the more settled Rabbit year, the Fire Ox's situation will now show a marked improvement and he will be able to catch up on some of what he has neglected in recent years. This could include devoting more time to his hobbies or to travel and carrying out projects that he has contemplated for a long time. In particular, the Fire Ox will greatly enjoy the time he spends on his personal interests over the year and would do particularly well to develop a new hobby or interest, ideally one unlike anything he has done before. He will find this will give him a satisfying and stimulating challenge as well as enable him to develop some new skills and talents. The Fire Ox can also look forward to a pleasing domestic life and will take much satisfaction in following and encouraging the progress of those around him. He will also find that those interests and activities he can share with family members will prove especially gratifying, as will family trips and holidays. As always, his family means much to him and throughout the year he will have good reason to value the love, support and encouragement he is given. He will also take much satisfaction in carrying out some projects on his home and garden, but rather than tackle too much single handed, he would do well to involve others and particularly seek help when dealing with complex matters. In many cases, he will find the project will benefit from the pooling of talents as well as bring more meaning for all concerned. In addition to the pleasure his domestic life will bring, the Fire Ox's social life will go well. During the year he can look forward to attending some memorable and sometimes unexpected parties and functions and will also have the opportunity to renew some old acquaintances. Any Fire Oxen who may have had some sadness or adversity over the last few years would do well to look on 1999 as the start of a new phase in their life and try to introduce some additional activities. This could include taking up different interests, enrolling on a course of study or joining a special interest group. The main thing for these Fire Oxen is to immerse themselves in new and stimulating activities; by doing so, they will reap the benefit as well as feel much better in themselves. The Fire Ox will also enjoy an improvement in his financial situation over the year, although he would do well to put any spare money he has to a specific use or to save it rather than allow it to tempt him into impulsive and sometimes reckless spending. Without a certain care, the Fire Ox could find he has spent a great deal on comparatively little and could come to rue some of his purchases. Fire Oxen, take note! Overall, however, 1999 will be a positive and enriching year for the Fire Ox. Most aspects of his life will go well and by using his time effectively, he will be delighted with what he is able to accomplish.

Over the last few years the *Earth Ox* will have made reasonable progress as well as gained much useful experience. However he still has many goals and aspirations and will be keen to make progress towards these and to put his skills to better and more effective use. Over the year his energy, drive and commitment will enable him to make good headway and in many cases take him towards some of his more cherished goals. Throughout, he should remain alert for opportunities to pursue as well as see if he can create some openings himself. Some enterprising thinking on his part could lead him towards some interesting possibilities which, in time, could develop in a most encouraging manner. During the Rabbit year the Earth Ox would do well to remember the old saying 'Nothing ventured, nothing gained' and it is those Earth Oxen who are prepared to be bold and adventurous in their outlook who will make the greatest progress. Also, if any of the Earth Ox's attempts to improve his position do not go his way, he should not allow this to deflect him from his goals. Rather, he should renew his determination and redouble his efforts. He knows he has it within him to accomplish much and his persistence and enterprise will ultimately be rewarded. As far as finance is concerned, the Earth Ox will enjoy an improvement in his situation. He is indeed adept in handling financial matters and will save or spend any additional money he receives wisely. In particular, the Earth Ox will take much satisfaction in acquiring some items that will add much to the comfort and quality of his home. In addition, he could well treat himself and his family to some luxuries that he may have been considering for some time. These could be an item of equipment that he and others can enjoy or alternatively he may decide to set a sum aside for a holiday later in the year. By planning his expenditure he will be well pleased with the decisions and purchases he makes, as will those around him. Also, any Earth Ox who is a keen collector and has a liking for antiques or memorabilia could be fortunate in making a shrewd purchase over the year, one which will, in time, become a useful asset. The Earth Ox's domestic life will also bring him much pleasure and he will take considerable delight in the companionship and successes of those dear to him. He should also involve those around him in his own activities and listen closely to any advice he is given. Over the year he will gain much from the input and encouragement of family members and close friends. His social life, too, will provide him with some most pleasurable occasions and for any Earth Ox who is unattached or seeking new friends, there will be some excellent opportunities to meet others. The spring months in particular could see a major development and upturn in his social life. Generally, the Earth Ox will fare well in the Rabbit year. He is blessed with many fine qualities and with his keen and determined nature he will be able to accomplish much, particularly in his work and in developing his future prospects. On a personal level, too, the Rabbit year will bring him considerable happiness and contentment.

FAMOUS OXEN

Madeleine Albright, Martin Amis, Hans Christian Andersen, Peter Andre, Johann Sebastian Bach, Warren Beatty, Tony Benn, Jon Bon Jovi, Napoleon Bonaparte, Rory Bremner, Benjamin Britten, Frank Bruno, Barbara Cartland, Charlie Chaplin, Martin Clunes, Natalie Cole, Bill Cosby, Tom Courtenay, Tony Curtis, Donald Dewar, Diana, Princess of Wales, Marlene Dietrich, Walt Disney, Patrick Duffy, Harry Enfield, Jane Fonda, Gerald Ford, Edward Fox, Michael J. Fox, Peter Gabriel, Richard Gere, William Hague, Handel, King Harald V of Norway, Robert

Hardy, Nigel Havers, Adolf Hitler, Dustin Hoffman, Anthony Hopkins, Saddam Hussein, Billy Joel, Lionel Jospin, King Juan Carlos of Spain, B. B. King, Mark Knopfler, Burt Lancaster, k. d. Lang, Jessica Lange, Angela Lansbury, Jack Lemmon, Nick Lowe, Nicholas Lyndhurst, Mary Tyler Moore, Kate Moss, Dr Marjorie Mowlam, Alison Moyet, Eddie Murphy, Benjamin Netanyahu, Paul Newman, Jack Nicholson, Leslie Nielsen, Billy Ocean, Oscar Peterson, Colin Powell, Robert Redford, Rubens, Greg Rusedski, Meg Ryan, Monica Seles, Jean Sibelius, Sissy Spacek, Bruce Springsteen, Rod Steiger, Meryl Streep, Elaine Stritch, Lady Thatcher, Mel Torme, Scott F. Turow, Dick van Dyke, Vincent van Gogh, Zoë Wanamaker, the Duke of Wellington, Barbara Windsor, Ernie Wise, W. B. Yeats.

8 FEBRUARY 1902 ～ 28 JANUARY 1903	*Water Tiger*
26 JANUARY 1914 ～ 13 FEBRUARY 1915	*Wood Tiger*
13 FEBRUARY 1926 ～ 1 FEBRUARY 1927	*Fire Tiger*
31 JANUARY 1938 ～ 18 FEBRUARY 1939	*Earth Tiger*
17 FEBRUARY 1950 ～ 5 FEBRUARY 1951	*Metal Tiger*
5 FEBRUARY 1962 ～ 24 JANUARY 1963	*Water Tiger*
23 JANUARY 1974 ～ 10 FEBRUARY 1975	*Wood Tiger*
9 FEBRUARY 1986 ～ 28 JANUARY 1987	*Fire Tiger*
28 JANUARY 1998 ～ 15 FEBRUARY 1999	*Earth Tiger*

THE
TIGER

THE PERSONALITY OF THE TIGER

Nothing great will ever be achieved without great men,
and men are great only if they are determined to be so.
— *Charles de Gaulle: a Tiger*

The Tiger is born under the sign of courage. He is a charismatic figure and usually holds very firm views and beliefs. He is strong-willed and determined, and sets about most of the things he does with a tremendous energy and enthusiasm. He is very alert and quick-witted and his mind is forever active. He is a highly original thinker and is nearly always brimming with new ideas or full of enthusiasm for some new project or scheme.

The Tiger adores challenges and loves to get involved in anything which he thinks has an exciting future or which catches his imagination. He is prepared to take risks and does not like to be bound either by convention or the dictates of others. The Tiger likes to be free to act as he chooses and at least once during his life he will throw caution to the wind and go off and do the things he wants to do.

The Tiger does, however, have a somewhat restless nature. Even though he is often prepared to throw himself wholeheartedly into a project, his initial enthusiasm can soon wane if he sees something more appealing. He can also be rather impulsive and there will be occasions in his life when he acts in a manner which he later regrets. If the Tiger were to think things out or to persevere in his various activities, he would almost certainly enjoy a greater degree of success.

Fortunately, the Tiger is lucky in most of his enterprises, but should things not work out as he had hoped, he is liable to suffer from severe bouts of depression and it will often take him a long time to recover. His life often consists of a series of ups and downs.

The Tiger is, however, very adaptable. He has an adventurous spirit and rarely stays in the same place for long. In the early stages of his life he is likely to try his hand at several different jobs and he will also change his residence fairly frequently.

The Tiger is very honest and open in his dealings with others. He hates any sort of hypocrisy or falsehood. He is also well known for being blunt and forthright and has no hesitation in speaking his mind. He can also be most rebellious at times, particularly against any form of petty authority, and while this can lead the Tiger into conflict with others, he is never one to shrink from an argument or avoid standing up for what he believes is right.

The Tiger is a natural leader and can invariably rise to the top of his chosen profession. He does not, however, care for anything too bureaucratic or detailed and he also does not like to obey orders. He can be stubborn and obstinate, and throughout his life he likes to retain a certain amount of independence in his actions and be responsible to no one but himself. He likes to consider that all his achievements are due to his own efforts and unless he cannot avoid it, he will rarely ask for support from others.

Ironically, despite his self-confidence and leadership qualities, the Tiger can be indecisive and will often delay making a major decision until the very last moment. He can also be sensitive to criticism.

Although the Tiger is capable of earning large sums of money, he is rather a spendthrift and does not always put his money to its best use. He can also be most generous and will often shower lavish gifts on friends and relations.

The Tiger cares very much for his reputation and the image that he tries to project. He carries himself with an air of dignity and authority and enjoys being the centre of attention. He is very adept at attracting publicity, both for himself and for the causes he supports.

The Tiger often marries young and he will find himself best suited to those born under the signs of the Pig, Dog, Horse and Goat. He can also get on well with the Rat, Rabbit and Rooster, but will find the Ox and Snake a bit too quiet and too serious for his liking, and he will also be highly irritated by the Monkey's rather mischievous and inquisitive ways. The Tiger will also find it difficult to get on with another Tiger or a Dragon – both partners will want to dominate the relationship and could find it difficult to compromise on even the smallest of matters.

The Tigress is lively, witty and a marvellous hostess at parties. She is usually most attractive and takes great care over her appearance. She can also be a very doting mother and while she believes in letting her children have their freedom, she makes an excellent teacher and will ensure that her children are brought up well and want for nothing. Like her male counterpart, she has numerous interests and likes to have sufficient independence and freedom to go off and do the things that she wants to do. She also has a most caring and generous nature.

The Tiger has many commendable qualities. He is honest, courageous and often a source of inspiration for others. Providing he can curb the wilder excesses of his restless nature, he is almost certain to lead a most fulfilling and satisfying life.

THE FIVE DIFFERENT TYPES OF TIGER

In addition to the 12 signs of the Chinese zodiac, there are five elements and these have a strengthening or moderating influence on the sign. The effects of the five elements on the Tiger are described below, together with the years in which the elements were exercising their influence. Therefore all Tigers born in 1950 are Metal Tigers, those born in 1902 and 1962 are Water Tigers, and so on.

Metal Tiger: 1950

The Metal Tiger has an assertive and outgoing personality. He is very ambitious and, while his aims may change from time to time, he will work relentlessly until he has obtained what he wants. He can, however, be impatient for results and also get highly strung if things do not work out as he would like. He is distinctive in his appearance and is admired and respected by many.

Water Tiger: 1902, 1962

This Tiger has a wide variety of interests and is always eager to experiment with new ideas or go off and explore distant lands. He is versatile, shrewd and has a kindly nature. The Water Tiger tends to remain calm in a crisis, although he can be annoyingly indecisive at times. He communicates well with others and through his many capabilities and persuasive nature he usually achieves what he wants in life. He is also highly imaginative and is often a gifted orator or writer.

Wood Tiger: 1914, 1974

The Wood Tiger has a very friendly and pleasant personality. He is less independent than some of the other types of Tiger and is more prepared to work with others to secure a desired objective. However, he does have a tendency to jump from one thing to another and can get easily distracted. He is usually very popular, has a large circle of friends and invariably leads a busy and enjoyable social life. He also has a good sense of humour.

Fire Tiger: 1926, 1986

The Fire Tiger sets about everything he does with great verve and enthusiasm. He loves action and is always ready to throw himself wholeheartedly into anything which catches his imagination. He has many leadership qualities and is capable of communicating his ideas and enthusiasm to others. He is very much an optimist and can be most generous. He has a likeable nature and can be a witty and persuasive speaker.

Earth Tiger: 1938, 1998

This Tiger is responsible and level-headed. He studies everything objectively and tries to be scrupulously fair in all his dealings. Unlike other Tigers, he is prepared to specialize in certain areas rather than get distracted by other matters, but he can become so involved with what he is doing that he does not always take into account the views and opinions of those around him. He has good business sense and is usually very successful in later life. He has a large circle of friends and pays great attention to both his appearance and his reputation.

PROSPECTS FOR THE TIGER IN 1999

The Chinese New Year starts on 16 February 1999. Until then, the old year, the Year of the Tiger, is still making its presence felt.

The Year of the Tiger (28 January 1998 to 15 February 1999) will have been an interesting one for the Tiger and in what remains of his own year, there is much that he can achieve.

The Tiger year is very much a year which favours enterprise and initiative and the ever-resourceful Tiger is well placed to benefit from the trends that prevail. In the closing months of the year he should continue to set about his activities in his usual enthusiastic manner, all the time remaining alert for possible opportunities to pursue and promoting his skills and ideas. The aspects will support him well in much of what he does and he should aim to make the most of this.

In his work the Tiger can make considerable progress and many Tigers will see important changes in their duties or be successful in obtaining a different position. Sometimes the tasks the Tiger will be given will be unlike anything he has done before but he will rise to the challenges and gain much useful experience in the process. For Tigers who are seeking work or are dissatisfied with their present duties, there will be opportunities to pursue right until the end of the year, with October and November being two especially productive months.

This is also a favourable year for the Tiger to extend his experience and if there are any skills or qualifications he feels he needs in order to progress, he should take steps to obtain these. This emphasis on development will continue in the Year of the Rabbit and courses and training started now could develop in an encouraging manner over the next 12 months.

Domestically and socially, the Tiger will be on top form. He can look forward to some splendid times with both family and friends and his personal life towards the end of the year promises to be both active and fulfilling. There will be a variety of social events for him to attend as well as the chance to meet some old acquaintances. For the unattached Tiger or for those seeking new friends, the aspects are especially favourable, with one or two new friendships made now becoming important over the next year.

In most respects the Tiger will support his own sign well and, by using his time and skills effectively, he can achieve some good results in his undertakings as well as lead a rich and fulfilling personal life.

The Year of the Rabbit begins on 16 February and will be another positive year for the Tiger. In 1999 he will be able to consolidate the gains and progress he has made over the last 12 months and will continue to make good headway. The year will also be quieter and less active than the last, leaving him better able to plan his activities with fewer interruptions and distractions to contend with.

Particularly well aspected are work matters and during the year the Tiger will be given many opportunities to demonstrate his wide-ranging skills as well as advance his ideas. Those around him will be much impressed by his versatility and innovative approach and useful progress can be made.

If the Tiger has recently taken on a new position or duties he should concentrate on familiarizing himself with his new role. As the year progresses he will find himself being given additional responsibilities, some of which will prove a stimulating challenge, giving him a fresh incentive to do his best and rise to all that is asked of him. What he is able to achieve will certainly impress others as well as do much to enhance his prospects.

However, if the Tiger feels he is currently not making as much of his abilities as he would like, is seeking work or would like to move to a different position, there will be several interesting opportunities to pursue over the year. The months from March to June will be a particularly positive time for work matters and the Tiger should remain alert not only for vacancies but also for information from others. A chance remark could lead to him learning of some interesting possibilities which would be well worth following up. For any Tiger who has been thinking of starting his own business, it would certainly be worth discussing his ideas and plans with those experienced enough to advise. The one thing these Tigers should avoid, however, is rushing into any new venture ill-prepared or without having considered all the implications of the undertaking. With care and sensible planning, the Tiger's venture could work out well, but it is important he attends to those often crucial early stages.

The Rabbit year also favours academic pursuits and, as with last year, if the Tiger should feel he would like to undertake further study or obtain new skills in order to progress this would be an excellent year in which to do so. The Tiger will find that extending his capabilities will be a satisfying and meaningful use of his time and will do much to help his prospects. If he finds himself eligible for any training courses to do with his work, he should take advantage of them. What he learns will prove most beneficial to him in the future.

Those Tigers in education will also have a successful year. They too will cover much useful material and if there are exams approaching, they will find they will fare much better and do themselves more justice by setting about their revision in a systematic and organized way rather than leaving it to the last moment. Also, if there are any aspects of his study or education which the Tiger does not fully understand or which are worrying him, he should not hesitate to tell others. Those around will be keen to assist and can do much to reassure him as well as provide helpful guidance.

As far as financial matters are concerned, this will also be a good year for the Tiger. Most Tigers will enjoy a noticeable upturn in their situation as well as experience several strokes of good fortune. However, despite this improvement, it would be in the Tiger's interests to decide how best he can use his money – whether to save, spend it on certain items or set some aside for holidays and travel. The one thing he should guard against is spending any spare money needlessly. Sometimes the Tiger can be just a little too lavish in his spending and without a certain restraint he could find he has spent far more than he intended. Tigers, take note and do give careful consideration to this when making large purchases!

As luck is on his side the Tiger would, however, do well to enter any competitions that interest him over the year, especially those of a more unusual nature. Several times in 1999 he can look forward to some pleasant surprises and winning a competition could well be one of them!

The Tiger's domestic life will also bring him much contentment. Those close to him will give him useful backing for his various activities and he would do well to listen closely to any advice they give. They do, after all, speak with his best interests at heart and sometimes think of aspects of his projects and enterprises that he might have overlooked. The Tiger will also gain much satisfaction from some household projects that he undertakes. These can range from decorating or redesigning parts of his accommodation to carrying out other alterations. However, the Tiger would do well to involve others rather than do the work single handed. The project will not only benefit from the pooling of skills but it will also be easier to complete as well as bring increased satisfaction for all involved.

The Tiger will also greatly enjoy the leisure time he spends with those around him and will find that joint interests, family holidays and local trips out will generally go well. Although the Tiger does like his independence, his family means much to him and the love that he has for them and they for him will be demonstrated many times over the year.

The Tiger's social life too will bring him considerable pleasure and he will enjoy the company of his friends and the several interesting parties and events that he attends. The late spring and late summer will both be active and promising times for social matters, with plenty of chances for the Tiger to make new friends and widen his circle of acquaintances. For the unattached Tiger, the Rabbit year is splendidly aspected for romance; many Tigers will meet their future partner, get engaged or married during the course of the year. Throughout the year, the Tiger's personal life will go well and, with his sociable and outgoing manner, he will find himself much in demand as well as greatly enjoy himself.

Generally, the Rabbit year will treat the Tiger well but, as with any year, problems can and do emerge. In the Tiger's case these could partly be self-inflicted. In his enthusiasm, the Tiger can sometimes commit himself to more than he can sensibly handle at any one time as well as set himself unrealistic deadlines. If he is not careful he could find himself being placed under increased and sometimes unnecessary pressure, as well as having to rush his activities just to get them finished. In 1999 it is better for him to plan and set about his activities at a steady pace rather than over-commit himself. However, unlike some years, which can bring many external pressures, the Rabbit year will give the Tiger a good chance to choose and conduct his activities in the way he wants. Because of this, he needs to curb his sometimes over-zealous manner and be realistic in what he agrees to undertake. Without care that precious free time that the Tiger so appreciates could all too quickly disappear!

Similarly, the Tiger should be wary of making important decisions on the spur of the moment or without consultation with those around him. Again, it could be a case of keeping his sometimes impulsive nature in check, but better this than regretting something done or agreed to in haste.

Overall, though, this will be a positive year for the Tiger. He can make good progress in his work and should actively pursue his goals and aspirations as well as add to his skills and knowledge. In many ways the Rabbit year is both a constructive and instructive year for him and by giving of his best he will do well. From a personal point of view, this will be a year he will much enjoy, with many pleasurable and meaningful occasions spent in the company of family and friends.

As far as the different types of Tiger are concerned, 1999 will be a most constructive year for the *Metal Tiger*. Over the last 12 months he will have accomplished and learnt much and in the Rabbit year he will be able to build on his gains and make further progress. Particularly well aspected is his work. Others will look favourably on his ideas and accomplishments and will encourage him in his endeavours. Several times over the year the Metal Tiger will be given additional responsibilities and while some of these may be of a challenging nature, by rising to all that is asked and expected of him, he will do much to impress and enhance his position. In 1999 he can make excellent headway and throughout the year should remain alert for chances to demonstrate his skills, promote his ideas and use his initiative. For those Metal Tigers desiring promotion, hoping to move to a different position or currently seeking work, the Rabbit year too will hold some interesting possibilities. These Tigers should actively follow up any openings that they see but also consider different ways in which they can put their past experience and skills to good use. Some enterprising thinking on their part could widen the range of positions open to them as well as make their quest easier. The Metal Tiger will also fare well in financial matters and, while he will enjoy this upturn, he should resist the sometimes great temptation of spending his money all too readily. As far as possible he should plan his purchases carefully and avoid impulse buying. Without a certain restraint and self-discipline he could come to regret some purchases made hurriedly and without proper consideration. This warning apart, the Metal Tiger will, however, be pleased with some items of furnishing and equipment that he buys, but again he would do well to look at the range of items on sale rather than proceed too hastily. The Metal Tiger's domestic and social life is also favourably aspected and he can look forward to some pleasing times with those around him. His home life will at times, though, be busy and there will be several occasions when he will despair of all he has to do, especially with lots of household chores mounting up! However, if he does feel under pressure, he should not hesitate to enlist the help of others rather than carry on unaided and he would also do well to decide upon his priorities rather than flit from one task to another. With fine organization and good use of his time he could end up pleasantly surprised at the considerable amount he is able to get done after just a few concerted efforts. The Metal Tiger would also do well to set some time aside over the year to sort out items and papers that have tended to accumulate and which are no longer needed. Again, he will take much satisfaction in just how much he is able to clear out and how much neater and better organized his home has become. Indeed, all Metal Tigers can benefit and take much pleasure from mounting an efficiency drive over the year! However, despite the often busy nature of his home life, the Metal Tiger can look forward to some splendid times with his family, including an opportunity to meet some relations or good family friends he has not seen for some time. He will also take much delight in the progress of a younger member of his family and any encouragement and advice he feels able to pass on will be warmly appreciated. The Metal Tiger's social life too will bring him much satisfaction and during the year he can look forward to attending some interesting and varied social events. For those Metal Tigers seeking new friends or hoping to build up their social life, the aspects are certainly promising, with the months of April and May marking a noticeable upturn. Overall, this will be a positive year for the Metal Tiger. The aspects will support him well in most of what he does, but to benefit from these favourable trends, he should aim to make the most of himself and his many talents. He has the ideas, the skills and the experience to accomplish much and the Rabbit year will certainly give him his chance.

This will be a satisfying year for the *Water Tiger*. Unlike more recent years, which have seen considerable activity, this will be a much quieter and more stable time. During the Rabbit year the Water Tiger will be able to proceed at his own pace, have more time for his interests and be given the chance to try out some ideas he has long been considering. The year holds much promise for him and by using his time effectively and taking advantage of the opportunities that occur, he can obtain some fulfilling and pleasing results. The many Water Tigers who have recently seen changes in their work or taken on new duties would do well to consolidate their position and familiarize themselves with the different aspects of their work. By setting about his duties in his usual diligent manner the Water Tiger will greatly impress and do much to enhance his reputation and future prospects. Indeed, from October onwards some new and excellent opportunities could become available to him, principally arising from what he has achieved earlier in the year. The Water Tiger should also actively promote his ideas; again, he will find these well received, with some developing in an encouraging manner. Those Water Tigers seeking work can also make good headway and many will be successful in obtaining a position in a rather unexpected and fortuitous way.

Sometimes this may be in a type of work they had not seriously considered before, but they will find they are not only well suited for the position but that it also contains some excellent chances for future progression. It would also be in the Water Tiger's interests to follow up any training opportunities that become available; again, any way he can add to his skills and enhance his prospects will be very much to his advantage, especially with the progressive trends that prevail both in this and the next year. As far as financial matters are concerned, the Water Tiger will enjoy a noticeable improvement in his situation and while he will welcome this, he would do well to manage his money with care. Ideally he should aim to set some aside for specific purposes, including saving, rather than succumb to too many immediate temptations. He will, however, decide to spend a lot on his accommodation, buying both furnishings and equipment, but before making any sizeable purchase he should take time to investigate the ranges and terms on offer. By looking around he could be successful in making some fine purchases at most reasonable prices. He will also devote some of his time over the year to carrying out practical projects on his home, but he should allow plenty of time for this as well as plan the work before commencing. Without proper preparation, he could find practical projects will not go as straightforwardly as he would like. Domestically, this will, however, be a generally pleasing year and the Water Tiger will be heartened by the encouragement he receives and the obvious care and interest others have for him and show in his activities. In view of this, he should remain mindful of their opinions and advice; they do, after all, speak with his interests at heart and with a genuine desire to see him succeed. In addition to the support he receives, the Water Tiger will also enjoy taking part in family activities, with mutual interests, joint projects, outings and breaks proving especially pleasurable. His social life too will go well, with many interesting and convivial occasions spent with his friends. For unattached Water Tigers or those seeking new friends, the early half of the year will bring a significant improvement in their social life with an important and long-lasting friendship being made. Overall, the Water Tiger will enjoy much of this favourably aspected year and by using his time wisely he will accomplish much as well as pave the way for the further successes and progress he will make in the not too distant future.

The Year of the Rabbit will be both a successful and important year for the *Wood Tiger*. During the course of it he will be able to make considerable progress in many of his activities as well as lead an agreeable domestic and social life. In his work the Wood Tiger will be able to draw on what he has learnt and achieved in recent years and make further gains. Over the last 12 months he will have greatly impressed others with his diligence and enterprise and this will lead him to greater responsibilities as the Rabbit year progresses. Throughout the year he should remain alert for ways in which he can best use his talents and experience and follow up any openings that he sees. Also, he should promote any ideas he has, especially those that are work and business related. He could find some of these will develop in a most encouraging manner, opening up some interesting possibilities for him. Similarly, many of those Wood Tigers looking for work or wanting to move from their current position will make good progress and will find their determination rewarded, with the spring months being an especially positive time. Many Wood Tigers who do take a new job over the year will find that their duties will change considerably and that one position will, in turn, lead to a better one in a comparatively short space of time, such are the auspicious trends that prevail. In addition to the progress the Wood Tiger will make now, he would also do well to reflect on his longer term goals and how he would like his career to develop over the next few years. If, in order to achieve his aims, he needs to obtain additional qualifications or experience, he should consider how best he can gain this. Much of what the Wood Tiger sets in motion in 1999 will have significant long-term implications. The Wood Tiger will also enjoy an improvement in his financial situation and any who may have been experiencing problems will find that these will ease during the year. However, despite this upturn, the Wood Tiger still needs to exercise care with his level of spending and not be tempted by too many indulgences. In 1999 he could still face some large expenses, especially connected with his accommodation, and should make full allowance for these in his budget. As far as his personal life is concerned, the Wood Tiger will be on splendid form. He can look forward to many happy and meaningful times with his loved ones and, for the unattached Wood Tiger, romance could come suddenly in 1999 and, in some cases, transform his life. Those around the Wood Tiger will also prove most supportive and at all times the Wood Tiger should be forthcoming over any ideas he may be nurturing or concerns he might have. In 1999 he will have good reason to be thankful for the assistance and encouragement he is given and should particularly listen to what he is told by a more senior relation. There will be some shrewd advice in their words, some of which may not be immediately apparent at the time. Although, with his various commitments, the Wood Tiger may sometimes feel he does not have too much time for his hobbies and interests over the year, it is important he does not neglect these, particularly any which he hopes may have relevance to his later life. Any Wood Tiger with creative aspirations should make a positive effort to develop his talents and reflect deeply on any feedback he is given. Again, what he learns now could have profound significance later. Wood Tigers who enjoy outdoor pursuits should also make sure they set time aside for these, as travel and sporting interests are particularly well favoured. In most respects this will be an enjoyable and satisfying year for the Wood Tiger, with his achievements having a favourable bearing on future years.

This will be a positive year for the *Fire Tiger*, with most aspects of his life bringing him much pleasure. Especially well aspected are hobbies, interests and cultural pursuits, and over the year the Fire Tiger should give serious thought to extending a current interest or taking up a new activity. He will find this will give him an interesting and fulfilling challenge for the year as well as lead to some absorbing times. In addition, the Fire Tiger will benefit from outdoor activities and for the many who take pleasure in travel, walking or gardening, or who follow sport, the year will contain some truly satisfying occasions. With the aspects supporting him so well, it is important that the Fire Tiger decides early on in 1999 just how he would like to spend his time rather than letting himself drift through the year without any particular goals in mind. For those Fire Tigers in education, this too will be a constructive year and they will cover much important material. Some subjects or topic work will, in particular, catch their imagination and lead to some excellent results and, in some cases, have a bearing on the study and work they select in later years. Also, throughout the year, the Fire Tiger will be encouraged and well supported by those around him and he should not hesitate to ask for assistance should he have any doubts or problems either at school or with his schoolwork. The Fire Tiger should not incur any undue financial worries over the year, although he should avoid being tempted into expensive transactions without careful consideration. Without some restraint, he could find he has spent money that could have been put to better purpose. Also, he should be wary of committing himself to any important agreement without checking all the implications beforehand. With good common sense the Fire Tiger can avoid problems and enjoy a comfortable life-style, but he should not allow himself to become complacent or careless when dealing with matters of finance and should also exercise care when completing forms, especially those related to finance, tax or any benefits he might be eligible for. Domestically and socially, this will, however, be a pleasant year. Those around the Fire Tiger will take a caring interest in all he does and throughout the Rabbit year he will have good reason to value their encouragement and advice as well as appreciate the obvious affection they have for him. The Fire Tiger can also look forward to some pleasing times with his friends and will have the opportunity to attend some interesting and varied social events, with the spring and early summer being an active and enjoyable time. Overall he will be content with how the year works out for him. However, early in 1999 he does need to give serious thought to what he wants to accomplish and plan his activities accordingly. In this he should bear in mind that cultural pursuits and personal interests are particularly well favoured and can bring him a considerable amount of pleasure and fulfilment over the year.

Much will have happened in the *Earth Tiger*'s life over the last 12 months. Some Earth Tigers will have retired, some taken on new duties, some moved or seen other changes in their personal life. This period of activity and the pressure that has sometimes been caused will ease early in 1999 and the Earth Tiger will be able to reflect on all that has occurred and take stock of his current position. For many Earth Tigers, the Rabbit year will be a time to heave a great sigh of relief and set about things at a more leisurely and orderly pace. In addition, it will also be a time for reaping the benefits of recent labours; for Earth Tigers who have moved or are moving this will allow them to settle into and enjoy their new accommodation and location, while others will be rewarded financially for work they have carried out or will see projects come to successful fruition. Indeed, the Rabbit year often represents the culmination of earlier efforts and, as such, will be a satisfying and heartening period. Also, with more time at his disposal, the Earth Tiger would do well to start some of the activities he has been considering for some time. If there has been an interest or subject that he has been wanting to take up, this would be an excellent year to do so (especially with the Rabbit year so supportive of cultural activities) or, if there is a destination he has been wanting to visit or special holiday that has been tempting him, he should explore the feasibility of carrying out his plans. This year holds a lot of promise for the Earth Tiger and it rests with him to decide what he wishes to do in it. Throughout the year those around the Earth Tiger will support him well and he will gain much by discussing his thoughts and ideas with others and listening to their views. Many times he will be given suggestions or advice that will help his activities go better as well as alert him to possible points he may have overlooked. Domestically, he can also look forward to some gratifying times, with mutual interests and projects that he can carry out with those around him proving especially satisfying. He will also take much pride in the progress of those around him and several times in 1999 there will be some splendid, and sometimes unexpected, news concerning family members. There is one word of warning, though. If the Earth Tiger tackles large and complex tasks in his home or garden he does need to take all the necessary precautions, especially when using potentially dangerous tools. Also, if moving heavy weights, he should seek assistance. Without care he could sprain himself and cause himself considerable discomfort. Earth Tigers, be warned! As far as his social life is concerned, however, the Earth Tiger can look forward to attending some interesting functions and events over the year as well as having some pleasant times with his friends. The spring and summer months will, in particular, be quite active for social matters. Any Earth Tigers who have recently moved and are looking to establish a new social life would do well to consider joining a local or special interest group where they will be able to meet others. By doing so they will soon find themselves building up new acquaintances, extending their interests and having some pleasant and enjoyable times. Similarly, any Earth Tiger who may be feeling lonely or who has had some recent adversity will find that positive action on his part – such as making the deliberate effort to go out more and engage in new and different activities – will bring its rewards, although it does rest with him to take those all-important initial steps. Financially this will be a generally satisfactory year, although the Earth Tiger should plan his major purchases carefully rather than be tempted to spend too hastily. Some carefully considered acquisitions, together with a certain patience, could result in him obtaining some excellent bargains, especially related to personal interests or equipment for his accommodation. Overall, 1999 will be a year that the Earth Tiger will greatly enjoy. At last he will have more time to spend in the way he would like and, as a result, he will find the year both satisfying and enriching.

FAMOUS TIGERS

Kofi Annan, Sir David Attenborough, Queen Beatrix of the Netherlands, Beethoven, Tony Bennett, Tom Berenger, Chuck Berry, Richard Branson, Garth Brooks, Mel Brooks, Isambard Kingdom Brunel, Agatha Christie, Phil Collins, Robbie Coltrane, Alan Coren, Tom Cruise, Paul Daniels, Emily Dickinson, David Dimbleby, Isadora Duncan, Dwight Eisenhower, Queen Elizabeth II, Enya, Roberta

Flack, E. M. Forster, Frederick Forsyth, Jodie Foster, Connie Francis, Charles de Gaulle, Crystal Gayle, Elliott Gould, Buddy Greco, Sir Alec Guinness, Naseem Hamed, Harriet Harman, Ed Harris, Tim Henman, William Hurt, Derek Jacobi, Stan Laurel, Louise, Karl Marx, Marilyn Monroe, Demi Moore, Eric Morecambe, Neil Morrissey, Marco Polo, Beatrix Potter, John Prescott, Renoir, Lionel Ritchie, Kenny Rogers, the Princess Royal, Dame Joan Sutherland, Dylan Thomas, Terence Trent-D'Arby, Liv Ullman, Jon Voight, Julie Walters, Oscar Wilde, Robbie Williams, Tennessee Williams, Terry Wogan, Stevie Wonder, Natalie Wood.

29 JANUARY 1903 ～ 15 FEBRUARY 1904   *Water Rabbit*

14 FEBRUARY 1915 ～ 2 FEBRUARY 1916   *Wood Rabbit*

2 FEBRUARY 1927 ～ 22 JANUARY 1928   *Fire Rabbit*

19 FEBRUARY 1939 ～ 7 FEBRUARY 1940   *Earth Rabbit*

6 FEBRUARY 1951 ～ 26 JANUARY 1952   *Metal Rabbit*

25 JANUARY 1963 ～ 12 FEBRUARY 1964   *Water Rabbit*

11 FEBRUARY 1975 ～ 30 JANUARY 1976   *Wood Rabbit*

29 JANUARY 1987 ～ 16 FEBRUARY 1988   *Fire Rabbit*

16 FEBRUARY 1999 ～ 4 FEBRUARY 2000   *Earth Rabbit*

THE
RABBIT

THE PERSONALITY OF THE RABBIT

It seems to me we can never give up longing and wishing
while we are thoroughly alive. There are certain things
we feel to be beautiful and good, and we must hunger
after them.

– George Eliot: a Rabbit

The Rabbit is born under the signs of virtue and prudence.
He is intelligent, well-mannered and prefers a quiet and
peaceful existence. He dislikes any sort of unpleasantness
and will try to steer clear of arguments and disputes. He is
very much a pacifist and tends to have a calming influence
on those around him.

He has wide interests and usually has a good appreciation of the arts and the finer things in life. He also knows
how to enjoy himself and will often gravitate to the best
restaurants and night spots in town.

The Rabbit is a witty and intelligent speaker and loves
being involved in a good discussion. His views and advice
are often sought by others and he can be relied upon to be
discreet and diplomatic. He will rarely raise his voice in
anger and will even turn a blind eye to matters which
displease him just to preserve the peace. The Rabbit likes to
remain on good terms with everyone, but he can be rather
sensitive and takes any form of criticism very badly. He
will also be the first to get out of the way if he sees any
form of trouble brewing.

The Rabbit is a quiet and efficient worker and has an
extremely good memory. He is very astute in business and

financial matters, but his degree of success often depends on the conditions that prevail. He hates being in a situation which is fraught with tension or where he has to make quick and sudden decisions. Wherever possible he will plan his various activities with the utmost care and a good deal of caution. He does not like to take risks and does not take kindly to changes. Basically, he seeks a secure, calm and stable environment, and when conditions are right he is more than happy to leave things as they are.

The Rabbit is conscientious in most of the things he does and, because of his methodical and ever-watchful nature, can often do well in his chosen profession. He makes a good diplomat, lawyer, shopkeeper, administrator or priest and he excels in any job where he can use his superb skills as a communicator. He tends to be loyal to his employers and is respected for his integrity and honesty, but if he ever finds himself in a position of great power he can become rather intransigent and authoritarian.

The Rabbit attaches great importance to his home and will often spend much time and money to maintain and furnish it and to fit it with all the latest comforts – the Rabbit is very much a creature of comfort! He is also something of a collector and there are many Rabbits who derive much pleasure from collecting antiques, stamps, coins, *objets d'art* or anything else which catches their eye or particularly interests them.

The female Rabbit has a friendly, caring and considerate nature, and will do all in her power to give her home a happy and loving atmosphere. She is also very sociable and enjoys holding parties and entertaining. She has a great ability to make the maximum use of her time and, although she involves herself in numerous activities, she always manages to find time to sit back and enjoy a good read or a chat. She has a great sense of humour, is very artistic and is often a talented gardener.

The Rabbit takes considerable care over his appearance and is usually smart and very well turned out. He also attaches great importance to his relations with others and matters of the heart are particularly important to him. He will rarely be short of admirers and will often have several serious romances before he settles down. The Rabbit is not the most faithful of signs, but he will find that he is especially well suited to those born under the signs of the Goat, Snake, Pig and Ox. Due to his sociable and easy-going manner he can also get on well with the Tiger, Dragon, Horse, Monkey, Dog and another Rabbit, but will feel ill at ease with the Rat and Rooster as both these signs tend to speak their mind and be critical in their comments, and the Rabbit just loathes any form of criticism or unpleasantness.

The Rabbit is usually lucky in life and often has the happy knack of being in the right place at the right time. He is talented and quick-witted, but he does sometimes put pleasure before work, and wherever possible will tend to opt for the easy life. He can at times be a little reserved and suspicious of the motives of others, but generally will lead a long and contented life and one which – as far as possible – will be free of strife and discord.

THE FIVE DIFFERENT TYPES OF RABBIT

In addition to the 12 signs of the Chinese zodiac, there are five elements and these have a strengthening or moderating influence on the sign. The effects of the five elements on the Rabbit are described below, together with the years in which the elements were exercising their influence. Therefore all Rabbits born in 1951 are Metal Rabbits, those born in 1903 and 1963 are Water Rabbits, and so on.

Metal Rabbit: 1951

This Rabbit is capable, ambitious and has very definite views on what he wants to achieve in life. He can occasionally appear reserved and aloof, but this is mainly because he likes to keep his thoughts and ideas to himself. He has a quick and alert mind and is particularly shrewd in business matters. He can also be very cunning in his actions. The Metal Rabbit has a good appreciation of the arts and likes to mix in the best circles. He usually has a small but very loyal group of friends.

Water Rabbit: 1903, 1963

The Water Rabbit is popular, intuitive and keenly aware of the feelings of those around him. He can, however, be rather sensitive and tends to take things too much to heart. He is very precise and thorough in everything he does and has an exceedingly good memory. He tends to be quiet and at times rather withdrawn, but he expresses his ideas well and is highly regarded by his family, friends and colleagues.

Wood Rabbit: 1915, 1975

The Wood Rabbit is likeable, easy going and very adaptable. He prefers to work in groups rather than on his own and likes to have the support and encouragement of others. He can, however, be rather reticent in expressing his views and it would be in his own interests to become a little more open and forthright and let others know how he feels on certain matters. He usually has many friends and enjoys an active social life. He is noted for his generosity.

Fire Rabbit: 1927, 1987

The Fire Rabbit has a friendly, outgoing personality. He likes socializing and being on good terms with everyone. He is discreet and diplomatic and has a very good understanding of human nature. He is also strong-willed and provided he has the necessary backing and support he can go far in life. He does not, however, suffer adversity well and can become moody and depressed when things are not working out as he would like. The Fire Rabbit is very intuitive and there are some who are even noted for their psychic ability. The Fire Rabbit has a particularly good manner with children.

Earth Rabbit: 1939, 1999

The Earth Rabbit is a quiet individual, but he is neverthe-less very shrewd and astute. He is realistic in his aims and is prepared to work long and hard in order to achieve his objectives. He has good business sense and is invariably lucky in financial matters. He also has a most persuasive manner and usually experiences little difficulty in getting others to fall in with his plans. He is held in very high esteem by his friends and colleagues and his views and opinions are often sought and highly valued.

PROSPECTS FOR THE RABBIT IN 1999

The Chinese New Year starts on 16 February 1999. Until then, the old year, the Year of the Tiger, is still making its presence felt.

The Year of the Tiger (28 January 1998 to 15 February 1999) will not have been the best of years for the Rabbit. He could have felt uneasy with some of its events as well as experienced times of considerable pressure. Tiger years are often times of upheaval and activity and the Rabbit is very much one who prefers gradual change, and at his own instigation. This will not always have been possible over the last 12 months.

However disquieting the Tiger year may be, the Rabbit can still gain much of value from it and this particularly applies to the closing stages. With the arrival of his own year, the Rabbit is about to experience a significant improvement in his fortunes and would do well to prepare himself for this upturn. In what remains of the Tiger year he should look closely at his current aims and aspirations and discuss these with others, particularly seeking out those with experience who are in a position to give expert advice. The ideas and plans the Rabbit formulates now will serve him well and also help him to direct his energies in a more purposeful way.

In his work the Rabbit should take advantage of any chance he gets to extend his experience or take on different duties as this again could do much to assist his future prospects. While he may currently have misgivings about some aspects of his work, he should still give of his best and remain his diligent and diplomatic self. By doing so he will continue to impress and this too will help when opportunities fall available. As the year draws to a close he should also make a concerted effort to deal with any outstanding matters, projects or correspondence and will find this will help relieve some of the pressure he has been under as well as leave him freer to attend to his plans and activities for the new year.

Domestically and socially the Rabbit will, however, enjoy some pleasant times with his family and friends in the closing stages of the Tiger year. Indeed, he will find himself much in demand and this activity in his personal life will certainly help to make up for, and take his mind off, some of his present concerns. Also, he should be forthcoming over any problems or anxieties he might have rather than keep them to himself; by doing so he will be helped as well as heartened by the advice he receives.

For all its problems and hassles, the Rabbit will have learnt much in the Tiger year and what he has achieved and the plans he has laid will all contribute to the excellent trends that await him in his own year.

The Year of the Rabbit starts on 16 February and will be a truly auspicious one for the Rabbit. Indeed, the Rabbit year does much to support and encourage its own and most areas of the Rabbit's life are positively aspected.

Almost as soon as the Rabbit year begins, the Rabbit will sense that his prospects are about to improve and this will give him an added incentive to set about his activities with a greater enthusiasm and commitment. As a result, he will find he will be achieving more in many areas of his life.

In the Rabbit's work, much progress is possible. If the Rabbit has been thinking of changing his present position, is seeking promotion or has some idea he wishes to pursue, he should keep alert for any opportunities. Often these will arise at short notice and occasionally in a surprising manner, and it rests with the Rabbit to seize them. Rarely have the aspects been so promising or positive changes so swift in coming.

The Rabbit will also find that it is possible to create some openings and opportunities himself. If there is a type of work he would particularly like to do, he would do well to approach organizations or contact those who might be able to assist and advise. In some cases a direct and enterprising approach will lead to some useful information which he can profit from. Similarly, if there is a business idea he would like to pursue, this is a good year to discuss it with others and explore the feasibility of setting it in motion. Again, with determination, much can be achieved.

Those Rabbits who are looking for employment will also make good progress and should actively follow up any openings that interest them. Most will find their persistence and commitment rewarded and once in a new position they will quickly impress and could find this will lead to further progress in a comparatively short space of time. The months from February to April and from September to the close of the Rabbit year are all positive for work matters, containing both opportunities and interesting developments.

The Rabbit year also favours learning and academic matters and is an excellent year for the Rabbit to undertake training or consider extending his skills in some way. He will find this will provide him with an interesting challenge as well as be a fulfilling use of his time. Those Rabbits in education too can make good progress. By setting about their studies in a careful and purposeful manner, they will be rewarded with some pleasing and worthwhile results. As all Rabbits will find in 1999, it really is worth making that little bit of extra effort – often substantial benefits will arise from what the Rabbit learns and achieves in his own year.

There are also many Rabbits who have some interest in the arts, either writing, painting, the theatre, music or some other area. Throughout the year these Rabbits will obtain considerable satisfaction in devoting time to their interest and for those with creative aspirations, it really would be to their advantage to bring their work and talents to the attention of others. They will be encouraged by the response they receive. While the Rabbit may not be the boldest of the Chinese signs, he should remember the saying 'Nothing ventured, nothing gained'. If he aspires to greater things, then he should overcome his reticence and be bold and promote himself. In this, his own year, he will find the aspects will support him well in what he does.

Again, if there is a hobby or interest that has been intriguing the Rabbit for some time, this is an ideal year in which to find out more. In 1999 the Rabbit can do much to make his life rich and fulfilling, but the initial steps do rest with him.

The Rabbit is usually careful when dealing with financial matters and over the year he will fare well. He could find any investments and savings he makes will perform well and build into a useful asset. He could also be fortunate in some of his purchases over the year, particularly in acquiring items that add to the decor and comfort of his accommodation. Rabbits who are collectors or have a fondness for art or antiques could be successful in making some fine acquisitions. As usual, the Rabbit's good taste and judgement will not let him down.

Domestically, this will be a pleasing year for the Rabbit. He will be encouraged by the support and affection he is given by those around him and at all times should be forthcoming with his thoughts and ideas. If he finds himself in any dilemma over the year, particularly concerning a possible career move or some projects he has in mind, he should discuss it with others rather than keep his thoughts to himself. Those around do so want to assist and the Rabbit will have good reason to value the advice given.

In addition to the support he receives, the Rabbit will also take much interest in the activities and progress enjoyed by those dear to him and any assistance he feels able to pass on will be much appreciated. There will also be several occasions which give rise to family celebrations over the year and at some point the Rabbit will play an active and central part. Family matters do mean a lot to the Rabbit and throughout the year his domestic life will provide him with much contentment and pleasure.

The Rabbit's social life too is splendidly aspected and he can look forward to being much in demand with his many good friends, as well as attending a variety of parties and social events. There will also be opportunities to make new friends and add to his circle of acquaintances and, for the unattached Rabbit, romance and matters of the heart have rarely been rosier. Many will find a friendship that starts quite casually will truly blossom and a large number of Rabbits will get engaged or married over the course of the year, such are the auspicious aspects that prevail.

Generally, this will be a year which the Rabbit will come to look back on with pride and satisfaction. He will enjoy good fortune and happiness in most areas of his life as well as make considerable progress in his work. Any problems that arise are likely to be small niggling irritations which can, with the support of others, be quickly dealt with. However, for the Rabbit to take maximum advantage of the trends that prevail, he does need to use his time wisely, decide upon his goals and priorities and work towards them. For the determined and active Rabbit, there are few better years than his own in which to make progress and he should not miss out on any opportunities by being too reticent. This is his own year and he really should make the most of it. It is a time for boldness, resolution — and some well-deserved success!

As far as the different types of Rabbit are concerned, this will be a significant year for the *Metal Rabbit*. The Metal Rabbit possesses a shrewd and alert nature and has a keen idea of his goals. He knows what he wants to achieve in life and where his natural strengths lie. This, together with his strong sense of purpose, will serve him admirably over the year and propel him to new heights. In 1999 he will be given every chance to build on his achievements and past experience and will make excellent headway. In his work he should follow up the opportunities that become available as well as keep a close eye on forthcoming developments. This way he will be able to prepare himself for any openings that are in the offing as well as make the most of changing situations. Indeed, for the enterprising and determined Metal Rabbit this will be a progressive time and he should capitalize on the considerable opportunities that the year will bring. The Metal Rabbit will also find that many of the openings will arise quickly and to benefit he will need to 'strike while the iron is hot'. This also applies to those Metal Rabbits seeking work. Again, opportunities will arise in a sudden and often unexpected manner and it is those who act quickly who will fare the best. The early and closing months of the year could be particularly active months for employment matters, but overall this is an excellent time to advance and the Metal Rabbit should take full advantage of the auspicious trends that prevail. In addition, many Metal Rabbits will also find that projects started in the previous year and ideas that they may have been nurturing could lead to some interesting developments now. The Metal Rabbit will also enjoy a significant upturn in his financial position and in many cases this will enable him to carry out plans and make purchases he has been considering for some time. This could include making changes to his accommodation, buying items of equipment and furnishing or, for some, moving. By looking around the Metal Rabbit will be able to make some fine and useful acquisitions and where decor is concerned, his judgement and taste will be much admired by those around him. The Metal Rabbit's home life will be active and satisfying. He can look forward to many happy and pleasurable family occasions and will take much interest in the activities and successes of those around him. In addition, he will be greatly encouraged by the support he is given and, as far as possible, should involve his loved ones in his various activities. Many times over the year he will benefit from their advice and assistance, particularly by being alerted to possibilities he may have overlooked or ways to make his work, projects and even household tasks easier. The Metal Rabbit's social life too will go well, with the spring and summer months being an active time. Over the year he can look forward to attending a wide variety of social events and having the opportunity to extend his circle of acquaintances, with some becoming firm friends over the next few years. Generally, 1999 will be a year that the Metal Rabbit will enjoy. He will be given the opportunity to progress, to show his true worth and develop his ideas. Indeed, some of the chances offered will be what he has been hoping for for a long time and he should seize the opportunities that the year will bring and make the most of the favourable trends that prevail. He knows he has it within him to do well and, helped by his own positive attitude, he will make good progress. Added to which, on a personal level, this will be a happy and fulfilling year.

This is a year which offers the *Water Rabbit* considerable potential. At the start of it he should take stock of his present position and recent achievements and consider just what it is he would like to accomplish next. Then, with some goals in mind, he should concentrate his efforts and energies towards achieving them. Over the year he will find his purposeful approach well rewarded and, with determination, almost all Water Rabbits will be able to substantially improve their position and enjoy a good measure of success. Throughout the year the Water Rabbit should also remain alert for any opportunities that become available and for ways in which he can most usefully draw on his skills and experience. This is a year for progress and, with the right attitude, he will achieve much. Over the year there will be some excellent chances for promotion or for taking on new and more varied responsibilities and the Water Rabbit will rise to the tasks and challenges given him. He should also advance any ideas he has, as he could find these favourably received, with some developing in an encouraging manner. However, when launching into any new activity, particularly a business idea, the Water Rabbit would do well to seek the advice of those who speak from experience and authority. He will find their words of great value as well as be alerted to possible pitfalls that could undermine his efforts. Many of those Water Rabbits seeking work will also be successful in their search for a position, although they should not allow any initial disappointments they face to weaken their resolve. Many will find success will follow on shortly after a setback and often in an unexpected and fortuitous way. The early months of the year could prove an active time for work matters and the many Water Rabbits who obtain a new position in the first quarter of the year will find it will develop well and lead to greater responsibilities as the year progresses. The Water Rabbit will also enjoy good fortune in financial matters. In addition to enjoying a noticeable increase in his income he could receive a useful sum of money from an unexpected but nevertheless welcome source. However, despite this upturn, the Water Rabbit would still do well to plan his purchases rather than succumb to too many indulgences or spending sprees. Certainly his careful and prudent nature will help, but without some restraint he could find he has spent more on certain items than he intended and that his money could have been put to better use. The Water Rabbit would also do well to consider setting something aside for his longer term future, either by investing or starting a savings scheme. In time this could build into a sizeable asset and be something he is glad he started sooner rather than later. On a personal level the Water Rabbit will be on good form. He will obtain much satisfaction from both his domestic and social life and can look forward to many meaningful and pleasurable times with those around him. He will also take much delight in playing a full part in family activities, particularly in encouraging and advising a younger relation. Both domestically and socially this will be an active and pleasant year for him but, despite his best intentions, he should be wary about taking on too many commitments at the same time. It is better to be honest and tell others he has not the time to attend or deal with something properly than put himself under too much pressure by over-committing himself. Also, if he finds he has many household matters and chores to deal with, he should not hesitate to ask for assistance. Help and support are available, but there may be occasions when the Water Rabbit has to prompt others into action! He will, however, greatly enjoy the travelling that he undertakes during the year and a holiday taken over the summer months could be one of the best he has had for a long time, especially if it is to a destination new to him. As usual, the Water Rabbit will get much pleasure from his personal interests and would do well to consider extending one in some way, perhaps by learning about another aspect or getting in contact with fellow enthusiasts. He could find this will give his interest added meaning as well as provide him with some fulfilling and satisfying times. Generally, 1999 can be an excellent year for the Water Rabbit. However, to take advantage of the positive trends he should act on the opportunities that become available as well as promote his ideas and talents. For the determined and enterprising Water Rabbit, these are great and significant times!

This will be an enjoyable and successful year for the *Wood Rabbit*. In 1999 he will make good progress and be able to achieve results that have for some time proved elusive. In particular, his work and career prospects are especially well aspected, with some positive developments taking place. However, to take advantage of the favourable aspects, the Wood Rabbit needs to decide early on in the year just what he would like to accomplish and then work purposefully towards it. If he is seeking work or promotion or wanting to change to a different type of work, he should actively follow up any openings that he sees. Determined and positive action on the Wood Rabbit's part will lead to good progress, with what he achieves now often having far-reaching implications. Throughout the Rabbit year the Wood Rabbit should also take advantage of any training courses that he might be eligible for or any chances to extend his skills. Again, what he learns now will do much to enhance his prospects. The Wood Rabbit will also see an improvement in his financial situation and while this may ease some of the financial pressures he may have been under, he still needs to exercise care with his outgoings, particularly with any important transactions that he enters into, especially when related to his accommodation. Fortunately the Wood Rabbit is usually adept at financial matters, but this is not a year for complacency or carelessness. On a personal level this will, however, be a splendid year. The Wood Rabbit's relations with those around him will go particularly well and throughout 1999 he will draw much comfort from the support and advice he receives and from the care and affection others show towards him. For the unattached Wood Rabbit, romance is splendidly aspected and a friendship started towards the end of 1998 or in the first quarter of 1999 could develop in a meaningful and significant way. Indeed, many Wood Rabbits will have good cause for some personal celebration over the year, either by getting engaged, married or by seeing an addition to their family. There will also be opportunities for the Wood Rabbit to travel and for any who have considered working in another country or who want to improve their language skills, 1999 could be a good year in which to do this. The Wood Rabbit will also obtain much satisfaction from his hobbies and interests and if there is one he is keen to develop he should make every effort to do so. The

Rabbit year does very much favour self-improvement and cultural activities. Generally, the Wood Rabbit can achieve a considerable amount over the year, with the progress he makes having a positive bearing on the next few years. Added to which, on a personal level, this will be a fulfilling year for him, with romance and his relations with others being a source of much happiness.

This will be a significant year for the *Fire Rabbit* and one which will see some positive changes taking place. For those Fire Rabbits born in 1987 this could involve a change of school or taking up a range of new subjects and activities. Initially these could prove daunting, but the Fire Rabbit will soon settle down and once in his stride he will truly impress. He will also find that the changes that occur will provide him with new interests and a greater incentive to get on and, as a result, he will do well and his upward progress will help set the pattern for the next few years. He will also be encouraged in his activities by those around him and if he has any worries or is troubled by what is being asked of him he should not hesitate to seek advice. For academic matters this will be a good and constructive year. Those Fire Rabbits born in 1927 will also see some positive changes take place, mainly concerning their accommodation. Some will move while others will have alterations carried out, some of which they may have been considering for some time. Admittedly this will cause inconvenience and extra burden for the Fire Rabbit, but in the end he will feel the effort and expense have been well worth while. Those Fire Rabbits who move will take much delight in settling into their new area, finding out about local amenities and attractions, and having the chance to build up a new social life. However, when the Fire Rabbit authorizes others to carry out work on his behalf, especially any tasks related to his accommodation, he should make sure that they understand his requirements and that he has a breakdown of all the costs involved. This could prevent some misunderstandings later. Also, if at any time the Fire Rabbit has heavy items to move or strenuous tasks to complete, he should seek assistance rather than perform them unaided. Help is readily available and all he has to do is ask. The Fire Rabbit will fare well in financial matters, with the likelihood of several strokes of luck, and he could also be successful in a competition he enters or receive a useful sum from an investment made earlier. However, with any financial upturn, the Fire Rabbit should consider carefully what he should do with money he does not immediately need rather than simply spend out too readily. A carefully planned holiday or some treats for himself and his loved ones could prove particularly meaningful as well as being appreciated by all concerned. Outdoor activities too will provide the Fire Rabbit with much pleasure and for the keen traveller, sports enthusiast or gardener, the year will contain some satisfying moments. The Fire Rabbit will also obtain much pleasure from his other hobbies over the year, especially any that allow him to use and extend his creative talents. Generally, this is a positive and rewarding time and any Fire Rabbits who may have experienced some recent misfortune or unhappiness should try to view the year as the start of a new chapter in their life. They could find it helpful to take up some new activities – with some providing a personal challenge – and get in contact with others, perhaps by joining a social group. The effort they make will certainly prove worthwhile. Overall, this will be a significant year for the Fire Rabbit with some important but beneficial changes taking place and, with his many talents and the support and affection that he receives, he is certain to make much of it as well as to enjoy the many pleasurable occasions that it will bring.

Much will have happened in the *Earth Rabbit*'s life over the last 12 months and 1999 will see the culmination of his efforts and hard work, together with the opportunity to put some of his ideas into practice. Indeed, this is the Earth Rabbit's own year and, as such, it will be a significant and rewarding time. Early in the year, though, the Earth Rabbit would do well to assess his present position and recent events and then set himself some goals and priorities for the year ahead. These could concern almost any area of his life, from his work or his accommodation to interests he would like to take up or places he would like to visit. But by planning his time in this way, the Earth Rabbit will be able to concentrate his efforts more profitably and achieve more as a result. The aspects will support him well and in some of his activities he will be able to build on previous successes and make good use of his experience. In his work this could involve the fruition of some projects he has been working on or lead to him being given increased responsibilities. Alternatively, some Earth Rabbits will opt to retire. Those who do so should consider how they intend to use the additional time that becomes available to them. As well as devoting attention to their existing interests, they would do well to consider taking up new ones, perhaps some they have been meaning to do for some time but have never had the chance or time to start. Similarly, the

Earth Rabbit could obtain a great deal of personal satisfaction from learning a new skill or subject. By doing something practical, he will make the year all the more fulfilling as well as set himself with some interesting personal challenges. In his activities he will enjoy the support and encouragement of those around him and should be forthcoming about his ideas. Over the year he will gain much from the input and sterling advice of others. Indeed, as far as his personal relations are concerned, the Earth Rabbit will be on sparkling form. He will thoroughly enjoy the various family activities and projects with which he is involved as well as take much pride in the achievements of those around him. On a social level, too, this will be an active year and, in addition to attending some interesting social occasions, the Earth Rabbit can look forward to many enjoyable times in the company of his friends. Any Earth Rabbit who may be feeling lonely or has recently moved will find that by going out more, getting in contact with others and joining local interest groups he will be able to form new friendships and will see an upturn in his social life. As all Earth Rabbits will find, by acting positively and making that all-important effort towards their goals, whatever they may be, they will quickly obtain results, such are the auspicious trends that prevail. There will also be good fortune in financial matters, with many Earth Rabbits receiving an additional sum of money over the year. With travel being well aspected, they would do well to consider putting some of this towards a special holiday, perhaps visiting a place that has long held a fascination for them. The Earth Rabbit will not only enjoy any holidays he is able to take over the year but will also benefit from the rest and change of scene that they give. In almost all respects this will be a positive year for the Earth Rabbit, but in order to profit from the favourable aspects that prevail, he must not allow himself to drift through it without any particular plans in mind. In 1999 he needs to give thought to what he wants to do and then go after his aims. It has been some time since the aspects have been so good for the Earth Rabbit and he really should make the most of them. This is a year of opportunity, for reaping the rewards of past efforts and for setting in motion his plans and ideas. And, for the determined and enterprising Earth Rabbit, this will also be a year he will savour and enjoy.

FAMOUS RABBITS

Paula Abdul, Bertie Ahern, Drew Barrymore, Cecil Beaton, Harry Belafonte, Ingrid Bergman, Melvyn Bragg, Gordon Brown, James Caan, Nicolas Cage, Lewis Carroll, Fidel Castro, John Cleese, Confucius, Christopher Cross, Dr Jack Cunningham, Marie Curie, Kenny Dalglish, Peter Davison, Johnny Depp, Albert Einstein, George Eliot, Peter Falk, W. C. Fields, Bridget Fonda, Peter Fonda, James Fox, Sir David Frost, James Galway, Cary Grant, Edvard Grieg, Oliver Hardy, Seamus Heaney, Paul Hogan, Bob Hope, Whitney Houston, John Howard, John Hurt, Chrissie Hynde, Clive James, Henry James, David Jason, Michael Jordan, Garry Kasparov, John Keats, Danny La Rue, Cheryl Ladd, Julian Lennon, Patrick Lichfield, Gina Lollobrigida, Robert Ludlum, Ali MacGraw, Trevor McDonald, George Michael, Arthur Miller, Colin Montgomerie, Roger Moore,

James Naughtie, Nanette Newman, Brigitte Nielsen, Tatum O'Neal, Christina Onassis, George Orwell, John Peel, Edith Piaf, John Redwood, Ken Russell, Mort Sahl, Elisabeth Schwarzkopf, Neil Sedaka, Jane Seymour, Neil Simon, Frank Sinatra, Dusty Springfield, Sting, Jimmy Tarbuck, Sir Denis Thatcher, J. R. R. Tolkien, Arturo Toscanini, Tina Turner, Luther Vandross, Queen Victoria, Terry Waite, Andy Warhol, Orson Welles, Walt Whitman, Kate Winslet, Tiger Woods, Yazz.

16 FEBRUARY 1904 ～ 3 FEBRUARY 1905   *Wood Dragon*

3 FEBRUARY 1916 ～ 22 JANUARY 1917   *Fire Dragon*

23 JANUARY 1928 ～ 9 FEBRUARY 1929   *Earth Dragon*

8 FEBRUARY 1940 ～ 26 JANUARY 1941   *Metal Dragon*

27 JANUARY 1952 ～ 13 FEBRUARY 1953   *Water Dragon*

13 FEBRUARY 1964 ～ 1 FEBRUARY 1965   *Wood Dragon*

31 JANUARY 1976 ～ 17 FEBRUARY 1977   *Fire Dragon*

17 FEBRUARY 1988 ～ 5 FEBRUARY 1989   *Earth Dragon*

THE
DRAGON

THE PERSONALITY OF THE DRAGON

If there is anything that a man can do and do well, I say let him do it. Give him a chance.

– Abraham Lincoln: a Dragon

The Dragon is born under the sign of luck. He is a proud and lively character and has a tremendous amount of self-confidence. He is also highly intelligent and very quick to take advantage of any opportunities that occur. He is ambitious and determined and will do well in practically anything he attempts. He is also something of a perfectionist and will always try and maintain the high standards he sets himself.

The Dragon does not suffer fools gladly and will be quick to criticize anyone or anything that displeases him. He can be blunt and forthright in his views and is certainly not renowned for being either tactful or diplomatic. He does, however, often take people at their word and can occasionally be rather gullible. If he ever feels that his trust has been abused or his dignity wounded he can sometimes become very bitter and it will take him a long time to forgive and forget.

The Dragon is usually very outgoing and is particularly adept at attracting attention and publicity. He enjoys being in the limelight and is often at his best when he is confronted by a difficult problem or tense situation. In some respects he is a showman and he rarely lacks an audience. His views and opinions are very highly valued and he invariably has something interesting – and sometimes controversial – to say.

He has considerable energy and is often prepared to work long and unsocial hours in order to achieve what he wants. He can, however, be rather impulsive and does not always consider the consequences of his actions. He also has a tendency to live for the moment and there is nothing that riles him more than to be kept waiting. The Dragon hates delay and can get extremely impatient and irritable over even the smallest of hold-ups.

The Dragon has an enormous faith in his abilities, but he does run the risk of becoming over-confident and unless he is careful he can sometimes make grave errors of judgement. While this may prove disastrous at the time, he does have the tenacity and ability to bounce back and pick up the pieces again.

The Dragon has such an assertive personality, so much will-power and such a desire to succeed that he will often reach the top of his chosen profession. He has considerable leadership qualities and will do well in positions where he can put his own ideas and policies into practice. He is usually successful in politics, show business, as the manager of his own department or business, and in any job which brings him into contact with the media.

The Dragon relies a tremendous amount on his own judgement and can be scornful of other people's advice. He likes to feel self-sufficient and there are many Dragons who cherish their independence to such a degree that they prefer to remain single throughout their lives. However, the Dragon will often have numerous admirers and there are many who are attracted by his flamboyant personality and striking looks. If he does marry, he will usually marry young and will find himself particularly well suited to those born under the signs of the Snake, Rat, Monkey and Rooster. He will also find that the Rabbit, Pig, Horse and Goat make ideal companions and will readily join in with many of his escapades. Two Dragons will also get on well together, as they understand each other, but the Dragon may not find things so easy with the Ox and Dog, as both will be critical of his impulsive and somewhat extrovert manner. He will also find it difficult to form an alliance with the Tiger, for the Tiger, like the Dragon, tends to speak his mind, is very strong-willed and likes to take the lead.

The female Dragon knows what she wants in life and sets about everything she does in a very determined and positive manner. No job is too small for her and she is often prepared to work extremely hard until she has secured her objective. She is immensely practical and somewhat liberated. She hates being bound by routine and petty restrictions and likes to have sufficient freedom to be able to go off and do what she wants to do. She will keep her house tidy but is not one for spending hours on housework – there are far too many other things that she feels are more important and that she prefers to do. Like her male counterpart, she has a tendency to speak her mind.

The Dragon usually has many interests and enjoys sport and other outdoor activities. He also likes to travel and often prefers to visit places that are off the beaten track rather than head for popular tourist attractions. He has a very adventurous streak in him and providing his financial circumstances permit – and the Dragon is usually sensible with his money – he will travel considerable distances during his lifetime.

The Dragon is a very flamboyant character and while he can be demanding of others and in his early years rather precocious, he will have many friends and will nearly always be the centre of attention. He has charisma and so much confidence in himself that he can often become a source of inspiration for others. In China he is the leader of the carnival and he is also blessed with an inordinate share of luck.

THE FIVE DIFFERENT TYPES OF DRAGON

In addition to the 12 signs of the Chinese zodiac, there are five elements and these have a strengthening or moderating influence on the sign. The effects of the five elements on the Dragon are described below, together with the years in which the elements were exercising their influence. Therefore all Dragons born in 1940 are Metal Dragons, those born in 1952 are Water Dragons, and so on.

Metal Dragon: 1940
This Dragon is very strong-willed and has a particularly forceful personality. He is energetic, ambitious and tries to be scrupulous in his dealings with others. He can also be blunt and to the point and usually has no hesitation in

speaking his mind. If people disagree with him, or are not prepared to co-operate, he is more than happy to go his own way. The Metal Dragon usually has very high moral values and is held in great esteem by his friends and colleagues.

Water Dragon: 1952

This Dragon is friendly, easy-going and intelligent. He is quick-witted and rarely lets an opportunity slip by. However, he is not as impatient as some of the other types of Dragon and is more prepared to wait for results rather than expect everything to happen that moment. He has an understanding nature and is prepared to share his ideas and co-operate with others. His main failing, though, is a tendency to jump from one thing to another rather than concentrate on the job in hand. He has a good sense of humour and is an effective speaker.

Wood Dragon: 1904, 1964

The Wood Dragon is practical, imaginative and inquisitive. He loves delving into all manner of subjects and can quite often come up with some highly original ideas. He is a thinker and a doer and has sufficient drive and commitment to put many of his ideas into practice. He is more diplomatic than some of the other types of Dragon and has a good sense of humour. He is very astute in business matters and can also be most generous.

Fire Dragon: 1916, 1976

This Dragon is ambitious, articulate and has a tremendous desire to succeed. He is a hard and conscientious worker and is often admired for his integrity and forthright nature. He is very strong-willed and has considerable leadership qualities. He can, however, rely a bit too much on his own judgement and fail to take into account the views and feelings of others. He can also be rather aloof and it would certainly be in his own interests to let others join in more with his various activities. The Fire Dragon usually gets much enjoyment from music, literature and the arts.

Earth Dragon: 1928, 1988

The Earth Dragon tends to be quieter and more reflective than some of the other types of Dragon. He has a wide variety of interests and is keenly aware of what is going on around him. He also has clear objectives and usually has no problems in obtaining support and backing for any of his ventures. He is very astute in financial matters and is often able to accumulate considerable wealth. He is a good organizer, although he can at times be rather bureaucratic and fussy. He mixes well with others and has a large circle of friends.

PROSPECTS FOR THE DRAGON IN 1999

The Chinese New Year starts on 16 February 1999. Until then, the old year, the Year of the Tiger, is still making its presence felt.

The Year of the Tiger (28 January 1998 to 15 February 1999) will have been a positive one for the Dragon and in what remains of it he can still accomplish a great deal. The Tiger year is one which supports innovation and enterprise and this will be very much to the Dragon's advantage. In the remaining months of the year he should actively promote his ideas and skills and if he sees any chance of advancement, no matter how small, he should pursue it. The period from September to November 1998 can be an especially important time for the Dragon's work and by taking advantage of the opportunities that become available, he could improve his situation, either by taking on further responsibilities or by attaining a new position.

In all he does, though, the Dragon should remain mindful of the views of those around him and of any advice he is given. Admittedly the Dragon has a tendency to do things his own way, and independently, but sometimes others can point out things he might have overlooked as well as provide tips and information which can be to his benefit.

In addition to the positive aspects concerning the Dragon's work, financial matters too will go well. However, the Dragon must not allow any financial good fortune to lull him into a false sense of complacency and become careless or extravagant in his spending. He should also be wary of any risky ventures that he might come across. This is a good time for money matters, but he cannot push his Dragon luck too far. Also, with the closing stages of the year being a traditionally expensive time, it would certainly be to the Dragon's advantage to monitor all he spends so that he can make adequate provision for this later.

Domestically and socially, however, the Dragon will be on top form and in the latter part of the Tiger year he can look forward to many enjoyable and meaningful occasions with his family and friends. For the unattached Dragon or for those seeking new friends, there will be a marked upturn from mid October onwards.

Generally, the Tiger year will be an active and positive time for the Dragon and in his usual resourceful and inimitable way, he is certain to get much of value from it, added to which, his personal life will bring him considerable pleasure.

The Year of the Rabbit starts on 16 February and will be a quiet but generally pleasant year for the Dragon. After the activity of the last 12 months it will provide a useful period of respite, allowing the Dragon to take stock of his present position and consider his future plans. The following year, 2000, is the Dragon's own year and holds great significance for him. What he accomplishes and sets in motion in 1999 will do much to prepare the way for the excellent trends he is soon to experience.

In his work the Dragon will be able to make reasonable headway, although his progress and level of achievement may not always be as great as he would like. Over the year there will be times when he will need to exercise patience as well as have obstacles to overcome. For the keen and ambitious Dragon, this could prove frustrating. However, annoying though this may be at the time, some of the delays and problems will turn out to be blessings in disguise. In some cases they will act as a brake on the Dragon and prevent him from being too hasty, thereby giving him a chance to think his plans through and to organize his activities.

Those Dragons who have recently moved to a new position or taken on different duties would do well to use this year to familiarize themselves with their new responsibilities, as well as take up any opportunity to add to their experience. Dragons who are seeking work or are dissatisfied with their present position should also keep alert for any openings to pursue. The quest for a new position may not always be as easy or as straightforward as the Dragon would like, but with determination he will eventually get what he wants. The months from March to early June could be significant for work matters, also the closing quarter of the year.

In addition to gaining experience in his work, if the Dragon feels he would benefit from acquiring a new skill, particularly if it would help him towards his future goals, he should take steps to attain it. The Rabbit year does favour academic matters and self-improvement and anything the Dragon can do now to enhance his prospects will be very much to his advantage as well as bring him considerable personal satisfaction.

Those Dragons in education will also make good progress over the year and could find that a new subject they take up will develop in an interesting way, possibly even influencing their future vocation. However, if he has important exams over the year, the Dragon would do well to set about his revision in a systematic way rather than leave everything to the last moment. Also, if he has any worries or problems concerning any educational matter, he should speak of his concerns to others rather than struggle on unaided. As he will find, those around are keen to help.

As far as financial matters are concerned, the Dragon will enjoy a modest upturn in his fortunes this year. Many Dragons will benefit from an increase in income and those who may have been experiencing financial problems will find that these gradually ease during the course of the year. The Dragon could also find that one of his special skills or interests could become quite lucrative and, if promoted, could develop in an encouraging manner. What the Dragon sets in motion during the Rabbit year will often bear sizeable fruit in the months and years ahead.

The Dragon's domestic life will generally go well. He can look forward to many meaningful times with his loved ones and will take much satisfaction in helping and encouraging them with their interests. Similarly, he too will be grateful for the support and advice he receives and would do well to listen closely to their views. They do, after all, speak with his best interests at heart. Also, if there is any matter that is particularly concerning him, he should let his feelings be known rather than keep them to himself. He will often find in 1999 that frank and open discussion will be more helpful than bottling up anxieties and pressures.

To help maintain the good relations and rapport he so values, the Dragon would also do well to encourage activities that all can enjoy, especially at busy or stressful times. A family treat, such as a trip or meal out, will be much appreciated and will help relieve any tension that might have built up. The Dragon's own interests, too, can be an important source of relaxation and he should not only devote adequate time to these but also encourage those around to join in. Travel too is favourably aspected and any family holidays or lengthy journeys the Dragon takes over the year will work out well, with his chosen destination often surpassing expectations.

The Dragon's social life will bring him considerable pleasure, with many opportunities on offer to meet others and attend some interesting parties and events. The spring months in particular will be an active time and for Dragons who are unattached or who would like additional friends, the period from April to June could prove auspicious. A romance started during the year could, in time, become significant.

Overall, the Dragon will fare well in the Rabbit year. Admittedly he may not realize all his aims, but he will gain much valuable experience and this, together with what he does achieve and the plans he makes, will help prepare the way for the excellent progress he will make in 2000. For the Dragon, the Rabbit year is, in many ways, a prelude to the better times ahead.

As far as the different types of Dragon are concerned, 1999 will be a significant year for the *Metal Dragon*. In recent times the Metal Dragon will have accomplished much and the Rabbit year will give him the opportunity to reap the rewards of his endeavours and savour some of what he has achieved. In many cases he will receive an additional financial sum for what he has carried out or find he now has more time for leisure pursuits. In either case he would do well to decide just what he intends to do with this extra benefit. With travel generally well aspected, he could find this is a good year to visit places he has longed to see or to arrange to meet up with relations or friends who live some distance away. Any holiday or break the Metal Dragon is able to take will bring him much pleasure as well as proving beneficial for him and those he goes with. The Metal Dragon is also likely to spend a great deal on his accommodation over the year, either in carrying out alterations or in moving. In this he should consider his options carefully and take his time rather than acting too hastily. Where considerable financial outlay is involved he should obtain several quotations and make sure he is aware of all the costs and obligations before proceeding. Fortunately, his usually shrewd nature will help avert problems, but this is not a year for complacency. Generally, the Metal Dragon will be pleased with how accommodation matters work out, but whether they involve alterations, redecoration or moving, he must allow adequate time and be prepared to be patient (not one of the Metal Dragon's strong points!) Another well aspected area concerns the Metal Dragon's own interests and he should make sure he sets a regular time aside for these. He could find it especially fulfilling to extend an existing interest in some way, perhaps by learning about a different aspect of it, or to take up a new one. Either way, his interests will provide him with many hours of pleasure and for those Metal Dragons who are creatively inclined or who enjoy outdoor pursuits, the year will hold many rewarding moments. The Rabbit year will also be significant for work matters and the Metal Dragon is likely to take several important decisions during it. Some Metal Dragons will choose to retire while others will see important, though sometimes initially daunting, changes in their duties. In both cases the Rabbit year will provide the Metal Dragon with fresh challenges and it rests with him to make the most of the situations in which he finds himself. In fact, with his diverse talents and tenacious nature, he is likely to enjoy rising to some of the challenges given him and will be able to set in motion ideas, projects or plans he has been contemplating for some time. He will also take much pleasure in his domestic and social life and can look forward to many happy and meaningful times with those around him. Over the year he will be well supported in his activities and when important decisions have to be taken, he should listen carefully to the views of those around him. Similarly, if he feels he can help and advise a close and younger relation who may be in a dilemma or have some problem to deal with, he should do so. Although the Metal Dragon may not want to appear interfering, his advice and interest will be appreciated and judgement respected. On a social level this will be a highly favourable year, with many pleasurable occasions to look forward to, particularly in the spring and summer. Any Metal Dragons who are seeking new friends or who have recently moved to a new area will soon find themselves building up a new and active social life if they go out and join in with group activities. Generally, the aspects will support the Metal Dragon well in 1999. However, to get the best from the year he needs to look positively at the opportunities that it will bring and to use his time wisely. Much of what he accomplishes now will have far-reaching implications and will help prepare the way for the even more improved times that await him in 2000.

This will be a year that the *Water Dragon* will greatly enjoy. After the activity of the previous 12 months, he will be able to adjust to any changes that have taken place and consolidate any gains made. If he has taken on new duties in his work he should concentrate on learning about them and rising to the new challenges, even though they may initially prove daunting. By giving of his best he will do much to impress and will add to his experience and this will help his progress in the latter part of 1999 and over the next year. The Water Dragon would also do well to take advantage of any training opportunities that become available to him and, if he feels he needs a particular skill or qualification, he should take steps to obtain it. He would do well to look on 1999 as a year for self-improvement and for widening his experience, with the results of his endeavours coming over the next few years. Those Water Dragons seeking work should remain active in following up any opportunities that become available and try not to get too discouraged by any disappointments. With every application he makes the Water Dragon will add to his experience and at some time in 1999 – perhaps when he least expects it – his quest will be rewarded. Again, if these Water Dragons find themselves eligible for training, they should follow this up as it could do much to enhance their long-term prospects. The Water Dragon will also enjoy good fortune in financial matters and would do well to consider putting any money he does not immediately need towards his future. Savings or investments made during the year could develop into a useful asset. The Water Dragon will also enjoy several strokes of luck in 1999 and should enter any competition that catches his eye – the Rabbit year will spring several surprises on the Water Dragon and winning a competition could be one of them! Domestically, this will be an active year for the Water Dragon, with some important events taking place. These could be a wedding in his family, the birth of a grandchild or someone moving out of his home, perhaps for the purposes of further education. This may cause moments of pressure, even anguish, but at the same time there will be much that will bring the Water Dragon pride and personal satisfaction. Also, if at any time he feels too great a burden is being placed on him, particularly with regard to household tasks, he should not hesitate to seek additional assistance. Others will be glad to help if asked. With work and domestic matters taking up much of his time, the Water Dragon may sometimes feel he is not always able to devote himself to his own interests or to socialize as much as he would like. However, it is vital he does not neglect these areas. His interests and social life do provide an important source of relaxation for him and to drive himself too hard without any respite could leave him tired, sometimes dispirited and also susceptible to minor ailments. Water Dragons, do take careful note. It could also be to the Water Dragon's advantage to consider taking up some form of exercise, particularly if he is sedentary for much of the day. Some additional walking, swimming or cycling could all prove beneficial for him and if he is reliant on convenience food, a more balanced diet could also help his well-being. Generally, 1999 will be an interesting year for the Water Dragon. Admittedly it may bring challenges, particularly in his work, but what he is able to achieve, together with any additional skills he is able to acquire, will do much to prepare for the marvellous opportunities and progressive times that lie ahead next year.

The *Wood Dragon* has much in his favour. He has a clear idea of where his chief talents lie and uses them and his time wisely. In addition, with his outgoing and amiable manner he is able to get on well with others. These abilities have enabled him to achieve a great deal and enjoy successes of which he can be truly proud. However, there are still many ambitions and goals that the Wood Dragon would like to attain, as well as ideas he is eager to try out. In 1999 he should give serious thought to what he wishes to accomplish next and discuss his ideas with those in a position to give informed advice. Then, having decided upon his objectives, he should set about achieving them. The ideas he formulates and plans he sets in motion now will have significant and far-reaching implications. Indeed, for some Wood Dragons, the Rabbit year will be one of the turning-points of their lives, a time when they instigate changes and prepare for new challenges ahead. Much of this planning will concern the Wood Dragon's career prospects and if there is a particular position he is seeking or type of work he would like to take up, maybe even an enterprise of his own, he would do well to look into this closely and take those all-important initial steps. Also, if he feels he needs additional training or experience in order to attain his objectives, he should take steps to attain this. What he is able to learn and accomplish now will stand him in good stead and he will find his efforts well rewarded, particularly with the progressive trends that await him at the end of the Rabbit year and in 2000. Those Wood Dragons seeking work could also enjoy several positive developments over the year and a position they obtain could turn out to be that all-important stepping-stone to greater things. The Wood Dragon will also fare well in financial matters and this will enable him to carry out some plans he has had involving the redecoration and refurnishing of his accommodation. In addition, any Wood Dragon who is building up a collection and has a penchant for art or antiques could, by keeping alert, make an excellent and unusual acquisition over the year. The Wood Dragon's home life too will bring him much pleasure and he will take considerable satisfaction in following and encouraging the activities of those around him. In particular, the progress of a younger relation will be a source of considerable delight. Throughout the year the Wood Dragon will be grateful for the support he receives from his loved ones and at all times will find it helpful to be open and forthcoming about his ideas, plans and activities. By doing so, he will be given much useful advice as well as be alerted to possible problems or snags he may have overlooked. On a social level the Wood Dragon can look forward to attending several interesting, and sometimes prestigious, social functions as well as enjoying some meaningful times with his friends. The summer will be a particularly active time for social matters and any Wood Dragon who may be feeling lonely or who would like additional company will enjoy a dramatic upturn in his fortunes, with new friendships and romance being well aspected. The Wood Dragon would also do well to consider taking up a new hobby or interest over the year, ideally something different from anything he has done before. He will not only enjoy the challenge this gives him, but will also find that it will add to his knowledge and could teach him some new and potentially useful skills. Generally, 1999 will be a positive year for the Wood Dragon, with some of what he starts now having important implications for the future. The Wood Dragon knows he has it within him to accomplish a great deal and in 1999 he will be preparing himself for what promises to be a new and important chapter in his life, one which will start late in 1999 and develop at a rapid pace in 2000.

This will be an interesting year for the *Fire Dragon* with much going in his favour. Personally it will hold some special and memorable times for him, with romance and new friendships to the fore. Many Fire Dragons will meet their future partner over the year, get engaged or married or see an addition to their family. The Fire Dragon himself will be in splendid form, helping to make this a memorable and enjoyable year. His social life, in particular, will bring him great pleasure and the many Fire Dragons who will find themselves moving and living in a new area will soon find themselves striking up new friendships. With his friendly and outgoing manner, the Fire Dragon is sure to impress. Any Fire Dragon who may have had a recent setback or adversity would do well to try and draw a line under this and regard the Rabbit year as the start of a new phase in his life. Indeed, with the glittering times that await him next year, this is but the start of a truly positive period for the Fire Dragon. Over the year, in addition to the favourable aspects in his personal life, he will make constructive progress in his work. In this, he should consolidate any gains he has recently made and concentrate on learning about the different aspects of his work. If there are any training courses he can go on or ways in which he can extend his skills, he should follow these up. What he learns and gains in experience now will do much to help his future prospects. Those Fire Dragons seeking work should also remain persistent. Admittedly it may take several attempts to get what they want but with each application they will be adding to their experience and improving their technique and presentation. Also, many Fire Dragons will find that the position they already have or one that they gain over the year will open up new possibilities for them, with the chance of promotion or different duties coming towards the end of the year. However, in his activities the Fire Dragon should be prepared to work closely with others rather than retain too independent an attitude. Admittedly, as a Fire Dragon he does have a tendency to set about things in his own way and to keep his own counsel, but in this and the next few years, better progress will be made by acting in conjunction with others. The Fire Dragon would also be helped by being forthcoming about his longer term objectives and seeking out those with experience in his chosen field. By doing so he will be given much useful advice as well as impress others with his foresightedness and initiative. As a Fire Dragon he has the abilities and ambition to make much of his life and in 1999 he will do much to lay the foundations for the success that lies ahead.

As far as financial matters are concerned, the Fire Dragon could face some large expenses concerning his accommodation and will need to watch his level of spending closely. With care, he should be able to avoid problems, but this is not a year for taking undue risks or for stretching his resources without making sure he can meet any obligations he is placed under. The Fire Dragon should also deal carefully with any important forms or paperwork he receives, particularly any related to his accommodation, and if he has any doubts about what is being asked of him, he should seek advice rather than jump to conclusions. Failure to do so could result in misunderstandings as well as waste a considerable amount of time. Overall, though, the Fire Dragon will fare well in the Rabbit year. He will make constructive progress in his work and do much to lay the foundation for the even better times ahead, while personally the year holds much promise, with the spring and latter part of the year being especially well aspected.

This will be a pleasant year for the *Earth Dragon*, with most areas of his life bringing contentment and satisfaction. As far as his family life is concerned, he will take much interest in following the progress and activities of those around him, as well as providing valuable support and encouragement to family members. Indeed, his views and judgement are highly regarded and several times over the year others will come to him for advice which, as always, he will be glad to give. He, too, will benefit from the support he receives for his own activities and throughout the year should be forthcoming over any plans he wishes to carry out as well as any concerns he might have. Just as others will benefit from his advice, so he too will gain from their input. The Earth Dragon will also spend time over the year in carrying out practical projects on his accommodation. In this he should involve others rather than try to do too much on his own. Not only will the project benefit from the pooling of talents, but it will also become all the more meaningful for all concerned. The Earth Dragon does, however, need to exercise care when moving heavy or bulky items and should take precautions when tackling anything of a complex nature. When in doubt he should seek assistance. The projects that he does carry out will do much to enhance his home and generally domestic and family matters will bring him considerable pleasure over the year. In addition, the Earth Dragon will get much satisfaction from his hobbies and interests, especially any which allow him to use and extend his creative skills or which take him out of doors. As the Rabbit year also favours cultural pursuits, if there is a subject that has been intriguing the Earth Dragon, he would do well to follow it up now; he could find it will provide him with a stimulating challenge and one which will lead to some absorbing and satisfying times. Those Earth Dragons born in 1988 could see some important changes over the year, which could include changing schools and starting a new range of subjects. While this will cause moments of anxiety, they will soon settle down, make new friends and acquit themselves well. Throughout the year they should also remember that if they have any problems or uncertainties there are many around who can help. As far as financial matters are concerned, this will be a generally favourable year, with many Earth Dragons receiving an additional sum of money, sometimes from an unexpected source. This will not only allow the Earth Dragon to enjoy some well deserved treats, but also to make some useful acquisitions for himself and his home. Those Earth Dragons who are collectors or who have a liking for art and antiques could make an attractive and reasonably priced purchase in the most unlikely of places. The Earth Dragon's good taste and eye for a bargain will certainly serve him well! Generally, this will prove a most satisfying year for the Earth Dragon and he will be content with what he achieves and with the many happy hours spent in the company of his friends and loved ones and in pursuing his interests.

FAMOUS DRAGONS

Clive Anderson, Maya Angelou, Jeffrey Archer, Joan Baez, Michael Barrymore, Count Basie, Pat Benatar, St Bernadette, James Brown, Neneh Cherry, James Coburn, Bing Crosby, Roald Dahl, Salvador Dali, Charles Darwin, Neil Diamond, Bo Diddley, Matt Dillon, Christian Dior, Frank Dobson, Placido Domingo, Fats Domino, Faye Dunaway, Prince Edward, Bruce Forsyth, Sigmund Freud, James Garner, Sir John Gielgud, Graham Greene, Che Guevara, David Hasselhoff, Sir Edward Heath, Joan of Arc, Tom Jones, Imran Khan, Martin Luther King, John Lennon, Abraham Lincoln, Queen Margrethe II of Denmark, Yehudi Menuhin, François Mitterrand, Bob Monkhouse, Hosni Mubarak, Florence Nightingale, Nick Nolte, Al Pacino, Elaine Paige, Gregory Peck, Pele, Sir Cliff Richard, Smokey Robinson, George Bernard Shaw, Ringo

Starr, Dave Stewart, Karlheinz Stockhausen, Mr T, Shirley Temple, Johnny Weissmuller, Raquel Welch, Mae West, Robin Williams, Frank Zappa.

4 FEBRUARY 1905 ～ 24 JANUARY 1906		*Wood Snake*
23 JANUARY 1917 ～ 10 FEBRUARY 1918		*Fire Snake*
10 FEBRUARY 1929 ～ 29 JANUARY 1930		*Earth Snake*
27 JANUARY 1941 ～ 14 FEBRUARY 1942		*Metal Snake*
14 FEBRUARY 1953 ～ 2 FEBRUARY 1954		*Water Snake*
2 FEBRUARY 1965 ～ 20 JANUARY 1966		*Wood Snake*
18 FEBRUARY 1977 ～ 6 FEBRUARY 1978		*Fire Snake*
6 FEBRUARY 1989 ～ 26 JANUARY 1990		*Earth Snake*

THE
SNAKE

THE PERSONALITY OF THE SNAKE

Be the change you want to see in the world.
— *Mahatma Gandhi: a Snake*

The Snake is born under the sign of wisdom. He is highly intelligent and his mind is forever active. He is always planning and always looking for ways in which he can use his considerable skills. He is a deep thinker and likes to meditate and reflect.

Many times during his life he will shed one of his famous Snake skins and take up new interests or start a completely different job. The Snake enjoys a challenge and he rarely makes mistakes. He is a skilful organizer, has considerable business acumen and is usually lucky in money matters. Most Snakes are financially secure in their later years provided they do not gamble – the Snake has the distinction of being the worst gambler in the whole of the Chinese zodiac!

The Snake generally has a calm and placid nature and prefers the quieter things in life. He does not like to be in a frenzied atmosphere and hates being hurried into making a quick decision. He also does not like interference in his affairs and tends to rely on his own judgement rather than listen to advice.

The Snake can at times appear solitary. He is quiet, reserved and sometimes has difficulty in communicating with others. He has little time for idle gossip and will certainly not suffer fools gladly. He does, however, have a good sense of humour and this is particularly appreciated in times of crisis.

The Snake is certainly not afraid of hard work and is thorough in all that he does. He is very determined and can occasionally be ruthless in order to achieve his aims. His confidence, will-power and quick thinking usually ensure his success, but should he fail it will often take a long time for him to recover. He cannot bear failure and is a very bad loser.

The Snake can also be evasive and does not willingly let people into his confidence. This secrecy and distrust can sometimes work against him and it is a trait which all Snakes should try to overcome.

Another characteristic of the Snake is his tendency to rest after any sudden or prolonged bout of activity. He burns up so much nervous energy that without proper care he can – if he is not careful – be susceptible to high blood pressure and nervous disorders.

It has sometimes been said that the Snake is a late starter in life and this is mainly because it often takes him a while to find a job with which he is genuinely happy. However, the Snake will usually do well in any position which involves research and writing and where he is given sufficient freedom to develop his own ideas and plans. He makes a good teacher, politician, personnel manager and social adviser.

The Snake chooses his friends carefully and, while he keeps a tight control over his finances, he can be particularly generous to those he likes. He will think nothing of buying expensive gifts or treating his friends or loved ones to the best theatre seats in town. In return he demands loyalty. The Snake is very possessive and he can become extremely jealous and hurt if he finds his trust has been abused.

The Snake is also renowned for his good looks and is never short of admirers. The female Snake in particular is most alluring. She has style, grace and excellent (and usually expensive) taste in clothes. A keen socializer, she is likely to have a wide range of friends and has a happy knack of impressing those who matter. She has numerous interests and her advice and opinions are often highly valued. She is generally a calm-natured person and while she involves herself in many activities, she likes to retain a certain amount of privacy in her undertakings.

The affairs of the heart are very important to the Snake and he will often have many romances before he finally settles down. He will find that he is particularly well suited to those born under the signs of the Ox, Dragon, Rabbit and Rooster. Provided he is allowed sufficient freedom to pursue his own interests, he can also build up a very satisfactory relationship with the Rat, Horse, Goat, Monkey and Dog, but he should try to steer clear of another Snake as they could very easily become jealous of each other. The Snake will also have difficulty in getting on with the honest and down-to-earth Pig, and will find the Tiger far too much of a disruptive influence on his quiet and peace-loving ways.

The Snake certainly appreciates the finer things in life. He enjoys good food and often takes a keen interest in the arts. He also enjoys reading and is invariably drawn to subjects such as philosophy, political thought, religion or the occult. He is fascinated by the unknown and his enquiring mind is always looking for answers. Some of the world's most original thinkers have been Snakes, and – although he may not readily admit it – the Snake is often psychic and relies a lot on intuition.

The Snake is certainly not the most energetic member of the Chinese zodiac. He prefers to proceed at his own pace and to do what he wants. He is very much his own master and throughout his life he will try his hand at many things. He is something of a dabbler, but at some time – usually when he least expects it – his hard work and efforts will be recognized and he will invariably meet with the success and the financial security which he so much desires.

THE FIVE DIFFERENT TYPES OF SNAKE

In addition to the 12 signs of the Chinese zodiac, there are five elements and these have a strengthening or moderating influence on the sign. The effects of the five elements on the Snake are described below, together with the years in which the elements were exercising their influence. Therefore all Snakes born in 1941 are Metal Snakes, those born in 1953 are Water Snakes, and so on.

Metal Snake: 1941

This Snake is quiet, confident and fiercely independent. He often prefers to work on his own and will only let a privileged few into his confidence. He is quick to spot opportunities and will set about achieving his objectives with an awesome determination. He is astute in financial matters and will often invest his money well. He also has a liking for the finer things in life and has a good appreciation of the arts, literature, music and good food. He usually has a small group of extremely good friends and can be generous to his loved ones.

Water Snake: 1953

This Snake has a wide variety of interests. He enjoys studying all manner of subjects and is capable of undertaking quite detailed research and becoming a specialist in his chosen area. He is highly intelligent, has a good memory, and is particularly astute when dealing with business and financial matters. He tends to be quietly spoken and a little reserved, but he does have sufficient strength of character to make his views known and attain his ambitions. He is very loyal to his family and friends.

Wood Snake: 1905, 1965

The Wood Snake has a friendly temperament and a good understanding of human nature. He is able to communicate well with others and often has many friends and admirers. He is witty, intelligent and ambitious. He has numerous interests and prefers to live in a quiet, stable

environment where he can work without too much interference. He enjoys the arts and usually derives much pleasure from collecting paintings and antiques. His advice
is often very highly valued, particularly on social and
domestic matters.

Fire Snake: 1917, 1977

The Fire Snake tends to be more forceful, outgoing and
energetic than some of the other types of Snake. He is
ambitious, confident and never slow in voicing his opinions
– and he can be very abrasive to those he does not like. He
does, however, have many leadership qualities and can win
the respect and support of many with his firm and resolute
manner. He usually has a good sense of humour, a wide
circle of friends and a very active social life. The Fire Snake
is also a keen traveller.

Earth Snake: 1929, 1989

The Earth Snake is charming, amusing and has a very
amiable manner. He is conscientious and reliable in his
work and approaches everything he does in a level-headed
and sensible way. He can, however, tend to err on the
cautious side and never likes to be hassled into making a
decision. He is extremely adept in dealing with financial
matters and is a shrewd investor. He has many friends and
is very supportive towards the members of his family.

PROSPECTS FOR THE SNAKE IN 1999

The Chinese New Year starts on 16 February 1999. Until then, the old year, the Year of the Tiger, is still making its presence felt.

The Year of the Tiger (28 January 1998 to 15 February 1999) will have been a challenging one for the Snake and he will have felt ill at ease with some of its events. The Tiger year is often characterized by activity and change and the Snake is very definitely one who prefers to proceed at a steadier and more reasoned pace. However, while the Tiger year will have brought moments of pressure and anxiety, it can still prove a positive and useful time for the Snake.

Certainly, the activity of the year will have helped keep the Snake on his toes rather than have allowed him to drift or develop a sense of malaise. In many cases this will have given him the added impetus to take action or decisions he might have been putting off. Sometimes the Snake does need such an incentive to get on and what he sets in motion during the Tiger year will certainly stand him in good stead for the more positive Year of the Rabbit.

In what remains of the Tiger year, though, the Snake should remain committed to his duties and objectives, take careful note of all that is happening around him and be prepared to make the most of the situations in which he finds himself. He would also do well to take advantage of any training opportunities or ways in which he can extend his experience, as this could prove useful to him over the next year.

Although the Snake is usually adept at dealing with financial matters, he does need to exercise care in the Tiger year. He should avoid unnecessary risks and be dubious about any 'get rich quick' schemes or speculative ventures that he may hear about. All is not as straightforward as it may appear and without care money could all too easily be lost.

More positively, however, the Snake can look forward to some pleasant and meaningful times with his family and friends, with the last quarter of the year being especially positive for personal matters. For the unattached Snake, a new friendship made in the latter part of the Tiger year could develop in a significant way over the next 12 months.

With the active and sometimes challenging nature of the Tiger year, it is also important that the Snake takes good care of himself. If he does not get much daily exercise, he could find some additional activity will do much to help his well-being. He should also allow time for his hobbies and interests, as these help him to unwind and restore lost energy, and this, for the Snake, is important.

The Tiger year may not have been the best of years for the Snake but in many cases its events will be far-reaching, as will become apparent in the next Chinese year.

The Year of the Rabbit begins on 16 February and will be a greatly improved one for the Snake. Although it will be busy, and sometimes demanding, the Snake will find himself more in control of events and will be able to set about his activities in a more systematic way. The Rabbit year will also give the Snake the opportunity to pursue some of his long-cherished ambitions and will therefore contain some truly fulfilling times for him.

In his work the Snake will make good progress. Although the events of the last year could have left him feeling unsettled and a little undecided about his future, in 1999 he will fare much better. As the Rabbit year starts the Snake will decide to make a conscious effort to overcome some of the obstacles that have been holding him back and 'make up lost ground'. He will find that by setting about his activities with a greater resolve and commitment he will be able to accomplish a considerable amount as well as enjoy a good level of success.

For Snakes who are keen to change their present work or who have a project or idea they would like to carry out, 1999 is the time to set about achieving this. As the old saying goes, 'There is no time like the present' and if the Snake wants results, he must act. In much of what he does this year, the aspects will support him well. The months from February to May are particularly encouraging for work matters and the Snake should remain alert for opportunities at this time or even see if he can create some himself. He possesses a fertile mind and in 1999 some of the ideas he comes up with will bring pleasing results.

Many of those Snakes seeking work will also be successful in their quest over the year. Admittedly there will be occasions when they get disheartened, but with each fresh application they will be adding to their experience and will eventually find that their persistence will be rewarded. Again, the early months of the year will hold some interesting possibilities, as will the months from September to early December.

The Year of the Rabbit also favours cultural activities and is an ideal year for the Snake to extend his current hobbies and skills. With his inquiring mind, there could well be certain subjects that have been intriguing him and left him wanting to find out more. This would be a good year in which to do so. Similarly, those Snakes with creative and artistic interests should aim to further their talents as well as promote any work they produce. Positive effort on their part could lead to an encouraging response but, as with most things in 1999, the initiative to act and make the most of his skills does rest with the Snake himself. For those who have the necessary drive, 1999 promises to be an exciting and progressive year.

The Snake is also very adept when dealing with matters of finance and in the Rabbit year these skills will bring him some notable successes. A carefully chosen savings scheme or investment could work out particularly well for him and he will also enjoy an increase in his income over the year. However, while an upturn in his financial situation is strongly indicated, the Snake must not permit his usually careful nature to slip and should avoid highly speculative ventures. If he has any doubts about a scheme, he would do well to avoid it or to obtain further details and clarification. Indeed, he will find it is better and safer for him to concentrate in financial areas that he does understand rather than take risks. He will, however, decide to spend a considerable amount on his accommodation over the year, particularly on furnishings and changing the decor. In this, though, he would do well to take his time and compare what is available. By doing so he will often end up with superior items, sometimes at more advantageous prices, than if he were to act too hastily. For household and practical projects the months of April, May, September and October are favoured.

Both domestically and socially this will be an active year for the Snake. He can look forward to many rewarding times with his family and will take much satisfaction in helping and encouraging them. He will also gain much by involving those around him in his own activities, particularly with regard to his own hobbies and interests, rather than keeping them his own preserve. Sometimes the Snake may feel that others are not interested in what he does, but such is not the case and by being more forthcoming he will be pleasantly surprised by their genuine concern. As far as personal interests are concerned, this will be a rich and rewarding year for the Snake.

In addition to the many pleasurable times the Snake will have with his family, travel is favourably aspected and a holiday he takes could surpass expectations, especially if to a destination he has not visited before.

The Snake's social life too will be busier than usual and for the unattached, a friendship started in the Tiger year or early in 1999 could develop in a meaningful way. Romance is truly well aspected and the year will certainly contain some enjoyable times. The Snake will also attend some interesting social parties and functions and these will allow him to extend his circle of friends and acquaintances. Even though the Snake is something of a private individual, by relaxing his reserve he will enjoy himself that much more.

However, while the Snake can look forward to many pleasing times in 1999, there could be temptations which he could find hard to resist and if these involve him in any form of duplicity or leave him open to censure, he should beware. There is a risk that the Snake could find himself embroiled in an embarrassing and awkward affair which could undermine his situation. These words of warning will only apply to a small number of Snakes, but to avoid any difficulty, in 1999 the Snake should strive to be his usual honourable self.

Overall, though, this will be a positive and fulfilling year for the Snake. He may be one of the quieter signs of the Chinese zodiac, but behind his placid exterior his mind is alert, constantly planning and creating ideas, and he is keen to make the most of himself. The prevailing trends will certainly lead him to some notable achievements and he should seize the opportunities that the Year of the Rabbit will bring.

As far as the different types of Snake are concerned, this will be a significant year for the *Metal Snake*. Over the last 12 months many Metal Snakes will have felt frustrated with their present situation and their inability to carry out some of their plans. Sometimes they will have found conditions against them or that others were less than enthusiastic about what they had in mind. However, in 1999 the Metal Snake's fortunes will show a marked improvement and he will, in his true inimitable style, once again be able to make the most of his ideas and wide-ranging talents. Indeed, as the Rabbit year begins, the Metal Snake will start to feel more positive in his outlook and be determined to overcome any obstacles that may have been holding him back. His renewed resolve will be recognized and this will help him to make significant headway. At the start of the

Rabbit year the Metal Snake would do well to decide upon his priorities and what he most wants to achieve over the next 12 months. Then, having clarified his thoughts, he should act. As he will find throughout the year, by actively following through his ideas and seizing the opportunities that arise, much can be accomplished. As far as work matters are concerned, this will prove a most constructive year, with significant changes taking place. Some Metal Snakes will decide to retire or move to less demanding positions, which will enable them to devote more time to their own activities, while others will seek new duties and be successful in transferring to a different position. Either way, the Metal Snake will be instrumental in making the changes, rather than having them foisted on him; indeed, once he has set his mind on a certain course of action, he will not rest until he has achieved it. Such a sense of purpose will pay off and by the end of the year the Metal Snake will be truly satisfied with what he has been able to achieve. Also, with some important decisions and actions to be taken, the Metal Snake would do well to speak to others about his thoughts and ideas rather than keep them too much to himself. Although he does tend to be guarded, sometimes evasive, others can do much to help him and he will find that discussing his options will often help to clarify his own thoughts as well as allow him to gain from the input and advice that others are so willing to give. The Metal Snake will also enjoy some success in financial matters over the year and his shrewd and canny knack of sensing good investments and bargains will be as keen as ever. The one word of warning, though, is not to let any piece of financial good fortune lull him into a false sense of complacency and tempt him to push his luck too far or to take unwise risks. In 1999 the Metal Snake needs to remain his usual careful and disciplined self when dealing with financial matters. If so, he will do well. He will also obtain much satisfaction from his own personal interests and, if possible, should aim to develop them in some way, perhaps learning about another aspect or getting in contact with fellow enthusiasts. This particularly applies to those Metal Snakes who retire over the year. By devoting time to their interests, they can look forward to some fulfilling and absorbing times. Travel too is well aspected and any holidays and journeys the Metal Snake takes will work out well for him. He will also find this a good year to visit friends and relations he has not seen for some time. He will be generally pleased with his domestic and social life and can look forward to many meaningful occasions with both family and friends. However, to help make these all the more enjoyable he should make every effort to be more forthcoming and involve those around him more readily in his activities. He will also be grateful for the practical help he receives, especially when undertaking projects in his home. In particular, he should not hesitate to seek assistance or advice if he is about to tackle a complex or strenuous task; it is far better to be safe than sorry. Generally, this will be an important year for the Metal Snake and by going after his objectives and setting in motion his plans he will achieve much. The Metal Snake is a doer and an achiever and his enterprise and determination will be well rewarded, making this a successful and significant year.

Two of the main qualities of the *Water Snake* are that he is patient and persevering. He knows he has it within him to achieve a great deal and is prepared to work long and hard for his objectives, sometimes making many sacrifices in the process. In 1999 he will reap his rewards. His years of patience, effort and determination will now bring him considerable success; indeed, over the year many Water Snakes will achieve at least one long-held ambition. This is a year of progress and at the start of it the Water Snake should redouble his efforts in order to achieve his goals. If there are any ideas he has been hoping to set in motion, now is the time to do so, or, if he has any particular objectives he would like to attain, again he should act. This will be a truly progressive year for him and he should make the most of the trends that prevail. He should also follow up any opportunities and even see if he can create some for himself. Enterprising thinking on his part could lead to some interesting possibilities and throughout the Rabbit year the Water Snake will find considerable truth in the saying 'Nothing ventured, nothing gained'. In his work he will make significant strides and many Water Snakes will be promoted or attain a position they have been seeking for some time. Alternatively, if the Water Snake has felt that he has become staid in his present line of work and would benefit from new challenges, he should regard the Rabbit year as the time to make that change. By setting his mind on a certain goal and working purposefully towards it, he will find that he can attain it, such are the favourable aspects that prevail. Those Water Snakes seeking work should continue their quest for a position with resolve; again, their determination will be rewarded, perhaps in an unexpected and fortuitous way. In addition to the success and headway that the Water Snake achieves in his work, he will also enjoy an upturn in his financial situation over the year. As usual, he will handle financial matters with his typical skill, although it would be in his interests to maintain records of his outgoings and transactions as well as check statements. Failure to do so could cause him considerable inconvenience as well as sometimes involve him in additional and unnecessary expense. Record-keeping and bureaucratic matters, although sometimes burdensome, should not be neglected. This is something all Water Snakes should bear in mind during the year. Domestically and socially, this will, however, be a splendid year and the Water Snake can look forward to many meaningful and pleasurable occasions with both family and friends. He will take particular satisfaction in following and encouraging the progress of a younger relation and will delight in their achievements. However, while domestically this will be a good year, it will also be a busy one. Should the Water Snake feel under pressure, he should not hesitate to seek assistance from those around him. Similarly, if there is any matter giving him anxiety, rather than brood over it by himself, he should discuss his concerns with others. In some cases, he could find he has simply let the matter get out of proportion and, as with most aspects of his life in 1999, he will benefit from being more open and forthcoming. In view of the activity of the year it is also important that the Water Snake does not neglect his own personal interests, for they do provide him with a valuable and necessary source of relaxation. If he does not get much exercise during the day, he will find some additional walking or some other suitable and appropriate physical activity beneficial. Overall, though, this will be a successful year for the Water Snake and by promoting himself and going after his aims, he will do well and realize some of his most cherished ambitions. The Water Snake has many talents as well as useful experience behind him and in the Rabbit year he should aim to put these to good use.

This will be a positive and interesting year for the *Wood Snake*. Over the last few years much will have happened and the Wood Snake will have made some useful progress and gained valuable experience, although there will also have been times of anxiety and sometimes disillusionment. However, the Wood Snake will have learnt a lot about himself and his abilities as well as gained much from life's rich learning process, difficult though this may sometimes be. In 1999 he will be able to draw on this experience, having learnt from any mistakes and setbacks that may have occurred but now with his sights set firmly on the present and future – and what a promising future it will be! As the new Chinese year starts the Wood Snake should give serious thought to what he wishes to accomplish and then set about achieving this with his customary resolve. In his work he can make considerable progress, but to make the most of the aspects that prevail, he needs to be sure in his own mind of the direction in which he is heading. Without any such plan, there is a risk that he could drift through the year, miss some excellent opportunities and not make as much of himself or his talents as he otherwise could. Much is possible in 1999, but it rests with the Wood Snake to take the initiative and proceed in a purposeful manner. Throughout the year he should actively follow up any opportunities that he sees and if he wants promotion or to move to a different type of work, he should remain alert for openings to pursue. The early and closing months of the year will be particularly promising for work matters. The aspects will also support those Wood Snakes seeking work and again they should follow up any opportunities. Their determination will be rewarded and many will find that one position they attain, though it may be different from what they were originally seeking, will develop in an encouraging manner, allowing them to learn new skills and uncover talents they did not realize they possessed. In many cases, the Wood Snake's achievements in the Rabbit year will set the pattern for the next few years, making this an important turning-point in his professional life. Another well aspected area is finance and the Wood Snake can look forward to an improvement in his situation over the year. With this upturn he will decide to go ahead with some projects that he has been wanting to carry out on his accommodation as well as buy some new items of furnishing and equipment. By taking his time and comparing what is on offer, he will be able to make some tasteful and well-chosen purchases, sometimes at most advantageous prices. The Wood Snake's home life will bring him much contentment over the year and he can look forward to many pleasurable occasions with his loved ones. However, he would do well to fully involve them in his activities as well as be forthcoming about his ideas. By doing so he will receive much useful encouragement and advice. The Wood Snake will also give some valued assistance to a close relation over the year and his thoughtfulness and the time he so willingly gives will be more appreciated and of more benefit than he may realize at the time. He will also find himself much in demand with his friends over the year and can look forward to some enjoyable occasions in their company. For the unattached, a friendship made over the last few years could now become significant. The Wood Snake should also make sure that he sets a regular time aside for his hobbies and interests, as these do provide a useful break for him. He could find creative and outdoor pursuits particularly fulfilling. Similarly, he should try to make sure he takes a proper holiday over the year. With travel favourably aspected, this could be a good year to visit a destination he has had in mind for some time. Overall, this will be a positive year for the Wood Snake. By setting about his activities in a disciplined and purposeful manner, he will enjoy a good level of success, added to which, domestically and personally the year will contain some truly pleasurable times.

This is a year which holds considerable potential for the *Fire Snake*, although just how much he achieves is very much dependent upon his attitude. He certainly possesses many commendable talents – he is quick-witted and determined and has a tremendous faith in both himself and his abilities. Over the years these qualities will serve him well and enable him to achieve much, but he also has his weaknesses and in 1999 these could, if not checked, undermine his progress. In particular, the Fire Snake will need to show some flexibility in his outlook rather than hold rigidly to his current plans, especially where his work is concerned. In the Rabbit year several openings could emerge for him which may be interesting but might not fit in with his present aims. However, if he passes them by he could lose out on getting further experience as well as future opportunities that could arise from them. Over the year the Fire Snake needs to be adventurous in his outlook and prepared to take full advantage of the situations in which he finds himself rather than wait for more specific opportunities that might still be some way off. This also applies to those Fire Snakes seeking work. They will fare better by following a wide variety of openings than by being too restrictive in their quest. Indeed, many Fire Snakes will find that one position they attain could lead to a better one in a comparatively short space of time. As far as financial matters are concerned, this will be a reasonable year and any problems that the Fire Snake may have been experiencing will ease considerably during it. However, if the Fire Snake enters into any large agreement or transaction, particularly involving accommodation, he should make sure he is conversant with any obligations he may be placed under and that he allows for any additional outlay in his budget. To make the most of his finances does call for careful financial management. On a personal level, however, this will prove an important and enjoyable year for the Fire Snake with a good cause for celebration. Unattached Fire Snakes may meet their future partner or get engaged or married during the year, such are the positive aspects that prevail, while others may see an addition to the family. The Fire Snake will also be well supported by his family and friends, but would do well to listen carefully to their views and any advice he is given. Although he does like to keep his own counsel, he will gain much by being more forthcoming and reflecting carefully on all he is told. Those around him do have his best interests at heart and some advice from a more senior relation will prove most pertinent as the year unfolds. The Fire

Snake will also get much satisfaction from the travelling he undertakes as well as from the time he devotes to his hobbies and interests. Outdoor pursuits will prove especially enjoyable and for Fire Snakes who engage in or follow sport, the year will contain some rewarding times. In most respects, 1999 will be a positive year for the Fire Snake. By taking advantage of the opportunities that the year will bring, even though these sometimes might be different from those he is seeking, he will make worthwhile progress, gain experience and stature and do much to advance his future prospects. Also, on a personal level, the year will bring him much happiness, with romance and his relations with others being particularly well aspected.

This will be a pleasing year for the *Earth Snake* with most of his activities going well. Several changes will take place over the year and while at the time these will put extra pressure on the Earth Snake, in the long term they will work in his best interests. Many of the Earth Snakes born in 1989 will change their school or class and start a new range of subjects. These may give the young Earth Snake moments of anxiety, particularly as he so wants to please and rise up to the expectations placed upon him. However, his worries will often be misplaced. With his diligent approach the Earth Snake will soon settle down and tackle the tasks given him. Indeed, he will find he will learn more and do better by being given more challenging work than by everything being kept on a comparatively simple level. Also, if he does have any uncertainties or worries, he should not hesitate to seek advice and guidance. As he will find, others can do much to assist and reassure. Those Earth Snakes born in 1929 will also see some important changes taking place during the year, mainly affecting their accommodation. Some of these Earth Snakes will move while others will decide to have alterations carried out to their home. In either case, the Earth Snake should proceed in his usual careful and measured way, considering and costing all the options available. The one thing he should avoid is acting too hastily or taking decisions with some uncertainties still in his mind. Time is on his side and he should only act or enter into agreements once he is sure of the right course of action. If he does so, by the end of the year he will be pleased with how the decisions that he has taken have worked out. The Earth Snake will, in any case, be well supported and advised by those close to him and should he have any doubts or concerns he should not hesitate to seek the opinions of those around him or, in the case of important forms and transactions, professional advice. The Earth Snake will also take much satisfaction in his hobbies and interests over the year, particularly any that allow him to draw on his creative talents. If he is able to extend a current interest in some way, perhaps by writing about it for fellow enthusiasts, he will find this will add to his pleasure as well as provide another outlet for his talents. The Earth Snake's domestic and social life will also go well and he can look forward to many meaningful times with his family and friends. In addition to the support he receives for his activities, he will take great delight in following the progress of some younger relations and any assistance and advice he feels able to give will be greatly appreciated. Those Earth Snakes who do move over the year and find themselves living in a new area, as well as those who are looking to build new friendships or have suffered some recent adversity, should make every effort to go out more and involve themselves in societies and special interest groups or join in with group-oriented activities. By taking action they will soon find themselves meeting others and forming what will become good friendships. The initiative does rest with the Earth Snake himself, but he will find that positive action on his part will lead to pleasing results. He will also enjoy any travelling that he undertakes and will benefit from any holiday or breaks he is able to go on. Overall, this will be an interesting year for the Earth Snake, with most of his activities bringing him pleasure and satisfaction. He will be well supported and advised in what he does and the changes that occur, disruptive though they may be at the time, will mostly work out in his favour and to his longer term advantage.

FAMOUS SNAKES

Muhammad Ali, Ann-Margret, Yasser Arafat, Paddy Ashdown, Ronnie Barker, Kim Basinger, Bjork, Tony Blair, William Blake, Heinrich Böll, Michael Bolton, Betty Boothroyd, Brahms, Pierce Brosnan, Casanova, Chubby Checker, Tom Conti, Randy Crawford, Jim Davidson, Bob Dylan, Elgar, Sir Alexander Fleming, Henry Fonda, Mahatma Gandhi, Greta Garbo, Art Garfunkel, J. Paul Getty, Dizzy Gillespie, W. E. Gladstone, Goethe, Princess Grace of Monaco, Stephen Hawking, Nigel Hawthorne, Audrey Hepburn, Jack Higgins, Paul Hogan, Michael Howard, Howard Hughes, Isabelle Huppert, Liz Hurley, James Joyce, Stacy Keach, Howard Keel, J. F. Kennedy,

Carole King, James Last, Cindi Lauper, Courtney Love, Dame Vera Lynn, Linda McCartney, Nigel Mansell, Mao Tse-tung, Robert Mitchum, Nasser, Bob Newhart, Alfred Nobel, Ryan O'Neal, Mike Oldfield, Aristotle Onassis, Jacqueline Onassis, Pablo Picasso, Mary Pickford, Brad Pitt, André Previn, Helen Reddy, Griff Rhys Jones, Franklin D. Roosevelt, Jean-Paul Sartre, Franz Schubert, Brooke Shields, Paul Simon, Delia Smith, John Thaw, Dionne Warwick, Charlie Watts, Ruby Wax, Oprah Winfrey, Victoria Wood, Virginia Woolf, Susannah York.

25 JANUARY 1906 ～ 12 FEBRUARY 1907 *Fire Horse*

11 FEBRUARY 1918 ～ 31 JANUARY 1919 *Earth Horse*

30 JANUARY 1930 ～ 16 FEBRUARY 1931 *Metal Horse*

15 FEBRUARY 1942 ～ 4 FEBRUARY 1943 *Water Horse*

3 FEBRUARY 1954 ～ 23 JANUARY 1955 *Wood Horse*

21 JANUARY 1966 ～ 8 FEBRUARY 1967 *Fire Horse*

7 FEBRUARY 1978 ～ 27 JANUARY 1979 *Earth Horse*

27 JANUARY 1990 ～ 14 FEBRUARY 1991 *Metal Horse*

THE
HORSE

THE PERSONALITY OF THE HORSE

To reach a port, we must sail – sail, not tie at anchor – sail,
not drift.

– Franklin Delano Roosevelt: a Horse

The Horse is born under the signs of elegance and ardour.
He has a most engaging and charming manner and is
usually very popular. He loves meeting people and likes
attending parties and other large social gatherings.

He is a lively character and enjoys being the centre of
attention. He has considerable leadership qualities and is
much admired for his honest and straightforward manner.
He is an eloquent and persuasive speaker and has a great
love of discussion and debate. The Horse also has a particularly agile mind and can assimilate facts remarkably
quickly.

He does, however, have a fiery temper and although his
outbursts are usually short-lived, he can often say things
which he will later regret. He is also not particularly good
at keeping secrets.

The Horse has many interests and involves himself in a
wide variety of activities. He can, however, get involved in
so much that he can often waste his energies on projects
which he never has time to complete. He also has a tendency to change his interests rather frequently and will
often get caught up with the latest craze or 'in thing' until
something better or more exciting turns up.

The Horse also likes to have a certain amount of
freedom and independence. He hates being bound by petty

rules and regulations and as far as possible likes to feel that he is answerable to no one but himself. But despite this spirit of freedom, he still likes to have the support and encouragement of others in his various enterprises.

Due to his many talents and likeable nature, the Horse will often go far in life. He enjoys challenges and is a methodical and tireless worker. However, should things work against him and he fail in any of his enterprises, it will take a long time for him to recover and pick up the pieces again. Success to the Horse means everything. To fail is a disaster and a humiliation.

The Horse likes to have variety in his life and he will try his hand at many different things before he settles down to one particular job. Even then, he will probably remain alert to see whether there are any new and better opportunities for him to take up. The Horse has a restless nature and can easily get bored. He does, however, excel in any position which allows him sufficient freedom to act on his own initiative or which brings him into contact with a lot of people.

Although the Horse is not particularly bothered about accumulating great wealth, he handles his finances with care and will rarely experience any serious financial problems.

The Horse also enjoys travel and he loves visiting new and far-away places. At some stage during his life he will be tempted to live abroad for a short period of time and, due to his adaptable nature, he will find that he will fit in well wherever he goes.

The Horse pays a great deal of attention to his appearance and usually likes to wear smart, colourful and rather distinctive clothes. He is very attractive to the opposite sex and will often have many romances before he settles down. He is loyal and protective to his partner, but, despite his family commitments, still likes to retain a certain measure of independence and have the freedom to carry on with his own interests and hobbies. He will find that he is especially well suited to those born under the signs of the Tiger, Goat, Rooster and Dog. The Horse can also get on well with the Rabbit, Dragon, Snake, Pig and another Horse, but he will find the Ox too serious and intolerant for his liking. The Horse will also have difficulty in getting on with the Monkey and the Rat – the Monkey is very inquisitive and the Rat seeks security, and both will resent the Horse's rather independent ways.

The female Horse is usually most attractive and has a friendly, outgoing personality. She is highly intelligent, has many interests and is alert to everything that is going on around her. She particularly enjoys outdoor pursuits and often likes to take part in sport and keep-fit activities. She also enjoys travel, literature and the arts, and is a very good conversationalist.

Although the Horse can be stubborn and rather self-centred, he does have a considerate nature and is often willing to help others. He has a good sense of humour and will usually make a favourable impression wherever he goes. Provided he can curb his slightly restless nature and keep a tight control over his temper, he will go through life making friends, taking part in a multitude of different activities and generally achieving many of his objectives. His life will rarely be dull.

THE FIVE DIFFERENT TYPES OF HORSE

In addition to the 12 signs of the Chinese zodiac, there are five elements, and these have a strengthening or moderating influence on the sign. The effects of the five elements on the Horse are described below, together with the years in which the elements were exercising their influence. Therefore all Horses born in 1930 and 1990 are Metal Horses, those born in 1942 are Water Horses and so on.

Metal Horse: 1930, 1990
This Horse is bold, confident and forthright. He is ambitious and also a great innovator. He loves challenges and takes great delight in sorting out complicated problems. He likes to have a certain amount of independence and resents any outside interference in his affairs. The Metal Horse has charm and a certain charisma, but he can also be very stubborn and rather impulsive. He usually has many friends and enjoys an active social life.

Water Horse: 1942
The Water Horse has a friendly nature, a good sense of humour, and is able to talk intelligently on a wide range of topics. He is astute in business matters and quick to take advantage of any opportunities that arise. He does, however, have a tendency to get easily distracted and can change his interests – and indeed his mind – rather

frequently, and this can sometimes work to his detriment. He is nevertheless very talented and can often go far in life. He pays a great deal of attention to his appearance and is usually smart and well turned out. He loves to travel and also enjoys sport and other outdoor activities.

Wood Horse: 1954

The Wood Horse has a most agreeable and amiable nature. He communicates well with others and, like the Water Horse, is able to talk intelligently on many different subjects. He is a hard and conscientious worker and is held in high esteem by his friends and colleagues. His opinions and views are often sought and, given his imaginative nature, he can quite often come up with some very original and practical ideas. He is usually widely read and likes to lead a busy social life. He can also be most generous and often holds high moral viewpoints.

Fire Horse: 1906, 1966

The element of Fire combined with the temperament of the Horse creates one of the most powerful forces in the Chinese zodiac. The Fire Horse is destined to lead an exciting and eventful life and to make his mark in his chosen profession. He has a forceful personality and his intelligence and resolute manner bring him the support and admiration of many. He loves action and excitement and his life will rarely be quiet. He can, however, be rather blunt and forthright in his views and does not take kindly to interference in his own affairs or to obeying orders. He is a flamboyant character, has a good sense of humour and will lead a very active social life.

Earth Horse: 1918, 1978

This Horse is considerate and caring. He is more cautious than some of the other types of Horse, but he is wise, perceptive and extremely capable. Although he can be rather indecisive at times, he has considerable business acumen and is very astute in financial matters. He has a quiet, friendly nature and is well thought of by his family and friends.

PROSPECTS FOR THE HORSE IN 1999

The Chinese New Year starts on 16 February 1999. Until then, the old year, the Year of the Tiger, is still making its presence felt.

The Year of the Tiger (28 January 1998 to 15 February 1999) is one which is characterized by change and activity and, for the most part, this will have suited the Horse. With his diligence, adventurous outlook and keenness to pursue new ideas, he will have found many interesting opportunities to pursue. In his work the Horse will have made good progress, perhaps taking on new and more varied responsibilities or switching to a different type of position. Even as the Tiger year draws to a close, further opportunities will emerge which the ever-eager Horse can turn to his advantage.

There is, however, one cautionary note that the Horse should bear in mind. Although he can accomplish much in the Tiger year, he should decide upon his immediate priorities and concentrate on these rather than over-commit himself or spread his energies too widely. The closing stages of the Tiger year can be a productive time, but the best results will come from an organized and systematic approach.

The Tiger year will, however, be an expensive time for the Horse and further expense is indicated in the closing months of the year. At this time, the Horse should watch his level of outgoings and exercise a certain restraint. Otherwise he could find he has spent more than he anticipated and could start the next Chinese year having to make some cutbacks. From October 1998 to the end of the Tiger year, financial matters do require care.

More positively, however, the Horse's domestic and social life will be a source of considerable pleasure and he will find himself much in demand with those around him. There will be parties, functions and social occasions to attend as well as the chance of meeting relations and friends he has not seen for some time. For the unattached Horse, romance continues to be strongly aspected right to the end of the year.

The Tiger year is a positive time for the Horse and he should take full advantage of the progressive aspects that prevail. For the earnest and industrious Horse, this can prove a most fulfilling and rewarding time.

The Year of the Rabbit starts on 16 February and will be a valuable one for the Horse. Although the Rabbit year may not always have the activity and bustle of the previous 12 months, it will allow the Horse to consolidate any recent gains he may have made, add to his experience and make pleasing progress. In addition, the Horse's personal life is favourably aspected.

As far as his professional life is concerned, the Rabbit year will offer the Horse several excellent opportunities to progress. However, to make the most of these aspects, the Horse would do well to concentrate on areas in which he is most familiar rather than launch into new and radically different ventures. If he attains a new position, or has recently taken one up, he should apply himself to learning his new duties rather than looking to move on quickly. Sometimes this may mean the Horse has to quench his restless spirit, but progress will come from solid and persistent application rather than from hasty and impulsive moves. Also, by concentrating on areas in which he is most skilled, the Horse is more likely to impress those around him, including those with influence, and this too will be to his advantage. Indeed, the Rabbit year will offer the Horse every opportunity to display his true worth and develop, but at the same time this does require patience, persistence and self-discipline on his part.

The Horse also needs to keep himself informed of all the developments around him as well as of the views of his colleagues. Sometimes, through his independent and self-willed nature, he tends to distance himself from what is going on or remain set on doing things in his own way, but to make progress he does need to work closely with others and show himself willing to involve them in his activities. To maintain a go-it-alone attitude could undermine his progress. If the Horse bears this in mind then he will do much to enhance his position and reputation during the year, with the second half of 1999 holding some particularly interesting developments for him.

Those Horses seeking work should also remain committed in their quest. They should not only continue to follow up any openings that they see but also consider the various ways in which they can put their training, experience and skills to good use. Some innovative thinking could open up interesting possibilities for them which may develop further over the year.

Overall, the Rabbit year is an encouraging time for the Horse with the months of March and April and the period from September to the end of the Rabbit year being especially positive for work matters.

Financial matters are also reasonably well aspected and many Horses will enjoy a noticeable improvement in their situation, especially in the second half of the year. With this upturn, the Horse would do well to think about what he wishes to do with any additional money he may have rather than allow it to slip through his fingers. He could, for instance, make some purchases in the home furnishings line which will greatly add to the comfort and decor of his home. Similarly, he would do well to set some money aside for any holidays and breaks that he may wish to take, as travelling too will bring him much pleasure over the course of the year. By managing his money in a careful way, the Horse will be able to make some pleasing and carefully considered purchases, enjoy himself and be generally satisfied with his financial situation.

As far as his domestic life is concerned, this too will be a pleasurable year, with the Horse taking much delight in the activities and successes of family members. Any encouragement he feels able to give will be greatly appreciated and, as always, his judgement and advice will be highly regarded. There will also be some notable family occasions over the year which will be a source of much pride to the Horse, with the summer months being a particularly active and rewarding time.

To preserve domestic harmony and good relations with those around him, the Horse would, though, do well to involve others in his activities and projects rather than carry them out single-handed. Admittedly he does like to retain a certain independence, but he will find that encouraging greater family involvement will do much to maintain the spirit of camaraderie that is so necessary for good relations. Similarly, if he faces any important decisions over the year, again he would find it helpful to discuss his options with those around him rather than mull them over just by himself.

The Horse can also look forward to a pleasing social life, with the summer and closing months of the year being times of great activity. There will be parties and other social gatherings he will enjoy attending and he can also look forward to some pleasurable occasions with his friends. For those Horses who have recently moved, who are for some reason feeling low or dispirited, or who would like to establish a new social life, the aspects will support them well. However, to take advantage of these trends, the Horse will need to take the initiative and make an effort to get in contact with others, perhaps by joining a local interest group or society. With his engaging manner and broad interests, he will soon find himself enjoying an upturn in his social life, but it does rest with him to take those all-important initial steps.

However, one of the more awkwardly aspected areas of the year is romance. This particularly applies to the younger and unattached Horse. Although there will be plenty of opportunities to meet others, the Horse would do well to let any new friendship or romance develop in its own time rather than rush into a commitment or build up high expectations too quickly. This way the friendship is more likely to be based upon a secure foundation and this could prevent subsequent anguish or heartbreak. Young Horses, take note! Enjoy the year, enjoy the company of those you meet, but avoid undue haste. Existing relationships and romances formed before the Rabbit year should continue to bring the Horse much joy, but for those formed in 1999, a certain care is needed.

The Horse's personal interests and hobbies will go well during the year, bringing him much satisfaction. He could also find that an existing interest will develop in an unexpected manner, bringing possible remuneration as well as credit for his skills and knowledge. This especially applies to those Horses who are musically, artistically or creatively inclined. In addition to the pleasure his interests give him, the Horse should also take advantage of any travel opportunities. Any holiday and break he is able to arrange – sometimes at short notice – will work out well.

Although the Rabbit year will be a quieter year than some, it will nevertheless bring the Horse much satisfaction. His personal life will generally go well and he will feel more inspired by the tasks and challenges given him, which in turn will lead to some positive achievements, some of which will have lasting value and far-reaching implications.

As far as the different types of Horse are concerned, 1999 will be a year which the *Metal Horse* will greatly enjoy. Most aspects of his life are well aspected, although to get the best from the year he would do well to consider what he would like to accomplish over the next 12 months. In particular he should consider any interests he is keen to develop, projects he would like to carry out or places he would like to visit. Then, having decided upon certain objectives, he should set his plans in motion. As he will find, by organizing and setting about his activities in a purposeful manner he will achieve much as well as make the year all the more satisfying. In planning his activities, the Metal Horse would do well to involve those around him and listen carefully to their views. Although he is strong and independent-minded and does have a fondness for doing things his own way, he really will gain a great deal of value from the input, advice and suggestions of others, as well as benefit from the practical assistance he is given. His personal interests and hobbies will prove most fulfilling and the Metal Horse should aim to set a regular time aside for them as well as consider ways of developing them. Some Metal Horses may consider writing about a long-held interest, passing on their knowledge to fellow enthusiasts, and this, in itself, could become another outlet for their talents. Also, if there has been a subject that has been intriguing the Metal Horse or a skill he would like to acquire, then this would be an excellent year in which to take this up, perhaps by enrolling on a suitable course.

Another well-aspected area is travel and all Metal Horses should take advantage of any opportunity to go away. They will find the holidays and breaks they take most pleasurable, especially any to destinations they have not visited before and which appeal to their liking of the unusual. On a domestic level, the Metal Horse will take much interest in following the activities of those around him and will take particular pride at the achievements of a younger relation. Several times during the year he will be prompted to give advice, and in some cases words of caution, and while he may not wish to appear interfering, his obvious concern will be appreciated. Indeed, others do think highly of the Metal Horse's judgement and will set great store by his views during the year. The Metal Horse will also busy himself with several projects on his home and garden. While he will be content with the finished result, he should be wary of rushing projects or of undertaking complex tasks for which he does not have the necessary experience or knowledge. If in doubt, he should seek professional advice. The Metal Horse will, however, enjoy an active social life in 1999, with the early summer and the closing months of the year being especially pleasing periods in which he will be able to spend time with his friends, renew acquaintances and attend various social gatherings. He will also enjoy good fortune in financial matters. Over the year many Metal Horses will receive an additional sum, either for work carried out in the past or as the fruition of an investment. However, the Metal Horse should think carefully about what to do with any extra money rather than be tempted into too many hasty spending sprees. Indeed, as with most of his activities, the more he plans, the better he will fare. Those Metal Horses born in 1990 will make pleasing headway in their education and if there is an additional subject or interest they wish to take up, this would be an ideal year in which to do so. For those who are musically inclined, this too would be a favourable year in which to further their skill or perhaps take up an instrument. However, while the year is well aspected for the Metal Horse, one potentially awkward area concerns bookkeeping and bureaucratic matters. Although the Metal Horse may sometimes lose patience with such matters, to be neglectful of or pay scant attention to important paperwork could lead to problems, protracted correspondence and even additional expense. Metal Horses, take note and do not let this spoil an otherwise pleasant and favourable year.

This will be a significant year for the *Water Horse*, offering him much scope to follow up ideas he has been considering as well as to come to important decisions about his future. However, to benefit from these supportive trends, at the start of the year the Water Horse would do well to reflect on his present position and on any changes he would like to bring about. Then, once he has clarified his thoughts, he should take steps to achieve his objectives. Positive action on his part will lead to some far-reaching results, but the initiative rests with him. When planning his activities he would also find it helpful to bear in mind the old saying 'There is no time like the present' rather than to delay too much in the hope of opportunities and openings that might still be some way off. The Water Horse's plans could concern almost any sphere of his life, from his work or accommodation to his interests or some personal objective, but whichever area he selects, important consequences will ensue. As far as his work is concerned, this will be a significant year, with changes indicated. Some Water Horses will be able to advance their position through promotion or taking on new duties while others will opt to take less onerous duties in order to develop other interests, with some even deciding to pursue their own business ideas. However, before taking any major and irrevocable decision, the Water Horse should discuss his options with those around him, seeking professional advice if need be. Once he is satisfied about the right course to take, then he should proceed. As far as work matters are concerned, the decisions and actions he takes now will often have far-reaching consequences. The Water Horse's domestic life will bring him much satisfaction. There will be times of great joy over the year, including possibly the birth of a grandchild or some other good cause for celebration, but there will also be matters that may give him concern. However, when he does have any anxieties, the Water Horse will find it helpful to be forthcoming and discuss these openly rather than allow them to linger in the background and mar an otherwise pleasing year. Some Water Horses will consider moving in 1999 and for those that do, it would be in their interests to proceed at a measured pace, taking the time to view and consider places they would like to live in rather than rush too hastily into any transaction. By the end of the year the Water Horse will be well pleased with how events have worked out, but he must allow himself time and be patient. Also, although financial matters are favourably aspected, it is important he checks the cost and terms of any important transaction or purchase that he enters into. Without such vigilance, he could find the cost greater than it need be. The Water Horse could, however, enjoy success with an investment that he makes in 1999 as well as have a stroke of good fortune in a competition that he enters. His social life and personal interests too will provide him with considerable pleasure and for any Water Horse who finds himself with additional time at his disposal, it really would be to his advantage to further a current interest or consider learning a new skill. By using his leisure time in a pleasurable but constructive way he will find himself enjoying some truly absorbing and fulfilling times. Overall, this will be an important year for the Water Horse, with some of the decisions he takes and plans he sets in motion now affecting the next few years. However, he will be well supported in all he does and should not hesitate to involve those around him in his activities as well as seek their views. He will be reassured and encouraged by the support he is given and heartened by the obvious affection others have for him. With his determined spirit and many fine skills, the Water Horse will not let them down.

The *Wood Horse* will enjoy much of the year, particularly as he will be able to progress at a steady rate as well as develop some long-held ideas. In his work he will have impressed others with his diligent and conscientious nature and this will lead to him being given additional responsibilities over the year. Although there may be occasions when he is daunted by some of what is asked of him, as well as by his workload, he will acquit himself well, gain valuable experience and do much to further his longer term prospects. In addition to their regular duties, many Wood Horses will also be encouraged to follow up some ideas of their own and this will bring them much personal satisfaction. The Wood Horse does possess a truly fertile mind and throughout the year he should take advantage of any opportunity he gets to promote his ideas, skills and any plans he may have been nurturing. Those Wood Horses who are hoping to change their present position or are seeking work will also fare well over the year. In their quest they would do well to reflect upon their strengths and accomplishments and consider different ways in which they can use their skills. Again, some innovative thinking could considerably widen the scope of positions they could try for and one they attain could develop in a significant manner over the next few years. The Wood Horse will also enjoy good fortune in financial matters and will see a noticeable upturn in his situation. If he feels in a position to make some investments or savings, these could build into a useful asset and be something he is grateful that he made now rather than later. He should also make sure that he sets a regular time aside for his hobbies and interests, as these will provide an important break from his usual daily preoccupations and will bring him much satisfaction over the year. Many Wood Horses will also decide to carry out some work on their home, particularly redecoration, and while this may sometimes take longer than envisaged, they will take pleasure in the finished result. As far as his domestic life is concerned, this will be an active year for the Wood Horse, with a variety of matters requiring his attention. There will be times of much happiness, but also matters that may cause him anguish and anxiety. Fortunately many of these will not be as bad as originally feared, but if there is anything that is particularly troubling the Wood Horse he should not hesitate to speak of his concerns to those around him as well as to his many good friends. Over the year he will find much truth in the saying 'A worry shared is a worry halved'. Also, if he feels too much is expected of him, especially with many household chores mounting up, he should ask for assistance. Help will be readily forthcoming. However, busy though his home life may sometimes be, the Wood Horse can look forward to many meaningful occasions with those around him and will find joint interests and projects will bring him and his loved ones much pleasure. Travel, too, is favourably aspected and all Wood Horses would do well to ensure they take a proper holiday over the year, ideally visiting an area new to them. They will not only find such destinations of great interest but will also benefit from the rest. Also, if the Wood Horse does not get much exercise during the day, he would do well to consider walking more or taking up swimming, cycling or some similarly suitable activity. This can do much to help his well-being and general level of fitness. Overall, however, the Wood Horse will be well satisfied with how events work out over the year. He has the skills and ideas to make much of himself and he will fare well in most of what he does.

The aspects will support the *Fire Horse* well in 1999 but to make the most of the year he needs to set about his activities in a disciplined and organized manner. The Fire Horse has wide interests and this, together with his tremendous energy, can sometimes lead him into pursuing a multitude of different activities at the same time as well as over-committing himself. Without a certain care, he could find he is involved in a great many things but is not making the progress he is capable of or would like. Throughout the year the Fire Horse should stick with his priorities and resist the sometimes great temptation of getting distracted into other and less important activities. With his enthusiasm, keen and alert mind and many good ideas, however, he will impress in his work and this will lead him to being given additional responsibilities. If he is currently dissatisfied with his current duties, is seeking work or wanting to broaden his experience, he should remain alert for opportunities to pursue. A positive and committed approach will bring him success and almost all Fire Horses will be able to substantially improve on their position over the year. Looking to the Fire Horse's long-term future, if there is a certain skill or qualification that he feels he needs in order to progress he should take steps to obtain it now, either by additional study or by enrolling on a training course. By taking positive action he will be doing much to enhance his prospects as well as obtaining personal satisfaction from what he learns and accomplishes. Indeed, the Rabbit year particularly supports matters connected with learning and self-improvement and the Fire Horse would do well to bear this in mind, particularly in view of some of his longer term ambitions. The Fire Horse will also enjoy a substantial upturn in his finances over the year and this will allow him to buy some equipment and items for himself and his home that he has been considering for some time. However, before proceeding with any large purchase, he would do well to check several different outlets and compare the prices and ranges on offer before making his final purchase. To rush large transactions could lead to him regretting his actions later, especially if he finds he could have got better and more suitable products else-where. He would also do well to consider making some provision for his future and in later years could be grateful for a savings plan started now. Similarly, a carefully chosen investment made over the year could yield a handsome profit but, if the Fire Horse does enjoy financial success, he should not allow this to tempt him into any risky and speculative investments. Again, a certain self-discipline is needed. However, in addition to the positive aspects concerning his work and finances, the Fire Horse's do-mestic life will bring him pleasure. Although he will be kept busy with many demands upon his time, he will take considerable satisfaction in encouraging those around him with their various activities. He will also take delight in carrying out practical projects on his home and garden, although again he should be wary of engaging in too many projects at the same time. Better results will be achieved by concentrating on specific activities rather than by trying to do too much. The Fire Horse will, though, be well sup-ported by his family and friends and should not hesitate to seek their assistance with practical undertakings or their views on any important decisions; by doing so, he will receive much useful input. The Fire Horse can also look forward to attending some interesting and sometimes unexpected social functions over the year. These will not only be pleasurable occasions but will also allow him to add to his circle of friends and acquaintances. For any Fire Horses who may be feeling lonely and perhaps seeking romance, a chance meeting could, in time, become signifi-cant. However it would be wise for the Fire Horse to let any new friendship progress in its own time rather than to rush into a too hasty commitment. Again, patience has its virtues. Overall, this can be a constructive and generally pleasing year for the Fire Horse, but to make the most of the favourable trends that prevail, he needs to decide upon his priorities and concentrate on these rather than spread his energies too widely. For Fire Horses who can do this, 1999 will prove a significant year, with their achievements and the experience they gain doing much to assist their longer term prospects.

This is a year which holds considerable promise for the *Earth Horse*. Almost all areas of his life are well aspected and during the year he will see some important developments, many of which will be a source of much pride and satisfaction. On a personal level he will enjoy some happy and meaningful times with his friends and his social life will prove especially active, particularly over the summer months. For those Earth Horses who have a partner, the year will go well, with several pieces of good personal and joint news indicated. For those who are unattached or seeking new friends, there will be many opportunities to meet others, with the summer being a significant time. However, as with all Horses, the Earth Horse should let any new friendship develop gradually, allowing each side to get to know the other better. To rush into a commitment or build up high expectations after just a short time could put undue pressure on the friendship and possibly lead to problems and misunderstandings. Earth Horses, take note! For those Earth Horses who may be feeling dispirited or are discontent with their current social life, it really would be in their interests to take positive action to bring about an improvement. They could, for instance, join a local interest group or society or just generally go out more. Whatever they do, by taking the initiative their efforts will be rewarded and their social life will show a marked improvement. In addition to the positive aspects concerning the Earth Horse's personal life, academic matters are also strongly favoured. Those Earth Horses in education will make good progress, with the time they devote to their studies being well rewarded. For those particularly keen on extending their language skills or who would like to widen their experience by working in another country, this would be a good year in which to do so. Similarly, if any Earth Horse feels he would benefit from obtaining another skill or qualification, he should take steps to obtain it now. By doing so he will do much to improve his situation and prospects. As far as the Earth Horse's work is concerned, the year will hold out several interesting possibilities. Many Earth Horses will be given new and greater responsibilities or offered a different position, one which will allow them to usefully extend their experience. Indeed, what the Earth Horse achieves and learns over the year will stand him in good stead for the future. Many of those Earth Horses seeking work will be successful in obtaining a position over the year, although this could be substantially different from what they were originally seeking. However, while the Earth Horse might be surprised at this turn of events, he should look on the duties he is given as an interesting challenge and could discover talents he did not realize he possessed and which he can develop further. As far as the Earth Horse's finances are concerned, he will face many outgoings, particularly with his social life being so active. To avoid problems he will need to watch his spending carefully and at times of great expense make sure he makes proper allowance in his budget. If he is tempted to stretch his resources too far, without making adequate provision, he could find himself having to make cutbacks and modifications later in the year. Generally, however, the Earth Horse will enjoy the Year of the Rabbit, with many areas of his life bringing him great pleasure. In addition, what he accomplishes and gains in experience over the year will do much to enhance his future prospects.

FAMOUS HORSES

Neil Armstrong, Rowan Atkinson, Margaret Beckett, Samuel Beckett, Ingmar Bergman, Leonard Bernstein, Sir John Betjeman, Karen Black, Cherie Blair, Helena Bonham Carter, Eric Cantona, Ray Charles, Chopin, Sean Connery, Billy Connolly, Catherine Cookson, Ronnie Corbett, Elvis Costello, Kevin Costner, Cindy Crawford, Michael Crichton, James Dean, Kirk Douglas, Clint Eastwood, Thomas Alva Edison, Britt Ekland, Chris Evans, Harrison Ford, Aretha Franklin, Sir Bob Geldof, Samuel Goldwyn, Billy Graham, Gene Hackman, Rolf Harris, Rita Hayworth, Jimi Hendrix, Bob Hoskins, Ted Hughes, Janet Jackson, Neil Kinnock, Calvin Klein, Helmut Kohl, Lenin, Annie Lennox, Desmond Lynam, Paul McCartney, Nelson Mandela, Princess Margaret, Curtis Mayfield, Spike Milligan, Ben Murphy, Jimmy Nail, Sir Isaac Newton, Louis Pasteur, Ross Perot, Harold Pinter, J. B. Priestley, Puccini, Rembrandt, Ruth Rendell, Jean Renoir, Theodore Roosevelt, Helena Rubenstein, Sinatra, Peter Sissons, Lord

Snowdon, Alexander Solzhenitsyn, Lisa Stansfield, Barbra Streisand, Kiefer Sutherland, Patrick Swayze, John Travolta, Kathleen Turner, Mike Tyson, Vivaldi, Robert Wagner, Billy Wilder, Andy Williams, the Duke of Windsor, Steve Wright, Tammy Wynette, Boris Yeltsin, Michael York.

13 FEBRUARY 1907 ～ 1 FEBRUARY 1908   *Fire Goat*

1 FEBRUARY 1919 ～ 19 FEBRUARY 1920   *Earth Goat*

17 FEBRUARY 1931 ～ 5 FEBRUARY 1932   *Metal Goat*

5 FEBRUARY 1943 ～ 24 JANUARY 1944   *Water Goat*

24 JANUARY 1955 ～ 11 FEBRUARY 1956   *Wood Goat*

9 FEBRUARY 1967 ～ 29 JANUARY 1968   *Fire Goat*

28 JANUARY 1979 ～ 15 FEBRUARY 1980   *Earth Goat*

15 FEBRUARY 1991 ～ 3 FEBRUARY 1992   *Metal Goat*

THE
GOAT

THE PERSONALITY OF THE GOAT

Twenty years from now you will be more disappointed by the things that you didn't do than by the ones you did do. So throw off the bowlines. Sail away from the safe harbor. Catch the trade winds in your sails. Explore. Dream. Discover.

– Mark Twain: a Goat

The Goat is born under the sign of art. He is imaginative, creative and has a good appreciation of the finer things in life. He has an easy-going nature and prefers to live in a relaxed and pressure-free environment. He hates any sort of discord or unpleasantness and does not like to be bound by a strict routine or rigid timetable. The Goat is not one to be hurried against his will but, despite his seemingly relaxed approach to life, he is something of a perfectionist and when he starts work on a project he is certain to give of his best.

The Goat usually prefers to work in a team rather than on his own. He likes to have the support and encouragement of others and if left to deal with matters on his own he can get very worried and tends to view things rather pessimistically. Wherever possible he will leave major decision-making to others while he concentrates on his own pursuits. If, however, he feels particularly strongly about a certain matter or has to defend his position in any way, he will act with great fortitude and precision.

The Goat has a very persuasive nature and often uses his considerable charm to get his own way. He can, however, be rather hesitant about letting his true feelings be known and if he were prepared to be more forthright he would do much better as a result.

The Goat tends to have a quiet, somewhat reserved nature but when he is in company he likes he can often become the centre of attention. He can be highly amusing, a marvellous host at parties and a superb entertainer. Whenever the spotlight falls on him, his adrenalin starts to flow and he can be assured of giving a sparkling performance, particularly if he is allowed to use his creative skills in any way.

Of all the signs in the Chinese zodiac, the Goat is probably the most gifted artistically. Whether it is in the theatre, literature, music or art, he is certain to make a lasting impression. He is a born creator and is rarely happier than when occupied in some artistic pursuit. But even in this, the Goat does well to work with others rather than on his own. He needs inspiration and a guiding influence, but when he has found his true *métier*, he can often receive widespread acclaim and recognition.

In addition to his liking for the arts, the Goat is usually quite religious and often has a deep interest in nature, animals and the countryside. He is also fairly athletic and there are many Goats who have excelled in some form of sporting activity or who have a great interest in sport.

Although the Goat is not particularly materialistic or concerned about finance, he will find that he will usually be lucky in financial matters and will rarely be short of the necessary funds to tide himself over. He is, however, rather indulgent and tends to spend his money as soon as he receives it rather than make provision for the future.

The Goat usually leaves home when he is young but he will always maintain strong links with his parents and the other members of his family. He is also rather nostalgic and is well known for keeping mementoes of his childhood and souvenirs of places that he has visited. His home will not be particularly tidy but he knows where everything is and it will also be scrupulously clean.

Affairs of the heart are particularly important to the Goat and he will often have many romances before he finally settles down. Although he is fairly adaptable, he prefers to live in a secure and stable environment and will find that he is best suited to those born under the signs of the Tiger, Horse, Monkey, Pig and Rabbit. He can also establish a good relationship with the Dragon, Snake, Rooster and another Goat, but he may find the Ox and Dog a little too serious for his liking. Neither will he care particularly for the Rat's rather thrifty ways.

The female Goat devotes all her time and energy to the needs of her family. She has excellent taste in home furnishings and often uses her considerable artistic skills to make clothes for herself and her children. She takes great care over her appearance and can be most attractive to the opposite sex. Although she is not the most well organized of people, her engaging manner and delightful sense of humour create a favourable impression wherever she goes. She is also a good cook and usually gets much pleasure from gardening and outdoor pursuits.

The Goat can win friends easily and people generally feel relaxed in his company. He has a kind and understanding nature and although he can occasionally be stubborn, with the right support and encouragement he can live a happy and very satisfying life. The more he can use his creative skills, the happier he will be.

THE FIVE DIFFERENT TYPES OF GOAT

In addition to the 12 signs of the Chinese zodiac, there are five elements, and these have a strengthening or moderating influence on the sign. The effects of the five elements on the Goat are described below, together with the years in which the elements were exercising their influence. Therefore all Goats born in 1931 and 1991 are Metal Goats, those born in 1943 are Water Goats, and so on.

Metal Goat: 1931, 1991

This Goat is thorough and conscientious in all that he does and is capable of doing very well in his chosen profession. Despite his confident manner, he can be a great worrier and he would find it a help to discuss his worries with others rather than keep them to himself. He is loyal to his family and employers and will have a small group of extremely good friends. He has good artistic taste and is usually highly skilled in some aspect of the arts. He is often a collector of antiques and his home will be very tastefully furnished.

Water Goat: 1943

The Water Goat is very popular and makes friends with remarkable ease. He is good at spotting opportunities but does not always have the necessary confidence to follow them through. He likes to have security both in his home life and at work and does not take kindly to change. He is articulate, has a good sense of humour and is usually very good with children.

Wood Goat: 1955

This Goat is generous, kind-hearted and always eager to please. He usually has a large circle of friends and involves himself in a wide variety of different activities. He has a very trusting nature but he can sometimes give in to the demands of others a little too easily and it would be in his own interests if he were to stand his ground a little more often. He is usually lucky in financial matters and, like the Water Goat, is very good with children.

Fire Goat: 1907, 1967

This Goat usually knows what he wants in life and he often uses his considerable charm and persuasive personality in order to achieve his aims. He can sometimes let his imagination run away with him and has a tendency to ignore matters which are not to his liking. He is rather extravagant in his spending and would do well to exercise a little more care when dealing with financial matters. He has a lively personality, many friends and loves attending parties and social occasions.

Earth Goat: 1919, 1979

This Goat has a very considerate and caring nature. He is particularly loyal to his family and friends and invariably creates a favourable impression wherever he goes. He is reliable and conscientious in his work but he finds it difficult to save and never likes to deprive himself of any little luxury which he might fancy. He has numerous interests and is often very well read. He usually gets much pleasure from following the activities of various members of his family.

PROSPECTS FOR THE GOAT IN 1999

The Chinese New Year starts on 16 February 1999. Until then, the old year, the Year of the Tiger, is still making its presence felt.

The Year of the Tiger (28 January 1998 to 15 February 1999) will have been a demanding one for the Goat. There will have been times when he will have despaired of all he has had to do, of the demands placed upon him and of the decisions he has had to make. However, the Goat can take heart. As the challenging influence of the Tiger year begins to wane, a new and more settled period is about to begin and the prospects for the Goat in the next Chinese year are excellent.

In what remains of the Tiger year, the Goat should set about his activities in an organized manner and keep his commitments to a manageable level. Sometimes this may require him to be firm and refuse when asked to take on something else, but better this than finding himself under even greater pressure and having to rush tasks just to get them done.

The Goat's domestic life will be particularly active, with various household matters, together with the usual chores, to deal with. At busy times, he should not hesitate to ask for assistance from others as well as try to share out some of the tasks he has to do. Those around can offer much practical assistance, but sometimes the Goat will need to ask for the help that he requires rather than soldier on in silence. Busy though his home life may be, it will still provide him with much satisfaction, with November and December being two enjoyable and gratifying months. Similarly, his social life will go well, with the Goat finding himself much in demand, with a variety of parties and social functions to attend.

Work-wise, too, the Tiger year will have brought times of pressure, with a sometimes heavy workload and daunting responsibilities. However, the problems, and indeed successes, of the year will have provided the Goat with some valuable experience and learning opportunities and he will be able to put these to good use in the more favourable Rabbit year.

As the Tiger year draws to a close, the Goat would do well to make a concerted effort to deal with any outstanding tasks as well as any jobs he might have been putting off, both in his work and his personal activities. He will be pleasantly surprised with just how much he is able to complete and this will leave him freer to enjoy himself at the end of the year as well as remove some of the pressures he may have been under.

Although the Tiger year will have brought some

challenging moments for the Goat, it will still have contained opportunities for him to develop as well as have allowed him to learn more about himself and his abilities. As the new year approaches, the Goat will start to feel more optimistic about his situation and be more determined than ever to make the next year a far better one.

The Year of the Rabbit begins on 16 February and will be a much improved year for the Goat, allowing him to proceed at his own pace and to concentrate on his own concerns. He will feel more at ease with the congenial atmosphere of the Rabbit year and will achieve some noticeable successes over the next 12 months.

As the Rabbit year starts, the Goat would do well to take stock of the many events of the past year and consider how he would now like his life to progress. In view of some of what has occurred, he may have to modify some of his plans, but he will think of new and interesting possibilities, some of which hold great potential. In this time of assessment the Goat would also do well to discuss his thoughts with others and listen carefully to all he is told. Others do want to see him make the most of himself and his abilities and will give him some shrewd words of advice. The Goat should also seek out those who have already achieved whatever it may be that he would like to do, whether in a professional or some other capacity. By taking the initiative he will again be given some valuable suggestions.

In his work the Goat will make substantial progress. He should draw on the lessons of the last few years, avoiding any mistakes he may have made but building on what he has already achieved. He should also consider the different ways in which he can use his experience and skills. With his creative and innovative mind the Goat does have much to offer and the Rabbit year will give him the opportunity, although it does rest with him to take positive action to attain his goals rather than just wait for the right circumstances to arise. For the determined Goat, the rewards of the year can be considerable.

If he is hoping to change his current position or obtain experience in another type of work, the Goat should pursue any opportunities he sees as well as approach companies and organizations he would like to work for, particularly laying stress on his experience and ideas, and ways in which he feels he could make a positive contribution. Such action will lead to some interesting developments and very often a suggestion made or a position the Goat is given will develop in a significant manner and will have a positive bearing not only on this year but on the next few years as well. The months of March, April, June and November could all prove significant for work matters, bringing opportunities, the chance of increased responsibilities or other favourable developments.

Many of those Goats seeking work will find their quest for a position rewarded over the year, and sometimes in an unusual and fortuitous way. The Goat could be given tasks unlike anything he has ever done before and while initially daunting, this could lead to him acquiring new skills, discovering talents he did not realize he possessed and developing his career in a positive, if unexpected manner. The Rabbit year will hold some interesting possibilities for the Goat and he should take full advantage of the events that occur, particularly with so many being in his long-term interests.

For those Goats whose work involves the creative arts or allows them to draw on their creativity, the Rabbit year will contain some singular opportunities which will bring them deserved success and recognition. However, to make the most of these aspects, the Goat should do all he can to promote his work and further his skills. For those prepared to be bold and enterprising, great opportunities and successes await!

These pleasing aspects will also extend to the Goat's interests and hobbies and, over the year, he should ensure that he sets a regular time aside for these. His interests will not only prove most fulfilling, but will also allow him to rest and unwind and will provide a valuable break from his usual everyday concerns. Again, any interests that draw on the Goat's creative talents will bring him especial pleasure and for those Goats who may have literary, artistic or musical aspirations, this would be an excellent year in which to bring their talents to a wider audience. Although some Goats may feel some reticence, even shyness, in promoting themselves, all Goats would do well to remember the old saying 'Nothing ventured, nothing gained'.

In addition to the satisfaction he will obtain from his interests over the year, if the Goat does not get much exercise during the day, he could find it beneficial to take up some additional physical activity such as walking or cycling. Similarly, if he tends to rely on fast or convenience food, switching to a more balanced diet could also prove beneficial.

As far as financial matters are concerned, the Goat can look forward to a noticeable upturn in his situation. This could arise from a salary increase, the fruition of an investment or from receiving some unexpected and additional funds. However, while the Goat will delight in this improvement, he should still exercise care when dealing with money matters. Although there will be strong temptations for him to spend, he would do well to exercise some restraint over the year, considering carefully any large purchases he wishes to make. He should also remember that money or savings spent too lavishly could take some time to replace. Goats can sometimes be extravagant and over-generous and a certain degree of care would certainly not come amiss this year.

The Goat's domestic and social life, however, will bring him much pleasure. Those around him will be supportive towards his activities and he should not only involve them in his plans but also be open about any concerns he might have. In 1999 he will gain a tremendous amount from consulting others, not only as regards useful information, but also through being heartened by the reassurance he receives.

The Goat himself will take much satisfaction in following and encouraging activities of those close to him and some joint family projects and mutual interests will bring him much pleasure. However, while his domestic life will go well over the year, there will still be occasions when he might be involved in a contretemps and have a difference of opinion with someone close to him. At such times the Goat should try to sort the matter out as quickly and amicably as he can, either reaching a compromise or just agreeing to disagree. To let any difference continue, and possibly escalate, could prove an unwelcome distraction and mar an otherwise auspicious year. In 1999 the Goat should also try not to allow his sometimes fickle nature cause acrimony. This is too good a year to spoil by petty squabbles or differences.

The Goat will also lead an active social life over the year and can look forward to many enjoyable occasions with his friends. The spring and the closing months of the year will be particularly rewarding times. For the unattached Goat, this will be a splendid year, with romance strongly aspected. Many young Goats will meet their future partner in 1999 or get engaged or married, such are the favourable aspects that prevail. Any Goat who may be feeling lonely or has had some recent sadness to cope with will find it very much in his interest to focus his attention firmly on the present and aim to build up his social life and perhaps develop some new interests. By taking positive action he will soon enjoy an upturn in his fortunes and over the year can establish some new and valuable friendships.

Generally, the aspects will support the Goat well in 1999 and it rests with him to make the most of himself and his skills and to take advantage of the opportunities that arise. This can be a truly positive and successful year for the Goat and will be one for him to enjoy.

As far as the different types of Goat are concerned, 1999 will be a positive and fulfilling year for the *Metal Goat*. For much of it he will be able to pursue his activities and interests in his own way, without being subject to some of the disruptive pressures of recent years. In this respect the Metal Goat can look forward to many absorbing hours spent on his hobbies, interests and other projects. With his strong artistic leanings he will obtain particular satisfaction in carrying out activities that draw on his creativity and imagination, and if he has a particular skill or talent which he can demonstrate to others, he should do so. He will not only find his work much appreciated, but in some cases he could be asked to guide others and this in itself will bring him much gratification. The Metal Goat will also obtain pleasure from outdoor activities and for those who enjoy gardening, walking, exploring the countryside or travel, the year will contain some special and memorable moments. With travel well aspected, the Metal Goat should aim to go away at least once over the year. A holiday taken in the summer months and to a destination new to him could surpass expectations and prove a truly happy occasion. The Metal Goat's domestic life will also bring him much pleasure. Those around him will be most supportive and throughout the year the Metal Goat should aim to involve them in his activities as well as ask for assistance and advice should he have any worrying or complex matter to deal with. One troublesome area could involve bureaucracy or a transaction he is trying to complete, and the help and advice he is given will prove invaluable. In 1999 it is important that the Metal Goat remembers that there are many he can turn to, if in need. In addition to the support he will be given, he will also delight in some pleasing family news over the year. This could include the engagement or marriage of a close relation or the birth of a grandchild. The Metal Goat's social life will go well and be more active than it has been of late. He will find himself much in demand with his friends and there will be some interesting and enjoyable social events to attend. Any Metal Goat who is looking for a more active social life should take steps to help bring this about, perhaps by joining a local society or group. By taking positive action these Metal Goats will soon find themselves meeting others and forming some new and in some cases important friendships. Financial matters will go reasonably well, although if the Metal Goat enters into any major transaction he does need to check the small print carefully and make sure he understands any obligations he may be placed under. Important matters concerning finance or paperwork cannot be rushed or embarked on lightly. Metal Goats, take note! Those Metal Goats in education will make good progress and could find themselves excelling in a subject they have recently started. However, if there is any aspect of his studies that is giving the young Metal Goat concern, he should not hesitate to tell others rather than keep it to himself. As he will find, those around can and will do much to help. In most respects, this will be a satisfying year for the Metal Goat, with most aspects of his life going well and bringing him pleasure and contentment.

The Rabbit year holds much promise for the *Water Goat*, although just how much he achieves is dependent upon his own attitude. The Water Goat has many admirable qualities and in 1999 he should resolve to make the most of these and set about his aims and activities with confidence and determination. Indeed, the year will hold some interesting possibilities for him and he should take full advantage of the favourable aspects that prevail. In his work he will be given the chance to undertake some projects that he has wanted to do for some time and this in itself will bring him much personal satisfaction. He will also be able to display and develop talents that he has not formerly had the chance to exploit, thereby impressing others and making good progress. If the Water Goat is currently dissatisfied with his present duties or is seeking work, he should actively pursue any openings that he sees as well as explore ways in which he can use his skills to better advantage. With his creative mind and innovative approach he is well placed to benefit from the general trends that prevail over the year and, for the enterprising Water Goat, this can be a truly successful and rewarding time. March and April could prove particularly significant for career matters, with some interesting developments. The Water Goat can also look forward to an improvement in his financial situation over the year and this will enable him to proceed with some projects and purchases he has had in mind for some time, especially items of equipment and home furnishings. By looking around, he could make some excellent purchases at highly favourable prices. Many Water Goats will also obtain much satisfaction in redecorating their home. Where decor is concerned, the Water Goat's eye for colour and detail will lead to impressive results. If, however, he does have funds that he does not immediately need, he would do well to set them aside for a specific purpose, such as travel and hobbies, as well as making some savings for the future. Although this will be a favourable year for financial matters, the Water Goat still needs to handle his finances with care and forethought. Domestically and socially this will, however, be a splendid year and the Water Goat can look forward to many happy and meaningful occasions with both family and friends. He will not only gain from the support and encouragement he is given but will also derive much pleasure from general family and social activities. Mutual interests and hobbies will give him particular joy and he will thoroughly enjoy the many gatherings, parties and events that he attends over the year. Also, any outings that he takes with his family and friends, especially those arranged at short notice and as something of a surprise, will go particularly well. For any Water Goat seeking new friends, a chance meeting in the first few months of the year could mark the start of a new and significant friendship. Another favourably aspected area concerns the Water Goat's own hobbies, especially those that allow him to use his artistic and creative talents. For those involved in the creative arts, whether professionally or as a hobby, the year will bring some notable and well-deserved successes and the creative Water Goat would do well to promote his work. In most respects, 1999 will go well for the Water Goat. With his skills, the experience he has built up and his ability to get on with others, he has much in his favour and he should use these talents well. The year will offer him the opportunities for which he has long been waiting and he should make the most of the excellent aspects that prevail. With commitment and resolve, this can be one of the most successful and rewarding years that the Water Goat has enjoyed for a long time.

Much will have happened to the *Wood Goat* in recent years, with some events being to his advantage, while others have been disappointing. He will have learnt much about himself, both from the mistakes he might have made and from life's rich learning experience. In 1999 he will be able to draw on this experience and be able to make some major strides, particularly in his work. Indeed, many Wood

Goats will have been giving considerable thought to how they would like their career to develop over the next few years, particularly in view of some of the recent changes and events. By giving thought to his future, the Wood Goat will find himself setting about his activities in a more purposeful manner and this in itself will lead him towards his goals. This is very much a year for positive action and with the aspects supporting him so well, the Wood Goat can achieve much. When opportunities arise in his work he should 'strike while the iron is hot' – to delay or hesitate could undermine his chances. Similarly, if there are ideas and plans he wants to try out, he should again take action. As well as benefiting from any opportunities, the Wood Goat will be greatly helped by the supportive attitude of those around him and throughout the year will gain much from the input, advice and encouragement of others. It would also be in his interest to contact those who have already achieved some of his own aims. This way he could be given some excellent advice and told of possibilities that he may not have realized were available. For Wood Goats anxious to improve their position or those seeking work, the year will bring many interesting openings. It does rest with the Wood Goat, however, to take action and make the most of his chances. This will also be a positive year for financial matters and if the Wood Goat feels able, he would do well to make some savings or investments for his longer term future. Over the years these could develop into a worthwhile sum. The Wood Goat will also enjoy several strokes of luck in 1999 and could enjoy some success in a rather unusual competition. His domestic and social life will be particularly active and a source of much pleasure.

The Wood Goat will enjoy many family occasions, including any holidays and breaks that he takes, and will also delight in the achievements of those around him. Any assistance and advice he feels able to give will be much appreciated and he too will be heartened by encouragement and support for his own activities. There is, however, one word of warning. In view of the active nature of some parts of the year, there will be times when the Wood Goat will feel tired and under pressure. In such situations he should try not to take out any feelings of tension or weariness on others; to do so could give rise to bickering and spoil the otherwise congenial atmosphere the Wood Goat so much values. It will be far better to discuss any concerns he has openly or to absorb himself in relaxing pursuits than let tension mar his relations with those around him. In addition to a full domestic life, his social life will, however, be a source of much pleasure, with some pleasant occasions being spent with his friends. For the unattached Wood Goat or for those seeking new friends, this will prove a splendid and happy year with a major upturn indicated. The months of April and May in particular could see some key developments. In almost all respects, this will be a positive and rewarding year for the Wood Goat and he should aim to take full advantage of the excellent aspects that prevail.

This will be an exciting year for the *Fire Goat*, with many positive and significant developments taking place. In his work he will be able to add to his experience and achievements while on a personal level he can look forward to many happy and meaningful times with his family and friends. Indeed, the Fire Goat sets great store by his relations with others and throughout the year he will find himself much in demand as well as heartened by the obvious esteem and affection others have for him. Domestically, this will indeed be a fine year. The Fire Goat will take much interest in the activities of those around him and any guidance he feels able to give will be greatly valued. In addition, the Fire Goat will take satisfaction in carrying out projects on his home and garden, and while these may sometimes take him longer to complete than he anticipated, he will be well pleased with what he is able to accomplish. In carrying out practical projects, however, he should not take risks with his personal safety and should follow all the recommended safety procedures. As far as DIY and complex tasks are concerned, it is better to be safe than sorry! The Fire Goat will also derive much satisfaction from any interests that he can share with others and, as far as possible, would do well to develop and encourage these. He will find mutual interests and joint family activities will lead to some happy and fulfilling occasions for all concerned. The Fire Goat's social life, too, is well aspected and he can look forward to attending a variety of parties and social gatherings over the year, with some proving especially pleasurable because of their surprise value. For Fire Goats seeking new friends this will be a truly excellent year, with some new and significant friendships being forged. Any Fire Goat who may have suffered some personal misfortune in recent times would do well to regard 1999 as the start of a new chapter in his life and to concentrate on the present and future rather than dwell too much on what has gone before. The Rabbit year holds considerable promise for the Fire Goat and he should aim to make the most of the favourable aspects that prevail. This will also be a good year for work matters and many Fire Goats will be able to improve substantially on their present position, either by taking on new duties, winning promotion or successfully transferring to another position. Throughout the year the Fire Goat should remain alert for opportunities to pursue and for different ways in which he can use his skills. With determination and a positive attitude he will be able to make pleasing headway. Also, if there is a particular position that he is seeking or an ambition he wishes to realize, he should make a determined effort to go after it this year. Again, his efforts will bring results, but it does lie with him to take the initiative and act in a positive manner. The advances that the Fire Goat will make in his work will also lead to an improvement in his financial position. This in turn will enable him to make some purchases for himself and his home over the year; some of these will be useful items which will add to the decor and comfort of his accommodation, while others will be more in the nature of treats and luxuries. However, when any sizeable outlay is involved, the Fire Goat should resist rushing his purchases. By comparing what is available in different outlets, as well as waiting for sale times and special offers, he could save himself a considerable amount. He would also do well to try and set some money aside for a holiday or break later in the year. In addition to the enjoyment this will give, he will greatly benefit from the rest and change of scene that a holiday will bring. In almost all respects, this will be a favourable year for the Fire Goat and by using his time and skills well, he can ensure it is significant, successful and personally rewarding.

This will be a pleasing year for the *Earth Goat*, bringing him happiness as well as enabling him to accomplish a great deal. Almost as soon as the Rabbit year starts, the Earth Goat will begin to feel more invigorated and more determined than ever to make the most of himself and the year, and his positive approach will repay him in many areas of his life. Personally, he will be on top form, with new friendships and romance to the fore. Indeed, many Earth Goats will meet their future partner over the year or get engaged or married, such are the auspicious trends that prevail. In addition to the considerable happiness he will enjoy with his partner or in developing a new friendship, the Earth Goat will also lead an active social life with a variety of parties and events to attend. Any Earth Goat who may start 1999 in low spirits will soon sense an upturn in his fortunes and become more hopeful in his outlook. However, to help bring this about, the Earth Goat should aim to go out more, particularly to places where he is likely to meet others. Positive action on his part will be quickly rewarded and with his amiable manner the Earth Goat is sure to impress. He will also be well supported by his family and although sometimes he may feel he does not want to bother them with his concerns or that they are not fully in tune with his thinking, this is not the case. The Earth Goat's family do genuinely want to assist and see him make the most of himself and if he has any uncertainties over any matter, he should not hesitate to seek their views. He will be given some helpful and reassuring advice, particularly by a more senior relation, even though some of the importance of their words may not always be apparent at the time. The Rabbit year is also very much one which favours cultural pursuits and self-improvement and any Earth Goat in education or taking exams can make good progress. However, when exams are approaching the Earth Goat does need to sort out his priorities. Even though this may mean he has to cut back on some of his social life, the sacrifices he makes will be worthwhile. Also, if any Earth Goat feels it would be useful to obtain a further qualification or skill in order to help his work prospects, he should try to obtain this. He will find that what he learns and accomplishes in 1999 will not only be to his future benefit but will also be a satisfying and constructive use of his time. There will also be some positive developments concerning the Earth Goat's work over the year. Those Earth Goats seeking a position could find their quest rewarded in an unexpected manner and although their new post might not be quite what they originally wanted, it will nevertheless allow them to develop new skills and provide them with useful experience and a platform from which to progress. Work-wise, the year holds much potential and the Earth Goat should take full advantage of the opportunities he is given and of the ways in which he can extend his experience. As far as financial matters are concerned, although this will not be an adverse year, there will be many expenses for the Earth Goat, particularly with all the socializing and general activity that is indicated. So, to avoid problems, he does need to watch his level of spending. He could be helped by setting certain amounts aside for specific purposes rather than trying to deal with his finances on an *ad hoc* basis and without any particular method or planning. Overall, 1999 will be a good year for the Earth Goat, with great personal joy and also significant and positive developments in his work and education. With so much in his favour, the Earth Goat owes it to himself to give of his best and take advantage of the truly auspicious conditions that prevail.

FAMOUS GOATS

Pamela Anderson, Isaac Asimov, W. H. Auden, Jane Austen, Anne Bancroft, Cilla Black, Ian Botham, Elkie Brooks, George Burns, Lord Byron, Leslie Caron, John le Carré, Coco Chanel, Mary Higgins Clark, Nat 'King' Cole, Harry Connick Jr, Angus Deayton, Catherine Deneuve, Charles Dickens, Angie Dickinson, Ken Dodd, Sir Arthur Conan Doyle, Umberto Eco, Douglas Fairbanks, Dame Margot Fonteyn, Anna Ford, Heinz-Harold Frentzen, Noel Gallagher, Paul Gascoigne, Bill Gates, Mel Gibson, Newt Gingrich, Paul Michael Glaser, Whoopi Goldberg, Mikhail Gorbachev, John Grisham, George Harrison, Sir Edmund Hillary, John Humphrys, Billy Idol, Julio Iglesias, Mick Jagger, Ben Kingsley, David Kossoff, Doris Lessing, Peter Lilley, Franz Liszt, John Major, Michelangelo, Joni Mitchell, Iris Murdoch, Rupert Murdoch, Mussolini, Randy Newman, Robert de Niro, Greg Norman, Edna O'Brien, Des O'Connor, Sinead O'Connor, Lord Olivier, Michael Palin, Eva Peron, Marcel Proust, Keith Richards, William Shatner, Freddie Starr, Jacques Tati, Lord Tebbit, Lana Turner, Desmond Tutu, Mark Twain, Rudolph Valentino, Vangelis, Lech Walesa, Barbara Walters, Andy Warhol, John Wayne, Fay Weldon, Bruce Willis, Debra Winger, Tom Wolfe, Paul Young.

2 FEBRUARY 1908 ～ 21 JANUARY 1909   *Earth Monkey*

20 FEBRUARY 1920 ～ 7 FEBRUARY 1921   *Metal Monkey*

6 FEBRUARY 1932 ～ 25 JANUARY 1933   *Water Monkey*

25 JANUARY 1944 ～ 12 FEBRUARY 1945   *Wood Monkey*

12 FEBRUARY 1956 ～ 30 JANUARY 1957   *Fire Monkey*

30 JANUARY 1968 ～ 16 FEBRUARY 1969   *Earth Monkey*

16 FEBRUARY 1980 ～ 4 FEBRUARY 1981   *Metal Monkey*

4 FEBRUARY 1992 ～ 22 JANUARY 1993   *Water Monkey*

THE
MONKEY

THE PERSONALITY OF THE MONKEY

'Where there is a will there is a way' is an old and true saying. He who resolves upon doing a thing, by that very resolution often scales the barriers to it, and secures its achievement.

– Samuel Smiles: a Monkey

The Monkey is born under the sign of fantasy. He is imaginative, inquisitive and loves to keep an eye on everything that is going on around him. He is never backward in offering advice or trying to sort out the problems of others. He likes to be helpful and his advice is invariably sensible and reliable.

The Monkey is intelligent, well read and always eager to learn. He has an extremely good memory and there are many Monkeys who have made particularly good linguists. The Monkey is also a convincing talker and enjoys taking part in discussions and debates. His friendly, self-assured manner can be very persuasive and he usually has little trouble in winning people round to his way of thinking. It is for this reason that the Monkey often excels in politics and public speaking. He is also particularly adept at PR work, teaching and any job which involves selling.

The Monkey can, however, be crafty, cunning and occasionally dishonest, and he will seize on any opportunity to make a quick gain or outsmart his opponents. He has so much charm and guile that people often don't realize what he is up to until it is too late. But despite his resourceful nature, the Monkey does run the risk of outsmarting even himself. He has so much confidence in his abilities that he rarely listens to advice or is prepared to accept help from anyone. He likes to help others but prefers to rely on his own judgement when dealing with his own affairs.

Another characteristic of the Monkey is that he is extremely good at solving problems and has a happy knack of extricating himself (and others) from the most hopeless of positions. He is the master of self-preservation.

With so many diverse talents the Monkey is able to make considerable sums of money, but he does like to enjoy life and will think nothing of spending his money on some exotic holiday or luxury which he has had his eye on. He can, however, become very envious if someone else has got what he wants.

The Monkey is an original thinker and, despite his love of company, he cherishes his independence. He has to have the freedom to act as he wants and any Monkey who feels hemmed in or bound by too many restrictions can soon become unhappy. Likewise, if anything becomes too boring or monotonous, the Monkey soon loses interest and turns his attention to something else. He lacks persistence and this can often hamper his progress. He is also easily distracted, a tendency which all Monkeys should try to overcome. The Monkey should concentrate on one thing at a time and by doing so will almost certainly achieve more in the long run.

The Monkey is a good organizer and, even though he may behave slightly erratically at times, he will invariably have some plan at the back of his mind. On the odd occasion when his plans do not quite work out, he is usually quite happy to shrug his shoulders and put it down to experience. He will rarely make the same mistake twice and throughout his life he will try his hand at many things.

The Monkey likes to impress and is rarely without followers or admirers. There are many who are attracted to him by his good looks, his sense of humour or simply because he instils so much confidence.

Monkeys usually marry young and for it to be a success their partner must allow them time to pursue their many interests and the opportunity to indulge in their love of travel. The Monkey has to have variety in his life and is especially well suited to those born under the sociable and outgoing signs of the Rat, Dragon, Pig and Goat. The Ox, Rabbit, Snake and Dog will also be enchanted by the Monkey's resourceful and outgoing nature, but he is likely to exasperate the Rooster and Horse, and the Tiger will have little patience for his tricks. A relationship between two Monkeys will work well – they will understand each other and be able to assist each other in their various enterprises.

The female Monkey is intelligent, extremely observant and a shrewd judge of character. Her opinions and views are often highly valued, and, having such a persuasive nature, she invariably gets her own way. She has many interests and involves herself in a wide variety of activities. She pays great attention to her appearance, is an elegant dresser and likes to take particular care over her hair. She can also be a most caring and doting parent and will have many good and loyal friends.

Provided the Monkey can curb his desire to take part in all that is going on around him and concentrate on one thing at a time, he can usually achieve what he wants in life. Should he suffer any disappointments, he is bound to bounce back. The Monkey is a survivor and his life is usually both colourful and very eventful.

THE FIVE DIFFERENT TYPES OF MONKEY

In addition to the 12 signs of the Chinese zodiac, there are five elements and these have a strengthening or moderating influence on the sign. The effects of the five elements on the Monkey are described below, together with the years in which the elements were exercising their influence. Therefore all Monkeys born in 1920 and 1980 are Metal Monkeys, those born in 1932 and 1992 are Water Monkeys, and so on.

Metal Monkey: 1920, 1980
The Metal Monkey is very strong-willed. He sets about everything he does with a dogged determination and often prefers to work independently rather than with others. He is ambitious, wise and confident, and is certainly not afraid of hard work. He is very astute in financial matters and usually chooses his investments well. Despite his somewhat independent nature, the Metal Monkey enjoys attending parties and social occasions and is particularly warm and caring towards his loved ones.

Water Monkey: 1932, 1992

The Water Monkey is versatile, determined and perceptive. He also has more discipline than some of the other Monkeys and is prepared to work towards a certain goal rather than be distracted by something else. He is not always open about his true intentions and when questioned can be particularly evasive. He can be sensitive to criticism but also very persuasive and usually has little trouble in getting others to fall in with his plans. He has a very good understanding of human nature and relates well to others.

Wood Monkey: 1944

This Monkey is efficient, methodical and extremely conscientious. He is also highly imaginative and is always trying to capitalize on new ideas or learn new skills. Occasionally his enthusiasm can get the better of him and he can get very agitated when things do not quite work out as he had hoped. He does, however, have a very adventurous streak in him and is not afraid of taking risks. He also loves travel. He is usually held in great esteem by his friends and colleagues.

Fire Monkey: 1956

The Fire Monkey is intelligent, full of vitality and has no trouble in commanding the respect of others. He is imaginative and has wide interests, although sometimes these can distract him from more useful and profitable work. He is very competitive and always likes to be involved in everything that is going on. He can be stubborn if he does not get his own way and he sometimes tries to indoctrinate those who are less strong-willed than himself. The Fire Monkey is a lively character, popular with the opposite sex and extremely loyal to his partner.

Earth Monkey: 1908, 1968

The Earth Monkey tends to be studious and well read, and can become quite distinguished in his chosen line of work. He is less outgoing than some of the other types of Monkey and prefers quieter and more solid pursuits. He has high principles, a very caring nature and can be most generous to those less fortunate than himself. He is usually successful in handling financial matters and can become very wealthy in old age. He has a calming influence on those around him and is respected and well liked by those he meets. He is, however, especially careful about whom he lets into his confidence.

PROSPECTS FOR THE MONKEY IN 1999

The Chinese New Year starts on 16 February 1999. Until then, the old year, the Year of the Tiger, is still making its presence felt.

The Year of the Tiger (28 January 1998 to 15 February 1999) will have been a challenging one for the Monkey. He will have found that some of its events will have delayed or disrupted his plans and that his progress will not have been all that he would have liked. The Monkey also prefers to be in control of a situation and this will not always have been possible during the year. This too will have caused him concern.

However, there are excellent reasons for the Monkey to take heart. From October 1998 onwards he will notice a gradual improvement in his situation and events will once more start to move in his favour. Some of the problems and obstacles that have hindered his progress will start to ease and the closing months of the Tiger year will be a much more favourable time, enabling the Monkey to finish tasks and settle some problems that have been hanging over him. Also, although some of the year will have been disheartening, the Monkey will have learnt much from what has occurred. He will have had cause to look at his objectives in the light of changing events and this will often have enabled him to form new and sometimes superior plans and ideas. Events will also have kept the Monkey on his mettle and prevented him from becoming staid or complacent; this, too, will have brought some benefit, helping prepare him for the better times that await in the Rabbit year. Often, before a period of growth and success, there is a time of reassessment, adjustment and overcoming obstacles and the Tiger year will have been such a time for the Monkey.

In what remains of the Tiger year the Monkey should continue to set about his activities and duties with care and, wherever possible, in conjunction with others. Admittedly he may like to do things in his own way, but the Tiger year is not a time when the Monkey can distance himself either from others or from the events going on around him.

Also, the Monkey needs to handle his relations with others with care. If he finds himself in a contentious situation, he should remain his tactful and diplomatic self rather than say things he may later regret. In his home life he should try not to take out any feelings of irritability or tenseness on others. At such times, the Monkey could be helped by being open about his true feelings. Others can assist and indeed sympathize over any awkward matters that he may have, as well as offer useful advice, but for this to happen the Monkey does need to adopt a spirit of openness.

Again, though, life for the Monkey will show a noticeable improvement as the Tiger year matures and domestically and socially some positive and happy times are indicated in the closing months of the year. The Monkey will sense that many of the pressures and troubles that the year may have brought are now behind him and will be able to relax and enjoy himself that much more.

The Year of the Rabbit starts on 16 February and, after the pressures and uncertainties of the Tiger year, the Monkey will once again be back to his usual self, benefiting from the more favourable aspects that prevail and making the most of the situations that arise. In addition, the Rabbit year will be a personally happy and fulfilling year for him with many pleasing times with both family and friends.

There will, though, be many Monkeys who start the year dissatisfied with their present situation and lack of recent progress. These Monkeys should despair no longer but actively seek to bring about the changes they desire. With his resourcefulness, personable manner and considerable abilities the Monkey can do much to attain his goals, but to do this he must act. He knows he is capable of a great deal and in 1999 he must rise to the challenges and aspirations he has set himself. By doing so, he will make significant headway.

In his work the Monkey will be able to make the progress that may have been eluding him of late and improve his position, either by being given new responsibilities or promotion or obtaining a different sort of employment. He should also set in motion some of the ideas and plans that he has been considering. Whereas conditions may have recently been against him and opportunities scarce, this will not be the case in the Rabbit year. The Monkey should now do all he can to advance his ideas and talents and, for the enterprising, the rewards of the year can indeed prove substantial.

In addition to pursuing the opportunities that arise the Monkey should also remain alert to all that is going on around him. Often, by chance, he will learn of openings and developments that he can turn to his advantage and April and May in particular could hold some interesting possibilities.

Many of those Monkeys seeking work will also be successful in their quest. Determination and persistence, together with their often resourceful approach, could lead these Monkeys to an interesting position and one which has good potential for development. Again, the spring could be a positive time.

As far as financial matters are concerned, 1999 will see a significant upturn in the Monkey's situation. This could arise through a salary increase or the fruition of a policy or successful investment or a gift, but most Monkeys will enjoy several pieces of good financial news over the year. With this upturn the Monkey will be able to make some purchases he has had in mind for some time. These can be for himself as well as his home. However, before making any sizeable purchase he should compare the ranges on offer as well as their suitability rather than acting too hurriedly.

There will also be many Monkeys who will consider moving over the year and again they should not act in undue haste. By taking time to choose their new location and accommodation, they will be delighted with what they acquire, but this is not something they should rush.

Another area which needs care is any important correspondence, forms and documents that the Monkey has to complete. Although he may regard such matters as wearisome, inattention to detail could result in some protracted correspondence as well as involve him in extra (and unnecessary) expense. The Monkey should also keep records of his transactions and receipts; failure to do so could again lead to problems. In 1999 efficient record-keeping could save the Monkey valuable time in the long run.

More positively, however, the Monkey will thoroughly enjoy his hobbies and interests, particularly those that take him out of doors and allow him to meet others. If there has been something that has recently been intriguing him, this would be an excellent time to find out more. The Rabbit year, with its emphasis on culture and self-development, will certainly be supportive towards those keen to develop their skills and interests.

Another favourably aspected area concerns the Monkey's domestic life. Although busy, it will contain many meaningful and pleasurable times. The Monkey will take much satisfaction in following and encouraging the activities of those around him and, as usual, will provide much useful guidance for others. Those around do think highly of his views and opinions and this will certainly be the case over the year. However, despite the considerable happiness family matters will bring, there will be lots for the Monkey to do and several times he will despair of the chores and tasks that appear to be mounting up. At such times he would find it helpful to set priorities and resist starting new projects until others are finished. Similarly, he should seek the assistance of others who, in many cases, will be delighted to help out. For those Monkeys who move over the year, it is important they plan and organize the moving process carefully. By doing so they will save themselves considerable time and hassle; indeed, in 1999, all Monkeys will gain much from organizing their activities properly and efficiently rather than proceeding without any sort of plan.

Socially, this will be an excellent year, with the Monkey being much in demand with his friends. He can look forward to attending some interesting social events over the year and these will enable him to add to his circle of friends and acquaintances. For the unattached Monkey, or for any Monkey seeking new friends, 1999 promises to be a splendid year, with new and often significant friendships being formed. The spring and late summer months will be two particularly happy and active periods for personal matters and for the unattached, romance will certainly beckon!

In almost all respects, the aspects will support the Monkey well over the year. He will make good headway in his work and what he accomplishes now will lead to even greater things in the year 2000. However, in the Rabbit year, he should aim to take advantage of the opportunities that arise and promote his ideas. For the enterprising Monkey this will be a truly excellent year. Domestic and social matters, too, are favourably aspected, although the Monkey may sometimes find he has difficulty in fitting in all he wants to do. But, busy though his personal life might be, this will be a year that will bring him considerable contentment.

As far as the different types of Monkey are concerned, this will be an auspicious year for the *Metal Monkey*. With his verve, enthusiasm and personable manner the Metal Monkey has much in his favour and, in 1999, he will be given every chance to use and develop his abilities. This is a year that holds considerable potential and one he will greatly enjoy. At the start of the Rabbit year the Metal Monkey would, however, do well to look closely at his present situation and at his more immediate and longer term goals. By giving thought to these he will find himself setting about the year in a more purposeful manner and taking advantage of the right opportunities, rather than allowing himself to drift or leaving events to chance. In all he does he will be helped by his determined and keen approach and those around him, recognizing his talents and drive, will also do much to help and encourage. As far as his work is concerned, there will be several significant developments. Whether in work or seeking work, the Metal Monkey should actively follow up any opportunities that he sees, particularly those that will enable him to add to his experience or help him towards his goals. Sometimes attaining what he wants will take several attempts, but with every application he makes he will be adding to his experience and improving his technique and this can only be to his future good. Also he could find himself being offered a different position from what he originally had in mind, but he will find that this will become a base from which to progress. Through his enterprise and initiative, the Metal Monkey will impress others and find himself being given more varied responsibilities as well as being encouraged to develop his skills. The Rabbit year will hold several important opportunities for him and it rests with him to seize them and give of his best. However, if the Metal Monkey feels he requires an additional skill for the type of career he wants to enter, he should take steps to obtain this. Again, positive action on his part will be rewarded and as far as preparing himself for the future or setting in motion his plans, he would do well to remember the old saying 'There is no time like the present'. For those Metal Monkeys in education this will also be a most favourable year and by setting about their studies in an organized and systematic way they will attain some pleasing results. Revision and exams may mean the young Metal Monkey has to make some sacrifices, but his results will reward him for his hard effort. The Metal Monkey has a great future ahead of him and what he learns and accomplishes in 1999 will help lead him to the successes that await. As far as his personal life is concerned, this will be a truly splendid year. He will be much in demand with his friends and can look forward to attending a variety of parties and functions. There will also be plenty of opportunities to make new friends, with April to August being a particularly active time socially. Romance, too, is favourably aspected and will bring the Metal Monkey much happiness over the year. In addition to the pleasure in his personal life, he will thoroughly enjoy the travel that he undertakes and for those Metal Monkeys who have been considering going on lengthy journeys, improving their language skills or obtaining work experience in another country, this would be a good year in which to do so. With all the activity indicated, the Metal Monkey would, however, do well to watch his financial situation. With care he should be able to avoid undue problems, but this is not a year in which he can afford to spend without regard to his financial situation or enter into risky ventures. While he may be anxious to improve his financial position, he should also be wary of what appear to be 'get rich quick' schemes. All may not be what it appears and without extra vigilance the Metal Monkey could find himself losing money. Metal Monkeys, take note. In most respects, though, this will be a splendid year for the Metal Monkey and, with his positive outlook, abilities and charm, he will make good progress and sow some important seeds for the future as well as greatly enjoy himself.

This is a year that will go well for the *Water Monkey*, with many positive developments taking place. In recent times the Water Monkey will have thought of several ideas and plans he would like to carry out but will not yet have had the chance to do so. This year will give him his opportunity. It is one which favours positive action and by setting in motion his ideas the Water Monkey can accomplish a great deal. These could concern a wide range of activities, although one particular area which will figure prominently over the year will be accommodation. Some Water Monkeys will decide to move and for those who do it would be worth their while to take their time in choosing their new location rather than acting too hastily. This way they will eventually find something that will meet their requirements perfectly, but it will take time and effort to discover and acquire. Also, if the Water Monkey has doubts over any aspect of the moving process, particularly the forms and paperwork, he should seek clarification rather than take risks. Another area which needs care – and this applies to all Water Monkeys – is the lifting or moving of heavy and cumbersome items. The Water Monkey should not undertake this without assistance, otherwise a strain could cause him considerable discomfort. Water Monkeys, be warned! The Water Monkey will, however, take much delight in some practical projects that he carries out on his accommodation and if there is something that he has had in mind for some time, such as making or installing a particular feature, this would be a good year in which to put his plans into practice. In all he does, though, the Water Monkey should act in close consultation with those around him and where practical tasks are involved, aim to share the workload. He will find this will not only make the projects quicker and easier to complete, but will also make them more meaningful for those concerned. As always, the Water Monkey's home life will prove important to him and, as well as joint undertakings and projects, he can look forward to many pleasant occasions with his loved ones. Mutual interests and hobbies, as well as trips out and holidays, are all favourably aspected. In addition, the Water Monkey will take considerable pride in the success and progress of a younger relation and the advice and encouragement he feels able to pass on will be greatly appreciated. The Water Monkey's social life will be more active than it has been for some time. Again, some interesting occasions are indicated and for those involved in clubs or societies, some honours or recognition of their efforts could be given during the year. Although there will be much that will keep the Water Monkey occupied in 1999, he would also do well to give serious thought to taking up a new interest, something completely different from anything he has done before, perhaps learning a new skill or musical instrument or enrolling on a study course. Whatever the Water Monkey chooses, he will find it will provide him with a stimulating challenge and could develop in a positive way over the next few years. The Water Monkey's financial situation will be sound over the year, although it would be in his interests to maintain proper financial records and check the terms and obligations of any large transaction that he enters into. Inattention to detail or lost receipts could cause problems later and involve him in some protracted correspondence. To avoid this, the Water Monkey should take care and time over his paperwork, tiresome though some of it may be. Overall, though, this will be a positive year for the Water Monkey and, by setting in motion some of his plans and ideas, he will enjoy some worthwhile achievements, particularly as far as his interests and accommodation are concerned. His home and social life will also bring him many rewarding times, helping to make this a rich and satisfying year.

A considerable amount will have happened to the *Wood Monkey* in recent years, with some events being to his advantage while some bringing times of anguish. However, in the Rabbit year the Wood Monkey will be able to draw on what has gone before, adding to previous successes and accomplishments and tackling some of the remaining problems. This will be a positive and constructive year and, with a determined attitude (and the aspects on his side), the Wood Monkey will be able to achieve much. Those Wood Monkeys who have recently taken on different responsibilities in their work should aim to familiarize themselves with their duties and establish themselves in their new role. With their conscientious and personable manner, they will quickly impress and will be given every opportunity to use and develop their skills. For Wood Monkeys who have been in the same position for some time and would like to move to more varied responsibilities, the Rabbit year will again bring some excellent and often unexpected opportunities. These Wood Monkeys should remain alert for openings to pursue and watch developments around them. By chance they could learn of some opportunities they had not realized were available or be alerted to changes that will give rise to new openings. In 1999 many Wood Monkeys will be the beneficiaries of some interesting developments that take place in the workplace. Similarly, those Wood Monkeys seeking work should remain active in following up any openings they see and would also do well to consider other ways in which they can use their skills and past experience. Some enterprising thinking could open up some significant doors for them; indeed, any Wood Monkey thinking of launching a business idea would do well to take further steps and test the initial reaction. This is very much a progressive year and the Wood Monkey should take full advantage of the favourable aspects that prevail. This will also be a positive year for financial matters and the Wood Monkey will enjoy several strokes of good fortune. This could include making a successful investment or receiving an unexpected financial bonus or gift. His good luck could even extend to winning a competition. The Wood Monkey's home life will be fairly active over the year, with many domestic matters to deal with. These will include attending to the interests of family members and carrying out some projects on his home, together with the usual household chores. Sometimes the Wood Monkey may despair of all he has to do and at busy times should aim to set himself some priorities, rather than try to do everything at once. He should also seek the assistance of those around him; help will be forthcoming, although there may be occasions when he has to prompt others into action. However busy and occasionally demanding his home life might be, those around will be a source of considerable pride and the Wood Monkey will follow their activities with a fond and caring interest. He will also enjoy some truly pleasurable occasions with his family and close friends, with trips and meals out and any breaks or a holiday he is able to take going particularly well. Indeed, the Wood Monkey has a good taste for the finer things in life and the Rabbit year will certainly contain many agreeable and meaningful occasions. Although the Wood Monkey may not always feel he has the time to devote to his own hobbies and interests, it is important he does not neglect these as they do give him the chance to relax and unwind. During the year he could find an interest in which he can use his imagination and creativity, such as photography, art or writing, particularly absorbing and therapeutic. Generally, the aspects that prevail will support the Wood Monkey well and give him the chance to put his skills and experience to good use. Provided he gives of his best and uses his time wisely, this will certainly prove a satisfying and rewarding year.

This is a year which holds considerable potential for the *Fire Monkey*. Almost all aspects of his life will contain some positive developments, although just how much he benefits from this most auspicious of years rests with him. Although the Fire Monkey is well-meaning and keen to give of his best, he does sometimes undermine his progress by two factors. Firstly he has a tendency to over-commit himself and engage in too many activities at the same time and secondly, he can get distracted all too easily and this can lead to the delay and even abandonment of some of his projects. Both traits can prove to the Fire Monkey's detriment and, if not watched, could reduce his level of success in 1999. To do well and to make the most of his considerable talents the Fire Monkey should decide upon his priorities for the year and concentrate on these. The best results and progress will come from persistent effort on specific activities rather than from attempting to be over-ambitious and spreading his energies too widely. Provided the Fire

Monkey bears this in mind and sets his sights on particular goals, however, he will enjoy some spectacular successes over the year. In his work he should continue to build on the progress he has made in recent years as well as promote and develop some of his plans and ideas. By doing so he will greatly impress and this can lead to further advances later in the year and in 2000. If the Fire Monkey is seeking promotion or desiring a change from his present duties, then this is also a year in which he should take positive action to achieve this rather than just hope for an opening to arise. Similarly, if he is seeking work, rather than just waiting for possible openings, he should consider making direct approaches to companies and organizations, laying particular stress on his skills and how he feels he can make a positive contribution. By being bold, enterprising and his resourceful self, the Fire Monkey's efforts will be noticed and can lead to some encouraging developments over the year. This will also be a much improved year for financial matters and while the Fire Monkey will face some large expenses connected with his accommodation and transport, by watching his outgoings and controlling his budget, these should not cause him undue problems. His home life will be busy and sometimes demanding over the year, with many matters requiring his attention. Being both considerate and caring he will worry too over the progress of some of those around him, but many times these worries will be misplaced. If he does have any concerns, he should let his views be known and although he may not wish to appear too interfering, any help and assistance he feels able to give, particularly to younger relations, will be appreciated more than he may realize at the time. Domestically, there may be pressures and anxieties, but overall these need not take away from the happiness and importance of his home life and during the year he can look forward to many pleasurable occasions with his loved ones. He would also do well to encourage some interests and activities that all can join in. Hobbies his family can share, visits to places of local interest, sporting activities, trips, treats and holidays will all produce some rewarding occasions. One other point the Fire Monkey would do well to consider is that if he does not get much exercise during the day, he could find it beneficial to take more physical activity, such as walking, cycling, swimming or something equally suitable. This way he could do much to help his own well-being. The Fire Monkey's social life will also be fairly active over the year and he will find himself much in demand with his friends, with the opportunity to attend some interesting parties and other social events. For any Fire Monkey seeking to build up his social life and make new friends, this will be a particularly favourable year, with a chance meeting in the spring or early summer leading to a new and significant friendship. Overall, 1999 can be a successful and fulfilling year for the Fire Monkey, but he does need to concentrate upon his priorities and act in his usual positive and determined way. The aspects will support him well in much of what he does and most Fire Monkeys will be pleased with what they are able to achieve in this most favourable of years.

After the events and activities of the last few years the *Earth Monkey* will be able to heave a great sigh of relief. For once he will not be so much a victim of events, many of which were outside his control, but will now be able to proceed in the way he wants as well as set in motion ideas and plans he has been considering for a long time. For the Earth Monkey 1999 will be a pleasant and rewarding year. As far as his work is concerned, he will be able to make constructive progress, often making the headway that has for some time been eluding him. This improvement in his situation will start to become apparent almost as soon as the Rabbit year begins and the Earth Monkey will begin to feel more optimistic about his future and able to set about his activities with greater confidence and resolve. His determination and renewed enthusiasm will lead to some pleasing results. Over the year he should aim to develop some of his ideas and if he has certain objectives connected with his work, whether obtaining a position, winning promotion or switching to a different field, then he should act. This is a year when the Earth Monkey can make good progress as well as benefit from the experience and gains he has made in recent years, but to do well he does need to seize the initiative and make the most of himself and the opportunities that occur. He knows he has it within him to achieve a great deal and during the year he will be given the chance to display his talents and show others his true and considerable worth. For work matters, late February to May could prove an important and significant time. The Earth Monkey will also enjoy an improvement in his financial situation as well as experience several strokes of luck. A carefully chosen investment could perform well and if the Earth Monkey feels able to put any money he does not immediately need towards saving for his longer term future he could find this will build into a useful asset in years to come. The Earth Monkey will also be keen to acquire several items for himself and his home over the year, although where expensive items are concerned, he would do well to investigate the ranges on offer and consider how best they meet his requirements rather than be too hasty with any purchase. In major transactions, care and patience are certainly required. The Earth Monkey's domestic and social life will be active over the year and he can look forward to many pleasurable occasions with family and friends. He will take a particularly keen interest in the progress and achievements of a younger relation and any assistance and encouragement he feels able to give will be greatly valued. Similarly, several times in 1999 family members and close friends will seek his views and advice on important matters and, as usual, the Earth Monkey's judgement and sound reasoning will do much to help. However, where his own personal interests are concerned, he should pay great heed to some advice given by a more senior relation. Although he may not fully agree with what he is told, or indeed appreciate its significance, there will be much wisdom in their words. The Earth Monkey can also look forward to a variety of interesting social events over the year and for those seeking romance, new friends or just a more active social life, this promises to be an excellent year. The spring months in particular will be a joyous time. Overall, the Rabbit year holds much promise for the Earth Monkey, but to benefit from the auspicious aspects that prevail he should actively pursue his goals and aspirations. In 1999 he can accomplish a great deal and, for the determined and committed Earth Monkey, this will prove a successful and fulfilling year.

FAMOUS MONKEYS

Gillian Anderson, Francesca Annis, Michael Aspel, Mike Atherton, J. M. Barrie, David Bellamy, Jacqueline Bisset, Victor Borge, Julius Caesar, Johnny Cash, Jacques Chirac, Chelsea Clinton, Joe Cocker, Colette, John Constable, Alistair Cooke, David Copperfield, Joan Crawford, Leonardo da Vinci, Timothy Dalton, Bette Davis, Phil de Glanville, Danny De Vito, Bo Derek, Jonathan Dimbleby, Celine Dion, Jason Donovan, Michael Douglas, Mia Farrow, Carrie Fisher, F. Scott Fitzgerald, Ian Fleming, Dick Francis, Fiona Fullerton, Paul Gauguin, Jerry Hall, Tom Hanks, Stephen Hendry, Martina Hingis, Harry Houdini, P. D. James, Pope John Paul II, Lyndon B. Johnson, Edward Kennedy, Nigel Kennedy, Don King, Gladys Knight, Patti LaBelle, Leo McKern, Walter Matthau, Kylie Minogue, Jack Nicklaus, Derek Nimmo, Peter O'Toole, Anthony Perkins, Robert Powell, Lisa Marie Presley, Debbie Reynolds, Tim Rice, Little Richard, Mickey Rooney, Diana Ross, Boz Scaggs, Michael Schumacher, Tom Selleck, Omar Sharif, Wilbur Smith, Rod Stewart, Jacques Tati, Elizabeth Taylor, Dame Kiri Te Kanawa, Harry Truman, the Duchess of Windsor, Bobby Womack.

22 JANUARY 1909 ~ 9 FEBRUARY 1910	*Earth Rooster*
8 FEBRUARY 1921 ~ 27 JANUARY 1922	*Metal Rooster*
26 JANUARY 1933 ~ 13 FEBRUARY 1934	*Water Rooster*
13 FEBRUARY 1945 ~ 1 FEBRUARY 1946	*Wood Rooster*
31 JANUARY 1957 ~ 17 FEBRUARY 1958	*Fire Rooster*
17 FEBRUARY 1969 ~ 5 FEBRUARY 1970	*Earth Rooster*
5 FEBRUARY 1981 ~ 24 JANUARY 1982	*Metal Rooster*
23 JANUARY 1993 ~ 9 FEBRUARY 1994	*Water Rooster*

THE
ROOSTER

THE PERSONALITY OF
THE ROOSTER

When schemes are laid in advance, it is surprising how
often the circumstances will fit in with them.
                    – *Sir William Osler: a Rooster*

The Rooster is born under the sign of candour. He has a
flamboyant and colourful personality and is meticulous
in all that he does. He is an excellent organizer and wherever possible likes to plan his various activities well in
advance.

The Rooster is highly intelligent and usually very well
read. He has a good sense of humour and is an effective
and persuasive speaker. He loves discussion and enjoys
taking part in any sort of debate. He has no hesitation in
speaking his mind and is forthright in his views. He does,
however, lack tact and can easily damage his reputation or
cause offence by some thoughtless remark or action. The
Rooster also has a very volatile nature and he should
always try to avoid acting on the spur of the moment.

The Rooster is usually very dignified in his manner and
conducts himself with an air of confidence and authority.
He is adept at handling financial matters and, as with most
things, he organizes his financial affairs with considerable
skill. He chooses his investments well and is capable of
achieving great wealth. Most Roosters save or use their
money wisely, but there are a few who are the reverse and
are notorious spendthrifts. Fortunately, the Rooster has

great earning capacity and is rarely without sufficient funds to tide himself over.

Another characteristic of the Rooster is that he invariably carries a notebook or scraps of paper around with him. He is constantly writing himself reminders or noting down important facts lest he forgets – the Rooster cannot abide inefficiency and conducts all his activities in an orderly, precise and methodical manner.

The Rooster is usually very ambitious, but can be unrealistic in some of the things that he hopes to achieve. He occasionally lets his imagination run away with him and, while he does not like any interference in the things he does, it would be in his own interests if he were to listen to the views of others a little more often. He also does not like criticism and if he feels anybody is doubting his judgement or prying too closely into his affairs, he is certain to let his feelings be known. He can also be rather self-centred and stubborn over relatively trivial matters, but to compensate for this he is reliable, honest and trustworthy, and this is very much appreciated by all who come into contact with him.

Roosters born between the hours of five and seven (both at dawn and sundown) tend to be the most extrovert of their sign, but all Roosters like to lead an active social life and enjoy attending parties and big functions. The Rooster usually has a wide circle of friends and is able to build up influential contacts with remarkable ease. He often belongs to several clubs and societies and involves himself in a variety of different activities. He is particularly interested in the environment, humanitarian affairs and anything affecting the welfare of others. The Rooster has a very caring nature and will do much to help those less fortunate than himself.

He also gets much pleasure from gardening and, while he may not always spend as much time in the garden as he would like, his garden is invariably well kept and extremely productive.

The Rooster is generally very distinguished in his appearance and, if his job permits, he will wear an official uniform with great pride and dignity. He is not averse to publicity and takes great delight in being the centre of attention. He often does well at PR work or any job which brings him into contact with the media. He also makes a very good teacher.

The female Rooster leads a varied and interesting life. She involves herself in many different activities and there are some who wonder how she can achieve so much. She often holds very strong views and, like her male counterpart, has no hesitation in speaking her mind or telling others how she thinks things should be done. She is supremely efficient and well organized and her home is usually very neat and tidy. She has good taste in clothes and usually wears smart but very practical outfits.

The Rooster usually has a large family and as a parent takes a particularly active interest in the education of his children. He is very loyal to his partner and will find that he is especially well suited to those born under the signs of the Snake, Horse, Ox and Dragon. Provided they do not interfere too much in the Rooster's various activities, the Rat, Tiger, Goat and Pig can also establish a good relationship with him, but two Roosters together are likely to squabble and irritate each other. The rather sensitive

Rabbit will find the Rooster a bit too blunt for his liking, and the Rooster will quickly become exasperated by the ever-inquisitive and artful Monkey. He will also find it difficult to get on with the anxious Dog.

If the Rooster can overcome his volatile nature and exercise more tact, he will go far in life. He is capable and talented and will invariably make a lasting – and usually favourable – impression almost everywhere he goes.

THE FIVE DIFFERENT TYPES OF ROOSTER

In addition to the 12 signs of the Chinese zodiac, there are five elements and these have a strengthening or moderating influence on the sign. The effects of the five elements on the Rooster are described below, together with the years in which the elements were exercising their influence. Therefore all Roosters born in 1921 and 1981 are Metal Roosters, those born in 1933 and 1993 are Water Roosters, and so on.

Metal Rooster: 1921, 1981
The Metal Rooster is a hard and conscientious worker. He knows exactly what he wants in life and sets about everything he does in a positive and determined manner. He can

at times appear abrasive and he would almost certainly do better if he were more willing to reach a compromise with others rather than hold so rigidly to his firmly held beliefs. He is very articulate and most astute when dealing with financial matters. He is loyal to his friends and often devotes much energy to working for the common good.

Water Rooster: 1933, 1993

This Rooster has a very persuasive manner and can easily gain the co-operation of others. He is intelligent, well read and gets much enjoyment from taking part in discussions and debates. He has a seemingly inexhaustible amount of energy and is prepared to work long hours in order to secure what he wants. He can, however, waste much valuable time worrying over minor and inconsequential details. He is approachable, has a good sense of humour and is highly regarded by others.

Wood Rooster: 1945

The Wood Rooster is honest, reliable and often sets himself high standards. He is ambitious, but also more prepared to work in a team than some of the other types of Rooster. He usually succeeds in life, but does have a tendency to get caught up in bureaucratic matters or attempt too many things all at the same time. He has wide interests, likes to travel and is very considerate and caring towards his family and friends.

Fire Rooster: 1957

This Rooster is extremely strong-willed. He has many leadership qualities, is an excellent organizer and is most efficient in his work. Through sheer force of character he often secures his objectives, but he does have a tendency to be very forthright and not always consider the feelings of others. If the Fire Rooster can learn to be more tactful he can often succeed beyond his wildest dreams.

Earth Rooster: 1909, 1969

This Rooster has a deep and penetrating mind. He is efficient, very perceptive and is particularly astute in business and financial matters. He is also persistent and once he has set himself an objective, he will rarely allow himself to be deflected from achieving his aim. The Earth Rooster works hard and is held in great esteem by his friends and colleagues. He usually gets much enjoyment from the arts and takes a keen and caring interest in the activities of the various members of his family.

PROSPECTS FOR THE ROOSTER IN 1999

The Chinese New Year starts on 16 February 1999. Until then, the old year, the Year of the Tiger, is still making its presence felt.

The Year of the Tiger (28 January 1998 to 15 February 1999) will have been a demanding one for the Rooster and in what remains of it, he will still need to exercise a certain care.

The Rooster is a great planner and likes to conduct his activities in a methodical and organized manner. However, the events of the year will not always have afforded him the opportunity to lay or keep to elaborate plans. There may have been moments of disruption, uncertainty and pressure and the Rooster will have felt ill at ease with some of the year's events. However, while the Tiger year will have brought its difficulties, it will have also brought some benefits which, while not always apparent at the time, can be to the Rooster's future advantage. Sometimes the changes that have occurred will have led to new opportunities and brought fresh challenges, some of which will have given the Rooster the incentive to take action and decisions which he may not have done otherwise. It will also have given him impetus to look afresh at his current situation and, as a result, will have led to him forming some interesting ideas. One or two of these could become significant over the next few years.

For what remains of the Tiger year, though, the Rooster will still need to show some flexibility and be prepared to make the most of new and developing situations. This is just not a time when he can be too independent in his approach or remain intransigent.

In his work the Rooster should continue to set about his duties in his usual thorough manner, but also look at ways in which he can usefully draw on his expertise and promote his ideas in the light of what is going on around him. A positive and imaginative attitude could lead to some interesting developments. Similarly, those Roosters seeking work will find that any experience they can obtain in the closing months of the year will prove valuable and could have a significant bearing in the next Chinese year. From October to the end of the Tiger year some interesting and often intriguing openings could arise, perhaps leading to greater things in the future.

The Rooster's domestic and social life will also see much activity and he can look forward to some pleasing times with both family and friends. Christmas will work out particularly well, giving him the chance to enjoy himself as well as rest and unwind after the exertions of the year. He will also enjoy any travelling that he undertakes and would do well to try and meet up with friends or relations he has not seen for some time. Such a meeting will bring pleasure to all concerned.

Although the Tiger year will not have been without its problems, it will still have contained some happy and meaningful times for the Rooster and he will have learnt much from its events. He will be able to put his experiences, plus some of the ideas he has formed, to good use in the next, more settled Chinese year.

The Year of the Rabbit starts on 16 February and will be an interesting year for the Rooster. He will be able to make useful progress in many of his activities as well as lead a rich and fulfilling personal life. Admittedly there will still be some problem areas, but generally the Rabbit year will herald the start of an improvement in the Rooster's fortunes, one which will gather pace as the millennium approaches.

In his work the Rooster should aim to build on any changes that have recently taken place. If he has taken on new responsibilities or moved to a different position he should concentrate on familiarizing himself with his various duties. His diligent and conscientious approach will greatly impress and this could lead to him making further progress and being given additional duties later in the year. However, the Rooster will find that he will fare considerably better by concentrating on areas in which he already has expertise than by attempting anything too diverse or initiating a major career change. In 1999 progress will come from steady and applied effort rather than from ambitious new ventures.

With its emphasis on culture and self-improvement, the Rabbit year is also an ideal time for the Rooster to obtain any further skills or qualifications he feels he might need to develop his career. He should take advantage of any courses that he might be eligible for or even undertake some private study. He will not only find this a satisfying use of his time but it will also do much to enhance his prospects. Indeed, the experience that the Rooster gains both in the Tiger and Rabbit years will serve him extremely well in the year 2000 and he would do well to view the present time as laying the foundations for his future progress.

For those Roosters who are frustrated in their current position or are seeking work, there will be several interesting openings to pursue. Admittedly these may not be plentiful, but those that do arise could prove significant. Whenever the Rooster does see an opportunity that he considers has potential, he should act quickly. To delay or hesitate could undermine his chances. He will also fare better by aiming for positions in which he can draw on his skills and past experience rather than by venturing into unfamiliar territory.

Although some months may appear slow and indifferent for career matters and the Rooster may despair at how long it takes to achieve results, there will also be more favourable times. March and May in particular could see important developments, while from mid September onwards there will be an upturn in the Rooster's situation, making his progress that much easier and finally rewarding his patience and persistence. This upturn will continue for some time, making the experience the Rooster has gained, including any new skills he has acquired, all the more meaningful.

One area which does require care over the year, however, is finance. This is just not a time when the Rooster can take risks or enter into speculative ventures; to do so could result in him losing money. He also needs to check the terms of any large transaction that he enters into and to make sure he is conversant with any obligations he may be placed under. Similarly, he should make due allowance for any large transactions in his budget – if not, problems could result. This is very much a year which calls for careful financial management and throughout the Rooster should not let his vigilance slip. Fortunately his meticulous nature will do much to help, but there are some Roosters who can be extravagant in their financial dealings and for these, great care and watchfulness are needed.

A more positive area, however, concerns the Rooster's relations with others. The Rooster sets great store by maintaining good relations with those around him and takes a genuine and caring interest in the activities of family and close friends. Many times in 1999 others will look to him for guidance and support and the assistance he feels able to give will be truly valued. However, while the Rooster will derive much satisfaction from helping others, this should not prevent him from seeking their opinions if he himself has any concerns or feels under pressure. As he will find, a worry shared is indeed a worry halved and to dwell too much over any awkward matter could sometimes cause him needless anguish as well as let the matter get out of all proportion. In 1999 the Rooster will do much to help others, but he must sometimes allow himself to be helped too.

The Rooster can, however, look forward to many meaningful occasions with his family and friends, with any mutual interests proving particularly satisfying. If he is contemplating any major project on his home or garden, he should aim to do this jointly rather than on his own. Not only will the project benefit from the pooling of talents, but it will also be quicker and easier to complete as well as be more fulfilling for all concerned. The year will also allow the Rooster to enjoy his fondness for the outdoors, with activities such as gardening, following sport or travelling providing much pleasure.

The Rooster's social life too will go well, with some enjoyable times spent in the company of friends and attending parties and other social events. For those who are unattached or would like to lead a more active social life, there will be a noticeable upturn in fortune from May onwards. However to assist with this, the Rooster should aim to go out more, particularly to places where he is likely to meet others. Positive input on his part will certainly be rewarded and some new friendships could become important and long lasting.

Overall, this will be a reasonable year for the Rooster. Personally, there will be much for him to enjoy and what he is able to achieve in his work will stand him in good stead for the progressive trends that will start to emerge in the last quarter of the Rabbit year and remain throughout 2000. Any skills and experience he is able to gain now will certainly prove helpful. The chief area of concern is finance and the Rooster should avoid over-spending or taking undue risks. Provided he bears this in mind, however, the year will bring him much contentment.

As far as the different types of Rooster are concerned, this will be both a pleasant and important year for the *Metal Rooster*. On a personal level it will go particularly well. The Metal Rooster will be much in demand with his friends and can look forward to attending many parties and social gatherings. He himself will feel on top form and the year will certainly contain some happy occasions. Some of the new friendships he makes now will become long lasting and for the unattached Metal Rooster, a new romance beckons, particularly in the period from May to September. However, the Metal Rooster would be well advised to let any romance develop gradually rather than build up high expectations after just a brief time. He will find it is better to get to know the other person well rather than rush into an all too hasty commitment. In addition to the pleasure his social life will give, the Metal Rooster will obtain much satisfaction from his various interests. Outdoor pursuits are particularly well aspected and for those Metal Roosters who enjoy sport or are keen travellers, the year will hold some special and memorable occasions. Any Metal Rooster who has been considering embarking on lengthy travels or who would like to improve his language skills by working in another country will find this a favourable year in which to do so. Academic matters are also favoured and by setting about his studies and revision in an organized manner, the Metal Rooster will make good progress. This may mean he occasionally has to forsake some more pleasurable activities, but the sacrifice will be worth his while and what he is able to achieve, either in qualifications or skills, will stand him in excellent stead for the future. Also, if he feels he needs another vocational skill to help his career prospects, again this is a good time to take steps to obtain this. In many respects, the Rabbit year is very much one of preparation for the major strides the Metal Rooster will make in 2000 and beyond. As far as his more immediate work prospects are concerned, he should follow up any opportunities that he sees, particularly any that would give him experience in the area in which he wishes to specialize. Admittedly his progress may not always be as easy or as automatic as he would like, but by persevering and keeping faith with himself and his abilities, he will eventually get what he wants. As far as financial matters are concerned, the Metal Rooster's outgoings will be quite considerable, especially with such an active social life indicated. To prevent problems, he would do well to keep a close watch over his level of spending and should steer clear of risky or speculative ventures. One other area which requires care is his relations with more senior members of his family. At some time over the year the Metal Rooster could find himself involved in a difference of opinion. If this occurs, he should try not to let the issue escalate or get out of all proportion. By all means he should put his case and explain his position, but at the same time he should also bear in mind that those senior to him do speak with experience and with his best interests at heart. With care, tact and a willingness to compromise, however, these differences can be settled amicably and should not mar the generally positive nature of the year. Overall, this will be a pleasant and constructive year for the Metal Rooster, with his accomplishments contributing to his longer term prospects.

This is a year that the *Water Rooster* will greatly enjoy. On a domestic level he can look forward to some pleasant and meaningful times with his family and will follow their progress and activities with interest. Several times those close to him will come seeking his views and advice and their faith in his judgement will be amply justified. Sometimes the Water Rooster may not realize just how much he is appreciated, but this will be made apparent to him over the year; he holds a very dear place in the affections of many and the support he is able to give, as well as receive, will hearten and encourage him as the year progresses. In addition, the Water Rooster can also look forward to some family celebrations, which could include a wedding or the birth of a grandchild. He will also spend time over the year in tackling some projects on his home. These will generally go well, especially any that relate to the decor and add to comfort of his home. However, when undertaking practical projects, the Water Rooster should allow plenty of time and take precautions when using potentially dangerous pieces of equipment or undertaking hazardous tasks. Although anxious to get things done, he most not allow this to compromise his personal safety. He will also lead a fulfilling social life, with some pleasant occasions spent in the company of his friends. Those Water Roosters who may have experienced some recent sadness, will be seeking new friends or find themselves living in a new area, should make every effort to go out more and join in with group-oriented activities, perhaps by joining a club. By taking the initiative they can bring about a considerable improvement in their social life and, as the year progresses, they will make some new and in some cases special friendships. The Water Rooster will also obtain much satisfaction from his personal interests over the year, particularly any that allow him to use creative skills or take him out of doors. The many Water Roosters who enjoy creative activities, whether writing, photography, music or some other aspect of the arts, should use the year to develop their interest and promote their work. They could be pleasantly surprised by the response and encouragement they receive and a new project started in 1999 could have a successful outcome in the next year. The Water Rooster will also enjoy any travelling he undertakes, especially as he could visit or revisit a destination he has wanted to see for some time. One area which does require considerable care, though, is finance. The Water Rooster will need to check carefully the terms and obligations of any new agreement he enters into as well as keep a close watch on his outgoings. This is not a year for risks, complacency or spending without regard to the current financial situation. Water Roosters, do take note! This warning apart, 1999 will be a fulfilling year for the Water Rooster, with some rewarding times spent with family and friends and in carrying out his hobbies and other projects.

Much will have happened in the *Wood Rooster*'s life in recent times and the Rabbit year will allow him to take stock of all that has taken place, consolidate any gains he may have made as well as develop some of his ideas. As such, this will be a personally satisfying year and one which will offer the Wood Rooster some interesting opportunities. One area which is likely to have seen considerable change in recent years is work. Many Wood Roosters will have changed their position or taken on other responsibilities. While this often means progression, some of the Wood Rooster's new duties may be daunting. However, it is often at these times that the Wood Rooster gives of his best, as the challenge is an impetus to make that special effort and rise up and tackle any complex tasks. The Wood Rooster knows he has many talents and strengths and the Rabbit year will give him the chance to show his true worth. Indeed, he will acquit himself well, winning the respect and admiration of others as well as doing much to enhance his future prospects. Although some of his work will be demanding, he can help himself by organizing and prioritizing what he has to do and resisting the temptation of getting distracted into inconsequential details, which is sometimes a weakness of the Wood Rooster. He will also be helped by his ability to get on well with others and will benefit from the input, advice and encouragement he receives. While many Wood Roosters will decide to concentrate on their present position and consolidate the progress they have recently made, there will still be some hankering for a new position or seeking work. For these, the Rabbit year will produce some interesting opportunities. The Wood Rooster should actively follow up any openings that he sees, but also consider different ways in which he can draw on his skills and experience. Some enterprising thinking could open up some possibilities for him as well as widen the scope of positions available. By being imaginative yet remaining determined and persistent, many Wood Roosters will be successful in their quest for work, with the spring and last quarter of the year being favourable times. The Wood Rooster is also an effective communicator and for those who enjoy putting pen to paper, it could be worth their while to consider writing about their experiences and interests; this will not only bring them much personal satisfaction but could also develop in a pleasing manner. The Wood Rooster's domestic life will go well for him over the year. In addition to benefiting from the supportive attitude of those around him, he can look forward to many gratifying times with family members. In particular, any projects and hobbies he can share will bring him, and those involved, much satisfaction and will help maintain the bond and spirit of closeness that he so appreciates. He will also find outdoor activities will go well and any trips out or visits to places of local interest he is able to arrange, sometimes as an unexpected treat, will lead to some enjoyable occasions. As always, the Wood Rooster will take a caring interest in the activities of his family and close friends and if at any time he feels he can help or advise, he should do so. Although he may not wish to appear interfering, his interest and views will be greatly valued. The Wood Rooster's social life too will be interesting and he can look forward to attending a variety of events over the year. As with all Roosters, the one area which could pose problems, however, is finance.

The Wood Rooster should avoid taking undue risks or entering into commitments without checking the small print and any obligations he might be placed under. Although he is usually meticulous with paperwork and financial matters, in 1999 he cannot afford to let his vigilance slip. Generally, however, this will be a pleasing year for the Wood Rooster with his domestic and social life and interests bringing him much satisfaction. Although work matters may sometimes be demanding, what he does achieve will have a positive bearing on the more successful and progressive times that await him in the closing months of the Rabbit year and particularly in 2000.

The *Fire Rooster* has many fine attributes. He is resolute, quick-witted and relates well to others. He also knows what he wants to achieve in life and uses his strengths and talents wisely. Over the years he will have accomplished much and further successes await. However, the Year of the Rabbit, while not an adverse one, will test the Fire Rooster's patience and there could be times when he will despair of achieving some of his more immediate aims and objectives. To avoid disappointment, he needs to keep his expectations to a more modest level and avoid launching ambitious new ventures. He will also find he will obtain the best results by concentrating on areas in which he has most experience and consolidating his present position. This way he will become even more familiar with and skilled in his line of work and will impress others, which in turn will add to his reputation and help his future prospects. He will also be given some interesting challenges over the year and by dealing with these will do much to prepare himself for the greater tasks that lie ahead. In many ways 1999 is a year of preparing the base from which to make further advances. Accordingly, all Fire Roosters, whether in work or seeking work, should take advantage of any opportunity they are given to go on courses or undertake further training and if there is a skill they would like to learn or subject that has been intriguing them, this would be an excellent time to follow this up. In addition to any training, those Fire Roosters seeking work should remain active in pursuing any openings that become available. Although they might not always be successful in attaining the exact position they were seeking, any post they do obtain will not only help to widen their experience but could also, in time, develop in a truly significant way. Again, what the Fire Rooster achieves in 1999 may not always meet his high expectations, but its bearing on his future cannot be underestimated. The Fire Rooster will, however, need to deal with financial matters with considerable care. In 1999 he could face some large expenses, especially connected with his accommodation and travel, and he must make suitable provision in his budget rather than stretch his resources too far. Although he may have been able to build up some savings in recent years, he should remember these are not limitless and to prevent problems emerging in 1999 he needs to monitor his outgoings continually as well as keep a tight control over the purse strings. The Fire Rooster's domestic life will, however, bring him considerable contentment. He will take much pride in the achievements of those around him and several times over the year will advise others on various matters and decisions they need to take. As usual, those around him will set great store by his views and some assistance he is able to give a more senior relation will be particularly appreciated. The Fire Rooster will also decide to carry out some improvements on his home and garden over the year and, while the eventual result will bring him much satisfaction, he could find practical projects will take him longer and cause more disruption than he originally anticipated. To avoid being placed under too much pressure, he should concentrate on one job at a time rather than spread his energies too widely. It is also important that he sets a regular time aside for his hobbies and interests. These do allow him to rest and unwind and provide him with an important break from his usual activities. Indeed, the Fire Rooster could find it helpful to consider extending an existing interest over the year or taking up a new one; this could lead to some fulfilling and personally rewarding times. Generally, the Year of the Rabbit will be a pleasant year for the Fire Rooster, with his accomplishments and the experience he gains doing much to help his longer term prospects.

Determined, dedicated and with good judgement, the *Earth Rooster* has a great future ahead of him. Already he will have accomplished and learnt much and his experiences, both good and bad, will have taught him much about himself and his strengths. In 1999 he will be given the opportunity to build on what he has achieved and, just as importantly, make some decisions about his future which will have far-reaching consequences. As far as his work is concerned, the Earth Rooster should consolidate any recent gains he has made as well as continue to set about his duties to the best of his abilities. He should also take advantage of any opportunity he gets to learn about other aspects of his work and extend his experience. Similarly, any training courses he is able to go on and skills he is able to acquire will also enhance his prospects. Generally, this will be a constructive time for the Earth Rooster and while his progress may not always be as swift or as smooth as he would like, he will be forming the basis of his future success and progression. The Earth Rooster would also do well to give some thought to how he would like his career to develop over the next few years and seek the guidance of those with experience of what he would like to do. By making such an approach, he will be given some valuable pieces of advice and told of openings and possibilities he may not have considered before. Indeed, some of the longer term plans he is able to set in motion in the Rabbit year will have significant consequences in future years. Also, by giving thought to his future, the Earth Rooster will be able to gain a clearer idea of the direction in which he is heading as well as the objectives he needs to set himself. Similarly, those Earth Roosters seeking employment will also see some interesting developments over the year. They should actively follow up any openings and could find that a position they obtain, perhaps in an unexpected and fortuitous manner, will lead to them learning new skills which will develop in an encouraging manner over the next few years. Work-wise, what the Earth Rooster accomplishes in the Rabbit year will often have far-reaching consequences. Financial matters, however, do need care and the Earth Rooster should avoid taking risks, particularly with money he can ill-afford to lose. He should also keep a close watch over his level of spending; otherwise he could find this all too easily creeps up and is far greater than he originally envisaged or budgeted for, forcing cutbacks later in the year. The Earth Rooster's domestic life, though, will be busy and fulfilling. The activities of those around him will keep him well occupied and while he may not always have the time to devote to his own pursuits, family matters and the progress of those close to him will be a source of much pride. One word of warning though – sometimes the Earth Rooster could feel under pressure from work activities or have matters that are preoccupying him. When this happens he should try not to allow any tensions or feelings of tiredness to spill over and affect his relations with those around him. He will find it easier – and comforting – to talk matters over rather than to brood or keep his thoughts to himself. Also, if any differences do arise, the Earth Rooster should show some flexibility and willingness to compromise. To be too stubborn or intransigent could again cause acrimony and sour what could otherwise be pleasant and meaningful times. Earth Roosters, do take careful note – domestic matters will, for the most part, go well but do not jeopardize them over what could be relatively trivial matters! The Earth Rooster can, however, look forward to leading a pleasing social life over the year, with the summer months being particularly active. For Earth Roosters who are seeking new friends or who are unattached, a new friendship that is formed out of a chance meeting could, in time, become significant and bring the Earth Rooster much happiness. There is also one other important consideration for the Earth Rooster over the year. If he does not get much exercise during the day or is reliant on convenience food, he would do well to try and exercise more and consider switching to a more balanced diet. He will find both could do much to help his well-being. Overall, 1999 will be an interesting and constructive year for the Earth Rooster, with his accomplishments often having important and positive implications for the future.

FAMOUS ROOSTERS

Adamski, Kate Adie, Francis Bacon, Dame Janet Baker, Severiano Ballesteros, Enid Blyton, Sir Dirk Bogarde, Barbara Taylor Bradford, Richard Briers, Michael Caine, Jasper Carrott, Enrico Caruso, Christopher Cazenove, Jean Chrétien, Eric Clapton, Joan Collins, Rita Coolidge, Cathy Dennis, Sasha Distel, the Duke of Edinburgh, Ernie Els, Gloria Estefan, Nick Faldo, Mohamed al Fayed, Bryan Ferry, Errol Flynn, Benjamin Franklin, Dawn French, Stephen Fry, David Gower, Steffi Graf, Melanie Griffith, Richard Harris, Goldie Hawn, Katherine Hepburn, Michael Heseltine, Glenn Hoddle, Quincy Jones, Alain Juppé, Diane Keaton, Dean Koontz, Bernhard Langer, D. H. Lawrence, Martyn Lewis, David Livingstone, Ken Livingstone, Jayne Mansfield, Steve Martin, James Mason, W. Somerset Maugham, Paul Merton, Bette Midler, Van Morrison, Willie Nelson, Paul Nicholas, Barry Norman, Kim Novak, Yoko Ono, Dolly Parton, Michelle Pfeiffer, Priscilla Presley, Nancy Reagan, Joan Rivers, Paul Scofield, Jenny Seagrove, George Segal, Carly Simon, Johann Strauss, Sir Peter Ustinov, Richard Wagner, Neil Young.

10 FEBRUARY 1910 ∼ 29 JANUARY 1911   *Metal Dog*

28 JANUARY 1922 ∼ 15 FEBRUARY 1923   *Water Dog*

14 FEBRUARY 1934 ∼ 3 FEBRUARY 1935   *Wood Dog*

2 FEBRUARY 1946 ∼ 21 JANUARY 1947   *Fire Dog*

18 FEBRUARY 1958 ∼ 7 FEBRUARY 1959   *Earth Dog*

6 FEBRUARY 1970 ∼ 26 JANUARY 1971   *Metal Dog*

25 JANUARY 1982 ∼ 12 FEBRUARY 1983   *Water Dog*

10 FEBRUARY 1994 ∼ 30 JANUARY 1995   *Wood Dog*

THE
DOG

THE PERSONALITY OF THE DOG

If you think you can win, you can win. Faith is necessary
to victory.

– William Hazlitt: a Dog

The Dog is born under the signs of loyalty and anxiety. He
usually holds very firm views and beliefs and is the cham-
pion of good causes. He hates any sort of injustice or unfair
treatment and will do all in his power to help those less
fortunate than himself. He has a strong sense of fair play
and will be honourable and open in all his dealings.

The Dog is very direct and straightforward. He is never
one to skirt round issues and speaks frankly and to the
point. He can also be stubborn, but he is more than prepared to listen to the views of others and will try to be as
fair as possible in coming to his decisions. He will readily
give advice where it is needed and will be the first to offer
assistance when things go wrong.

The Dog instils confidence wherever he goes and there
are many who admire him for his integrity and resolute
manner. He is a very good judge of character and can often
form an accurate impression of someone very shortly after
meeting them. He is also very intuitive and can frequently
sense how things are going to work out long in advance.

Despite his friendly and amiable manner, the Dog is not
a big socializer. He dislikes having to attend large social
functions or parties and much prefers a quiet meal with
friends or a chat by the fire. He is an excellent conversationalist and is often a marvellous raconteur of amusing

stories and anecdotes. He is also quick-witted and his mind is always alert.

The Dog can keep calm in a crisis and although he does have a temper, his outbursts tend to be short-lived. He is loyal and trustworthy, but if he ever feels badly let down or rejected by someone, he will rarely forgive or forget.

The Dog usually has very set interests. He prefers to specialize and become an expert in a chosen area rather than dabble in a variety of different activities. He usually does well in jobs where he feels that he is being of service to others and is often suited to careers in the social services, the medical and legal professions and teaching. The Dog does, however, need to feel motivated in his work. He has to have a sense of purpose and if ever this is lacking he can quite often drift through life without ever achieving very much. Once he has the motivation, however, very little can prevent him from securing his objective.

Another characteristic of the Dog is his tendency to worry and to view things rather pessimistically. Quite often these worries are totally unnecessary and are of his own making. Although it may be difficult, worrying is a habit which the Dog should try to overcome.

The Dog is not materialistic or particularly bothered about accumulating great wealth. As long as he has the necessary money to support his family and to spend on the occasional luxury, he is more than happy. However, when he does have any spare money he tends to be rather a spendthrift and does not always put his money to its best use. He is also not a very good speculator and would be advised to get professional advice before entering into any major long-term investment.

The Dog will rarely be short of admirers, but he is not an easy person to live with. His moods are changeable and his standards high, but he will be loyal and protective to his partner and will do all in his power to provide a good and comfortable home. He can get on extremely well with those born under the signs of the Horse, Pig, Tiger and Monkey, and can also establish a sound and stable relationship with the Rat, Ox, Rabbit, Snake and another Dog, but will find the Dragon a bit too flamboyant for his liking. He will also find it difficult to understand the creative and imaginative Goat and is likely to be highly irritated by the candid Rooster.

The female Dog is renowned for her beauty. She has a warm and caring nature, although until she knows someone well she can be both secretive and very guarded. She is highly intelligent and despite her calm and tranquil appearance she can be extremely ambitious. She enjoys sport and other outdoor activities and has a happy knack of finding bargains in the most unlikely of places. She can also get rather impatient when things do not work out as she would like.

The Dog usually has a very good way with children and can be a loving and doting parent. He will rarely be happier than when he is helping someone or doing something that will benefit others. Providing he can cure himself of his tendency to worry, he will lead a very full and active life – and in that life he will make many friends and do a tremendous amount of good.

THE FIVE DIFFERENT TYPES OF DOG

In addition to the 12 signs of the Chinese zodiac, there are five elements and these have a strengthening or moderating influence on the sign. The effects of the five elements on the Dog are described below, together with the years in which the elements were exercising their influence. Therefore all Dogs born in 1910 and 1970 are Metal Dogs, those born in 1922 and 1982 are Water Dogs, and so on.

Metal Dog: 1910, 1970
The Metal Dog is bold, confident and forthright, and sets about everything he does in a resolute and determined manner. He has a great belief in his abilities and has no hesitation about speaking his mind or devoting himself to some just cause. He can be rather serious at times and can get anxious and irritable when things are not going according to plan. He tends to have very specific interests and it would certainly help him to broaden his outlook and also become more involved in group activities. He is extremely loyal and faithful to his friends.

Water Dog: 1922, 1982
The Water Dog has a very direct and outgoing personality. He is an excellent communicator and has little trouble in persuading others to fall in with his plans. He does, however, have a somewhat carefree nature and is not as

disciplined or as thorough as he should be in certain matters. Neither does he keep as much control over his finances as he should, but he can be most generous to his family and friends and will make sure that they want for nothing. The Water Dog is usually very good with children and has a wide circle of friends.

Wood Dog: 1934, 1994

This Dog is a hard and conscientious worker and will usually make a favourable impression wherever he goes. He is less independent than some of the other types of Dog and prefers to work in a group rather than on his own. He is popular, has a good sense of humour and takes a very keen interest in the activities of the various members of his family. He is often attracted to the finer things in life and can get much pleasure from collecting stamps, coins, pictures or antiques. He also prefers to live in the country rather than the town.

Fire Dog: 1946

This Dog has a lively, outgoing personality and is able to establish friendships with remarkable ease. He is an honest and conscientious worker and likes to take an active part in all that is going on around him. He also likes to explore new ideas, and providing he can get the necessary support and advice, he can often succeed where others have failed. He does, however, have a tendency to be stubborn. Providing he can overcome this, the Fire Dog can often achieve considerable fame and fortune.

Earth Dog: 1958

The Earth Dog is very talented and astute. He is methodical and efficient and is capable of going far in his chosen profession. He tends to be rather quiet and reserved but has a very persuasive manner and usually secures his objectives without too much opposition. He is generous and kind and is always ready to lend a helping hand when it is needed. He is also held in very high esteem by his friends and colleagues and he is usually most dignified in his appearance.

PROSPECTS FOR THE DOG IN 1999

The Chinese New Year starts on 16 February 1999. Until then, the old year, the Year of the Tiger, is still making its presence felt.

The Year of the Tiger (28 January 1998 to 15 February 1999) will have been a positive one for the Dog, although just how much he will have achieved is partly dependent upon himself and his attitude. For the determined and enterprising Dog, much useful headway can be made during a Tiger year. The encouraging aspects remain right to the end of the year, so there is still time for the Dog to benefit from them.

In his work the Dog should remain committed to the tasks before him, while using any opportunity he gets to extend his experience, promote his ideas or further his position. He will have done much to impress during the year and what he accomplishes in the last quarter can lead to further headway as well as have a favourable bearing on the next Chinese year. Some of those Dogs seeking work will also find their determination rewarded at this time. Sometimes a chance remark they overhear or an intriguing advert will alert them to an interesting possibility which they would do well to follow up. October and November 1998 in particular will contain some interesting developments and again what the Dog is able to achieve can have far-reaching implications. Similarly, any training or new skills that the Dog can acquire at this time will also be to his future advantage.

As far as financial matters are concerned, the Dog should not experience any undue problems, although with the last months of the year being a traditionally expensive time, he could find it helpful to spread some of his purchases out rather than making them all at once.

Both domestically and socially, however, the closing months of the Tiger year will be a positive time for the Dog. His family and friends will be most supportive and if at any time he has any worries or concerns, he should not hesitate to seek the opinions of others. Throughout the Tiger year, the Dog will benefit greatly from the input and encouragement of those around him and should listen to their words carefully. They do, after all, speak with his best interests at heart.

For the unattached Dog, or those seeking new friends and romance, the aspects are excellent towards the end of the year and a friendship started at this time could blossom in the next Chinese year.

By giving of his best and making the most of the chances that arise, the Dog will have good cause to be pleased with his accomplishments in the Tiger year, and in many cases he will be able to build on these in 1999.

The Year of the Rabbit starts on 16 February and is one which holds much promise for the Dog. Most areas of his life are well aspected, with his personal life bringing especial pleasure.

However, to make the most of this favourable year, the Dog needs to decide upon his objectives and then set about realizing them with his customary resolve. This is a time when a bold and enterprising approach will lead to some pleasing developments and, for those prepared to be tenacious in the pursuit of their aims, considerable success awaits.

To make the best headway, though, the Dog should concentrate his efforts on areas in which he has greatest interest and expertise, building on what he has already learnt and accomplished and making the most of his skills. Should he face any setbacks or disappointments, he should not let them get the better of him. Rather than get disheartened, he should learn from the experience and set forth with even greater determination. The Dog possesses many wonderful talents and the Rabbit year will certainly give him every encouragement to make the most of himself.

In his work the Dog will be given the chance to take on different responsibilities, which will provide him with new challenges and the chance to put his experience and skills to good use. Admittedly some of what is asked of him may initially appear daunting, but this will often give the Dog the stimulus to make that extra effort and show his true capabilities. As a result, he will certainly impress others and do much to enhance his reputation and prospects.

Throughout the year the Dog should also use any chance he gets to promote his ideas; some of these will be favourably received and could develop in an encouraging manner. If he has been considering launching a business idea, now is also a good time to advance his plans, seek the opinions of those qualified to advise and gauge the initial response. Again, it is those who are prepared to take decisive steps towards their aspirations who will fare the best over the year.

There will also be positive developments for those Dogs seeking work. Again, they should follow up any openings that they see, but would also do well to consider different ways in which they can use their skills and past experience. This could lead to new openings and possibilities which could result in some interesting opportunities. As before, an enterprising and innovative approach can achieve much.

Also, with the Rabbit year favouring cultural activities and self-development, all Dogs would do well to take advantage of any opportunity they get to go on training courses or add to their skills. If there has been a subject that has been intriguing the Dog for some time, this will be an excellent year to find out more. Anything constructive the Dog can do will not only help his prospects but will also be a source of much personal satisfaction.

This will be a positive year for financial matters, with many Dogs enjoying a noticeable improvement in their financial situation. For some, this will allow them to buy items for themselves and their accommodation that they have long been considering. By looking at various outlets and comparing what is on offer, they will be able to make some excellent acquisitions over the year and at keen prices. However, if the Dog should find himself with funds he does not immediately need, he would do well to set these aside for specific purposes rather than allow them to 'burn a hole in his pocket'. For instance some could be put aside for holidays and travel, some for future contingencies and some saved for the long term. By managing his money the Dog will have more to show for it than if he were to succumb to too many indulgences and temptations.

Another area which is well aspected is travel and the Dog should try to make sure he goes away at least once over the year. He will not only enjoy his time away, particularly if it allows him to visit places new to him, but will also greatly benefit from the rest and break a holiday will bring. For Dogs particularly keen on travel or any who would like to improve their language skills or work in another country, the year will contain some opportunities that would certainly be worth following up, particularly as some may not arise again for a long time.

As far as the Dog's personal and domestic life is concerned, this will be an enjoyable year. As always, the Dog's family means a great deal to him and over the year he will have good reason to value the encouragement and support they give as well as the obvious care and affection they show towards him. If he is ever in a dilemma or has any matters concerning him, he will find it helpful to seek the views of those around him. Often their opinions will be able to put the matter in true perspective, raise points that the Dog might have overlooked or just help to put his mind at ease. Throughout the year the Dog should remember that help, advice and practical assistance are on hand and he should not hesitate to avail himself of them.

The Dog can also look forward to some notable occasions with his family over the year. Not only will his own progress and success be a source of much family pleasure, but there could also be other reasons for celebration, such as a wedding, an addition to his family, academic success or some other achievement. The Rabbit year will certainly contain several memorable events, with the months from April to late September being particularly finely aspected for family and personal activities.

In addition to the undoubted pleasure his family life will bring the Dog, this will also be an active year for social matters. The Dog selects his friends with care and in 1999 he will forge some friendships that will become significant in the months ahead. For the unattached Dog, romance is well aspected, with a friendship made in the previous Chinese year or early in the Rabbit year bringing much happiness. On a personal level, 1999 will be a year of much joy, with many unattached Dogs getting engaged or married, such are the splendid aspects that prevail.

However, while much of the year will go well for the Dog, there are certain points that he should bear in mind. During 1999 there will be times of considerable activity, with pressures at work plus numerous household matters to deal with. At such times the Dog should prioritize his tasks rather than spread his energies too widely. Also, he should be realistic in his level of commitments. Although he may not want to disappoint, it is best for him to be honest and say if he cannot properly attend to something, or ask for additional help with it, rather than put himself under needless pressure or rush his activities just to get them done.

Also, the Dog does have a tendency to drive himself hard, and while his efforts will be appreciated and will bring him credit over the year, it is important that he takes good care of himself and allows himself time to relax and unwind. If not, he could find he is becoming tired and stressed and not making as much of himself or the year as he otherwise might. Fortunately, his family, social life and interests will all help, but there are certainly some Dogs who could be tempted to overdo things and if not checked, this tendency could cause problems. In 1999 it is important that the Dog keeps his life and activities in balance.

Overall, however, this will be a positive and constructive year for the Dog and by setting his mind on certain objectives and working steadily towards them, he will make good progress, especially where work and travel are concerned. Personally, the year is superbly aspected, with the Dog's family and social life bringing him much happiness. In almost all respects, this is a year in which the Dog will prosper and will be one for him to enjoy.

As far as the different types of Dog are concerned, 1999 is a year which holds considerable promise for the *Metal Dog*. He has a strong faith in his abilities and commendable determination to do well, and his drive, motivation and enterprise throughout the year will be recognized and rewarded. In 1999 he will be able to build on past successes and accomplishments and make even greater headway. However, to take full advantage of his abilities and the progressive trends that prevail, the Metal Dog should give some thought to what he would like to accomplish over the next 12 months. By setting himself some objectives he will find himself proceeding in a more purposeful way and achieving more than if he were to leave things to chance.

In the Metal Dog's work there will be some particularly good opportunities to progress, ones which will allow him to put his skills to more effective use. When he sees openings to pursue or has any ideas which he feels would help his position, he should actively follow these up. In 1999 his progress will often come as a direct result of some decisive and enterprising action on his part. Many Metal Dogs seeking work will also find their perseverance rewarded and, while sometimes they may find a position with slightly different duties from those they were seeking, often this will allow them to add to their experience and it may develop in a meaningful way in a comparatively short space of time. The aspects for work activities are very positive and the Metal Dog should do all he can to take advantage of these excellent trends. He will also enjoy an upturn in his financial position and this will enable him to carry out some improvements on his accommodation or perhaps to move altogether. In either case, the Metal Dog should proceed carefully rather than too hastily. By considering his options and taking his time he will often obtain more satisfactory results. For those Metal Dogs who do decide to move, choosing their new accommodation and location could take some time, but the wait will be worth their while and they could finally find the place they decide upon by a curious twist of fate. On a personal level, this will be a happy and fulfilling year for the Metal Dog. His domestic life will be busy and sometimes demanding, but despite the often high level of activity, these will still be rich and rewarding times. The Metal Dog will take a deep and caring interest in the activities of those around him as well as do much to assist and encourage. As usual, his advice and opinions will be sought and valued by his loved ones. The Metal Dog will also have good reason for a celebration over the year; this may be a personal achievement, a birth in his family or an engagement or marriage. Both personally and professionally, the Rabbit year will contain some memorable occasions. However, with parts of it being busy, it is important that the Metal Dog does not neglect his own interests or drive himself so hard that he becomes tired or over-stressed. To prevent this, he should aim to set a regular time aside for his own interests, especially those that give him a chance to unwind and provide a break from his usual daytime concerns. Any Metal Dogs who are sedentary for much of the day could also benefit from taking a little more exercise. In addition, the Metal Dog should ensure that he takes a proper break or holiday over the year and, with travel well aspected, this could be a good year in which to visit a destination he has had in mind for some time. In almost all respects, this will be a favourable year for the Metal Dog, with his personal life bringing much happiness and constructive progress indicated in his work. In 1999 the Metal Dog has much going in his favour and, with his keen and determined nature, he is certain to make the most of the opportunities that the year will bring.

This will be an important year for the *Water Dog*, with some of what happens and some of the decisions he takes having far-reaching consequences. However, throughout the year the Water Dog will be well supported and most of what he undertakes will work out well for him. On a personal level this will be a particularly favourable time. The Water Dog can look forward to leading a busy and active social life, with several parties and other functions to attend. There will also be the opportunity to make new friends and those Water Dogs who move over the year, either as a result of their education or work, will soon establish a new and pleasing social life. With his ability to get on so well with others the Water Dog will find himself fitting in wherever he goes and some of the friendships he forms will become significant and long lasting. Any Water Dog who may have experienced some personal misfortune or be feeling lonely should regard the Rabbit year a new start and should concentrate on the present and future rather than dwell heavily on what has gone before. To help with this, these Water Dogs should aim to go out more, involve themselves in group activities and consider joining a local society or interest group. Positive action on their part will certainly help to bring about an improvement in their social life as well as greater contentment. For the Water Dog in education this will be an important and favourable year. Some of the material he covers and exams he takes will have a major bearing on his future and it would certainly be in his interests to set about his studies in a disciplined and organized manner. When exams are approaching he may have to modify his social life as well as not succumb to too many other distractions, but the sacrifice he makes and effort he puts into his work will be well worth his while. Also, if there are any aspects of his studies that are giving him difficulty, he should not hesitate to seek additional guidance. As he will find, those around are keen for him to make the most of his abilities and can do much to help and to put his mind at ease on certain points. In addition to what the Water Dog accomplishes academically, he should also give some thought to his future vocation and consider any training and qualifications that he might need. If appropriate, he would again do well to approach those in a position to advise and take steps to secure the necessary training or enrol on appropriate courses. Again, some of what the Water Dog sets in motion over the year will have important implications for the future. For those Water Dogs who are already in work or seeking work, the year will hold some interesting developments. Many will be successful in gaining a new position and while sometimes their duties will be different from those they were originally seeking, they should regard this as a way of gaining useful experience. In addition, the Water Dog should take advantage of any courses he is offered or ways in which he can extend his skills, as again this will do much to help his prospects. He will enjoy any travelling that he undertakes during the year, although he will need to keep a close watch over his level of spending and as far as possible avoid dipping too heavily into any savings he has built up. These could take some time to replenish! In most respects, though, 1999 is a year which holds much promise for the Water Dog. He has a good future ahead of him and what he accomplishes now will do much to pave the way for the considerable progress and success that await him.

This will be a positive year for the *Wood Dog*, with many of his activities bringing him much pleasure. However, to get the full benefit from this most favourable of years, he needs to plan his activities well and use his time wisely. If there are projects he wishes to carry out or ideas he is keen to put into practice, he should take steps to achieve them, as this is very much a year for action; otherwise he could so easily find that the year has passed him by and he has little to show for his efforts. One area which will prove especially fulfilling for the Wood Dog concerns his accommodation. Some Wood Dogs will decide to move to a different location entirely and while the moving process will take a lot of time, the end result will be well worth it and once installed, the Wood Dog will delight in discovering the amenities and attractions of his new area. In some respects, these Wood Dogs will consider the Rabbit year as the start of a new chapter in their life. Wood Dogs who decide to stay where they are will also spend much time planning and setting about projects on their home. Again, some of these will be time-consuming, but these Wood Dogs will be delighted with what they are able to accomplish, particularly as some of it will add a great deal to the comfort and decor of their home. However, while practical projects will bring the Wood Dog considerable satisfaction, he does need to take care with his personal safety. If he has to undertake any hazardous task he should follow all the recommended safety procedures and should be wary of tackling anything complicated that he does not fully understand. When in doubt he should seek professional help. Also, he should be careful when lifting or moving heavy weights; without care he could all too easily strain himself. Wood Dogs, take note and take care! In addition to what the Wood Dog accomplishes with regard to his accommodation, his own personal hobbies and interests will bring him considerable delight and he should make sure he sets a regular time aside for these. If he is able to extend a current interest in some way, perhaps by learning about another aspect of it, it could become all the more fulfilling. The Wood Dog's domestic and social life too will bring him much contentment. Both his family and friends will take a keen interest in all he does and many times during the year he will be heartened by the encouragement and advice he receives, as well as by the obvious affection he is shown. Also, if at any time there is any matter concerning him, he should not hesitate to seek the opinions of those around him. He will find others can do much to put his mind at ease as well as offer valuable assistance. The Wood Dog will also take much pleasure in following the achievements of those close to him and although he may not want to appear interfering, any advice he feels able to pass on to a younger relation, particularly as a result of his own experience, will be much appreciated. Another area which is well aspected is travel and the Wood Dog should try to go away at least once over the year, perhaps visiting a place he has wanted to see for some time or relations and friends he has not seen for some while. In addition, visits to local places of interest will also provide some happy and memorable occasions. Generally, the Rabbit year will bring the Wood Dog considerable satisfaction. However, to benefit from its favourable aspects, he needs to decide just what he wants to achieve over the year and how he wishes to spend his time. Then, once he has made his decision, he should set his thoughts and plans in motion and will find that much of what he does will work to his advantage.

The *Fire Dog* has tremendous drive and whenever he is committed to a certain task he gives his all. His will-power, enthusiasm and wide-ranging abilities will have served him well in recent years and allowed him to achieve a great deal. This year will give him the chance to consolidate his more recent achievements, savour his accomplishments and take stock of his position, thereby bringing him much contentment and satisfaction. As far as his work is concerned, the Fire Dog will be able to build on any recent gains and if he has taken on a different position or been given new responsibilities, he will content himself with learning and making the most of his new role. While not all the tasks he is given will be straightforward, his tenacity and ability to rise up to the challenges will do much to enhance both his reputation and prospects. While many Fire Dogs will decide to build on the position they already hold, for those keen to move to another type of work or those seeking work the year will contain some excellent opportunities. These Fire Dogs would do well to consider just what type of position they would like and then pursue any openings that arise. It could also be in their interests to approach companies or organizations they would like to work for, setting out their past experience and ideas. A positive and enterprising approach could give rise to some interesting and helpful developments. This is also a favourable year for the Fire Dog to advance any business idea he has and those who have been considering setting up their own business would find it worth their while to gauge the initial response and seek the opinions of qualified advisers. Again, positive action on the Fire Dog's part will bring results, while failure to do anything will leave him looking back and wondering 'What if?' This will also be a positive year for financial matters, although the Fire Dog would do well to save or put any spare money he does not immediately need towards a specific purpose rather than to succumb to too many temptations or extravagances. With travel well aspected, he should also try to ensure that he takes a holiday or break over the year. Not only will he benefit from the rest and change of scene this will give, but his chosen destination could also exceed expectations. The Fire Dog will gain much satisfaction from his hobbies and interests, too, and should set a regular time aside for these. In particular, outdoor activities and pursuits that draw on his practical and creative abilities will go especially well. The Fire Dog can also look forward to leading an active domestic and social life and throughout the year will find himself much in demand with both family and friends. In addition to the many meaningful occasions he will have with those around him, his views and advice will often be sought and over the year he will do much to support others. The assistance he gives, together with the important role he plays in the lives of those around him, will be truly underlined over the year and this will hearten the Fire Dog. However, while he will help others, he too can benefit from seeking advice on any matters that might be concerning him. Those he asks will often be delighted to reciprocate his kindnesses and will give him some sterling advice and support. One other point that the Fire Dog needs to consider concerns his level of commitments – he should avoid taking on new projects and activities that he does not really have time to deal with properly. Without a certain care in this regard, he could find himself under increased and sometimes unnecessary pressure and with some of the free time he would have liked to set aside for more pleasurable activities already taken up. Overall, though, this will be a positive and constructive year for the

Fire Dog. By using his skills well and making the most of the situations in which he finds himself, he can make good progress, added to which, his domestic and social life will be a source of much happiness and pleasure.

The *Earth Dog* will have accomplished much in recent years and can be justifiably proud of his many achievements, both personal and professional. However, despite all he has attained, there will still be many goals that he would like to reach and the Rabbit year will give him the chance to pursue some of his long-held ambitions. In order to do this, though, the Earth Dog would do well to reflect on his current situation and consider the best way for him to progress. As far as work is concerned, some Earth Dogs will decide to remain where they are and use this as a base from which to develop, knowing that their skills, reputation and knowledge will stand them in good stead. However, other Earth Dogs will feel the time is right for a career change and that they would benefit from new challenges. For these Earth Dogs the year will contain some splendid opportunities, but to benefit from the favourable aspects the Earth Dog does need to have a reasonably clear idea of the direction in which he is heading. It is one thing to desire change, but another to know the change he wants. However, once he has decided on the line of work he wishes to pursue, the Earth Dog should go after his objective with determination, leaving no stone unturned. His efforts, energy and sheer determination will bring him positive results. Those Earth Dogs seeking work will also make headway and should persist in following up any opportunities that interest them. They could find that once they are able to get a foothold in a company, there is

considerable scope for progression. For almost all Earth
Dogs, what they accomplish in 1999 will have positive and
far-reaching implications, such are the important and beneficial aspects that prevail. The Earth Dog will also enjoy
an improvement in his financial situation over the year,
although he would do well to plan his purchases carefully
rather than go through the year without any sort of financial planning or control. He would do particularly well to
consider saving or investing any money that he does not
immediately need, or putting some money towards items
and equipment for his home. By keeping alert at sale times
he could find he is able to obtain some excellent bargains,
especially in the clothing and home furnishings line. With
travel well aspected, he should also aim to take a proper
holiday or break and will greatly enjoy visiting destinations new to him. Domestically, this will be an active and
sometimes demanding year for the Earth Dog, with many
calls upon his time and matters to deal with. Occasionally
he will despair of all that is being asked of him and at these
times he should not hesitate to ask for help rather than
shoulder too many domestic jobs and responsibilities
himself. Also, he should try not to start or engage in too
many household projects all at once; he would do better
to concentrate on a few tasks at a time and do them well
rather than to put himself under pressure by attempting
too much. However, busy though his home life will be,
these will still be meaningful times for the Earth Dog and
he will take much pride and satisfaction in the achievements, progress and successes enjoyed by those dear to
him. The help and encouragement he is able to give to
others will also be genuinely appreciated. At busy times,

the Earth Dog will find it in everyone's interest to suggest activities all can enjoy, perhaps a local outing or special meal, rather than driving on relentlessly. Not only will this bring pleasure to all concerned, but it will also help to relieve any pressures that might have built up. Similarly, the Earth Dog's social life will provide him with some enjoyable occasions and for those Earth Dogs who may, for some reason, find themselves dispirited or lonely, the Rabbit year will certainly mark an upturn, with some new and important friendships being formed. To assist this upturn, though, these Earth Dogs would do well to go out more, especially to places where they are likely to meet others. Their efforts will certainly pay off. Generally, this will be a favourable year for the Earth Dog and by pursuing his goals and aspirations, he will achieve a great deal as well as sow the seeds for even greater accomplishments in the future.

FAMOUS DOGS

André Agassi, Jane Asher, Zoë Ball, Brigitte Bardot, Gary Barlow, Dr Christiaan Barnard, Candice Bergman, David Bowie, Michael Buerk, Kate Bush, Max Bygraves, Naomi Campbell, Mariah Carey, King Carl Gustaf XVI of Sweden, Belinda Carlisle, José Carreras, Paul Cézanne, Cher, Sir Winston Churchill, Petula Clark, Bill Clinton, Leonard Cohen, Robin Cook, Jamie Lee Curtis, Charles Dance, Daniel Day-Lewis, Claude Debussy, Frankie Dettori, Blake Edwards, Sally Field, Robert Frost, Ava Gardner, Judy Garland, George Gershwin, Lenny Henry, O. Henry,

Patricia Hodge, Victor Hugo, Barry Humphries, Michael Jackson, Felicity Kendal, Sue Lawley, Maureen Lipman, Sophia Loren, Joanna Lumley, Shirley MacLaine, Madonna, Norman Mailer, Winnie Mandela, Barry Manilow, Rik Mayall, Golda Meir, Freddie Mercury, Liza Minnelli, David Niven, Gary Numan, Sydney Pollack, Elvis Presley, Priscilla Presley, The Artist formerly known as Prince, George Robertson, Paul Robeson, Linda Ronstadt, Gabriela Sabatini, Sade, Carl Sagan, Susan Sarandon, Jennifer Saunders, Claudia Schiffer, Norman Schwarzkopf, Dr Albert Schweitzer, Alan Shearer, Clare Short, Sylvester Stallone, Robert Louis Stevenson, Sharon Stone, Jack Straw, David Suchet, Donald Sutherland, Chris Tarrant, Mother Teresa, Ben Vereen, Voltaire, Paul Weller, Prince William, Shelley Winters, Ian Woosnam.

30 JANUARY 1911 ~ 17 FEBRUARY 1912	*Metal Pig*
16 FEBRUARY 1923 ~ 4 FEBRUARY 1924	*Water Pig*
4 FEBRUARY 1935 ~ 23 JANUARY 1936	*Wood Pig*
22 JANUARY 1947 ~ 9 FEBRUARY 1948	*Fire Pig*
8 FEBRUARY 1959 ~ 27 JANUARY 1960	*Earth Pig*
27 JANUARY 1971 ~ 14 FEBRUARY 1972	*Metal Pig*
13 FEBRUARY 1983 ~ 1 FEBRUARY 1984	*Water Pig*
31 JANUARY 1995 ~ 18 FEBRUARY 1996	*Wood Pig*

THE
PIG

THE PERSONALITY OF THE PIG

For the resolute and determined there is time and
opportunity.

— Ralph Waldo Emerson: a Pig

The Pig is born under the sign of honesty. He has a kind
and understanding nature and is well known for his abilities
as a peacemaker. He hates any sort of discord or unpleasantness and will do all in his power to sort out differences of
opinion or bring opposing factions together.

He is also an excellent conversationalist and speaks
truthfully and to the point. He dislikes any form of falsehood or hypocrisy and is a firm believer in justice and the
maintenance of law and order. In spite of these beliefs,
however, the Pig is reasonably tolerant and often prepared
to forgive others for their wrongs. He rarely harbours
grudges and is never vindictive.

The Pig is usually very popular. He enjoys other people's
company and likes to be involved in joint or group activities. He will be a loyal member of any club or society and
can be relied upon to lend a helping hand at functions. He
is also an excellent fund-raiser for charities and often a
great supporter of humanitarian causes.

The Pig is a hard and conscientious worker and is particularly respected for his reliability and integrity. In his early
years he will try his hand at several different jobs, but he is
usually happiest where he feels that he is being of service to
others. He will unselfishly give up his time for the common
good and is highly valued by his colleagues and employers.

The Pig has a good sense of humour and invariably has a smile, joke or whimsical remark at the ready. He loves to entertain and to please others, and there are many Pigs who have been attracted to careers in show business or who enjoy following the careers of famous stars and personalities.

There are, unfortunately, some who take advantage of the Pig's good nature and impose upon his generosity. The Pig has great difficulty in saying 'No' and, although he may dislike being firm, it would be in his own interests to say occasionally, 'Enough is enough.' The Pig can also be rather naïve and gullible; however, if at any stage in his life he feels that he has been badly let down, he will make sure that it will never happen again and will try to become self-reliant. There are many Pigs who have become entrepreneurs or forged a successful career on their own after some early disappointment in life. And although the Pig tends to spend his money quite freely, he is usually very astute in financial matters and there are many Pigs who have become wealthy.

Another characteristic of the Pig is his ability to recover from setbacks reasonably quickly. His faith and his strength of character keep him going. If he thinks that there is a job he can do or has something that he wants to achieve, he will pursue it with a dogged determination. He can also be stubborn and, no matter how many may plead with him, once he has made his mind up he will rarely change his views.

Although the Pig may work hard, he also knows how to enjoy himself. He is a great pleasure-seeker and will quite happily spend his hard-earned money on a lavish holiday or an expensive meal – for the Pig is a connoisseur of good food and wine – or taking part in a variety of recreational activities. He also enjoys small social gatherings and, if he is in company he likes, can very easily become the life and soul of the party. He does, however, tend to become rather withdrawn at larger functions or when among strangers.

The Pig is also a creature of comfort and his home will usually be fitted with all the latest in luxury appliances. Where possible, he will prefer to live in the country rather than the town and will opt to have a big garden, for the Pig is usually a keen and successful gardener.

The Pig is very popular with the opposite sex and will often have numerous romances before he settles down. Once settled, however, he will be loyal and protective to his partner and he will find that he is especially well suited to those born under the signs of the Goat, Rabbit, Dog and Tiger, and also to another Pig. Due to his affable and easy-going nature he can also establish a satisfactory relationship with all the remaining signs of the Chinese zodiac, with the exception of the Snake. The Snake tends to be wily, secretive and very guarded, and this can be intensely irritating to the honest and open-hearted Pig.

The female Pig will devote all her energies to the needs of her children and her partner. She will try to ensure that they want for nothing and their pleasure is very much her pleasure. Her home will either be very clean and orderly or hopelessly untidy. Strangely, there seems to be no in between with Pigs – they either love housework or detest it! The female Pig does, however, have considerable talents as an organizer and this, combined with her friendly and open manner, enables her to secure many of her objectives.

She can also be a caring and conscientious parent and has very good taste in clothes.

The Pig is usually lucky in life and will rarely want for anything. Provided he does not let others take advantage of his good nature and is not afraid of asserting himself, he will go through life making friends, helping others and winning the admiration of many.

THE FIVE DIFFERENT TYPES OF PIG

In addition to the 12 signs of the Chinese zodiac, there are five elements and these have a strengthening or moderating influence on the sign. The effects of the five elements on the Pig are described below, together with the years in which the elements were exercising their influence. Therefore all Pigs born in 1911 and 1971 are Metal Pigs, those born in 1923 and 1983 are Water Pigs, and so on.

Metal Pig: 1911, 1971

The Metal Pig is more ambitious and determined than some of the other types of Pig. He is strong, energetic and likes to be involved in a wide variety of different activities. He is very open and forthright in his views, although he can be a little too trusting at times and has a tendency to accept things at face value. He has a good sense of humour and loves to attend parties and other social gatherings. He has a warm, outgoing nature and usually has a large circle of friends.

Water Pig: 1923, 1983

The Water Pig has a heart of gold. He is generous and loyal and tries to remain on good terms with everyone. He will do his utmost to help others, but sadly there are some who will take advantage of his kind nature and he should, in his own interests, be a little more discriminating and be prepared to stand firm against anything that he does not like. Although he prefers the quieter things in life, he has a wide range of interests. He particularly enjoys outdoor pursuits and attending parties and social occasions. He is a hard and conscientious worker and invariably does well in his chosen profession. He is also gifted in the art of communication.

Wood Pig: 1935, 1995

This Pig has a friendly, persuasive manner and is easily able to gain the confidence of others. He likes to be involved in all that is going on around him and can sometimes take on more responsibility than he can properly handle. He is loyal to his family and friends and he also derives much pleasure from helping those less fortunate than himself. The Wood Pig is usually an optimist and leads a very full, enjoyable and satisfying life. He also has a good sense of humour.

Fire Pig: 1947

The Fire Pig is both energetic and adventurous and he sets about everything he does in a confident and resolute manner. He is very forthright in his views and does not mind taking risks in order to achieve his objectives. He can, however, get carried away by the excitement of the moment and ought to exercise more caution with some of the enterprises in which he gets involved. The Fire Pig is usually lucky in money matters and is well known for his generosity. He is also very caring towards the members of his family.

Earth Pig: 1959

This Pig has a kindly nature. He is sensible and realistic and will go to great lengths in order to please his employers and to secure his aims and ambitions. He is an excellent organizer and is particularly astute in business and financial matters. He has a good sense of humour and a wide circle of friends. He also likes to lead an active social life, although he does sometimes have a tendency to eat and drink more than is good for him.

PROSPECTS FOR THE PIG IN 1999

The Chinese New Year starts on 16 February 1999. Until then, the old year, the Year of the Tiger, is still making its presence felt.

The Year of the Tiger (28 January 1998 to 15 February 1999) will have been a tricky one for the Pig. His progress will not have been as easy or as straightforward as he would have liked and he could have met with setbacks in carrying out some of his plans. It will also have been quite an expensive year for him and this, together with some of the challenges he will have met, will have added to his concerns. However, there are now excellent reasons for the Pig to take heart. As the influence of the Tiger year wanes, the aspects will slowly start to swing back in his favour and in the last quarter of the year his prospects and situation will gradually improve.

To help with this, for the remainder of the Tiger year the Pig will need to watch developments around him and be prepared to adjust to new and changing situations. The one thing he should avoid is appearing too inflexible in his attitude or approach and thereby distancing himself from events or others. The next Chinese year will be much better for him and in what remains of this one the Pig must not undermine or jeopardize his future chances.

Also, while the Tiger year will have brought its difficulties, the Pig will have learnt much from the challenges he has had to meet and the experience he has gained. This will serve him well over the forthcoming year as well as give him an added incentive to improve his situation and make more of his potential. The Pig will also find it helpful to use the remaining weeks of the year to finish off any outstanding matters he might have, particularly any unanswered correspondence or any tasks he may have been putting to one side. With a concerted effort he will be pleased with just how much he is able to complete, as well as be relieved that some of these matters are now out of the way.

While the Tiger year will have been a testing time for the Pig, one area which will have brought him much happiness is his domestic and social life. This trend will continue and in the closing months of the year the Pig can look forward to some truly enjoyable times with those around him and will find himself very much involved in some events and gatherings that take place. Also, the holiday period at the end of the year will give him a good chance to relax and unwind and by January 1999 he will feel ready and more determined than ever to make the most of the year ahead. As has so been often shown, periods of success and growth follow on from more difficult and challenging times and this will now be the case for a large number of Pigs.

The Year of the Rabbit starts on 16 February and will be a highly favourable one for the Pig. After the challenges of the Tiger year, the aspects will now move firmly back in the Pig's favour and this will be a year in which he will make considerable progress as well as enjoy himself.

Almost as soon as the Rabbit year begins the Pig will sense an important change in his fortunes is taking place and will set about his activities with greater enthusiasm and resolve, determined to make up for past setbacks and realize his true potential. His energy, strong sense of purpose and faith in his abilities will all help propel him to new heights.

As regards work, those Pigs who start the Rabbit year dissatisfied with their present position should consider early on in the year just what it is they would like to do. Some might consider the time is right for a career change or for setting up their own business, while others will want to progress in their current line of work and build on their expertise. Whatever the Pig decides, he should remain alert for openings to pursue as well as see if he can create some opportunities himself. If he acts in a positive and enterprising way, his efforts will be rewarded and will bring results. As the Pig himself knows, to get what he wants does require him to seize the initiative; in this respect, however, the aspects will support him well.

Many of those Pigs seeking work will also find their persistence rewarded over the year, often in a surprising and unexpected manner. Not only should they remain active in following up any openings that they see but they should also consider different ways in which they can use their skills and experience. Some enterprising thinking could widen the range of positions available to them and make their quest easier. Some of these Pigs could also be successful in obtaining a position which is unlike anything they have done before but which has the potential of developing in a positive manner over the next few years.

Work-wise, the Rabbit year contains some pleasing and encouraging trends for the Pig and it rests with him to promote himself and pursue his goals. He has the talents, capabilities and character to achieve much and with the right attitude he can set himself on course for success not only in 1999 but in succeeding years as well. For work opportunities, the early months of the year, from mid February to mid April and then from September to the end of November could all see important developments.

As far as financial matters are concerned, the Pig's money-making abilities will be on top form this year. In addition to looking forward to an increase in income, many Pigs could receive or earn money from other sources. This could be through using a special skill the Pig has acquired, promoting an interest or furthering a business idea. The Pig has a very keen business sense and some enterprising thinking on his part could bring him financial reward. However, while a financial upturn is indicated, this should not lead the Pig into taking undue risks or becoming complacent. In 1999 he will have the chance to make money and add to his assets, but he must not push his good fortune or luck too far.

In many cases the financial improvement the Pig will enjoy will lead him to making changes in his accommodation. Some Pigs will decide that it is now the right time for them to move and while the moving process will take up much of their time, they will be pleased with their new accommodation and with the opportunities that living in a new area will bring. Other Pigs will, however, decide to spend time and money on their existing home. Redecorating, new equipment and alterations could all be on the agenda and, while again these will take some time to plan and complete, the Pig will be pleased with what he is able to accomplish. Generally, accommodation matters, while time-consuming, will go well for the Pig, with many improvements taking place.

The Pig also has a strong affinity with the outdoors and for those who enjoy gardening the year will contain many satisfying moments, with many Pigs taking pleasure in adding to or redesigning their garden.

The Pig's personal life will also be a source of considerable joy to him, with some significant events indicated.

Some Pigs could see an addition to their family, the wedding of a close relation or have some other cause for personal and family celebration. The summer, in particular, is well aspected and will bring some memorable occasions.

In addition, the Pig will be heartened by the support and encouragement he is given by those around him and at all times he should bear in mind any words of advice he receives from his loved ones. They do speak with his best interests at heart and want him to make the most of himself and his abilities. Also, if he finds himself under undue pressure over the year, particularly should household projects and chores mount up, the Pig should not hesitate to ask for assistance rather than try to do too much single-handed. At busy times he would also find it helpful to set himself certain priorities rather than spread his energies too widely.

With his friendly and outgoing nature, the Pig's social life is also important to him and throughout the Rabbit year he will be on top form. There will be meals and trips out, parties, functions and other events for the Pig to attend and enjoy and he can look forward to some splendid times in the company of his friends. For the unattached Pig, romance is splendidly aspected and many Pigs will get engaged or married over the year, such are the favourable trends. For personal matters, the months of April, May, August and September are especially well aspected.

Any Pig who may have had some recent personal sadness to bear or be looking to build up his social life should view the Rabbit year as the start of a new phase and, by going out more and getting involved group-oriented activities, will soon find himself building up some new and important friendships. By making the effort, even though in some cases this may understandably be difficult, these Pigs will be able to bring some happiness back into their life.

In most respects the Rabbit year will be a highly favourable one for the Pig. However, as with any year, problems can and do occur, and one which will concern a few Pigs will involve legal matters. If the Pig finds himself in any dispute or has a legal problem, he needs to proceed with great care and make sure he obtains proper legal advice. If not, greater difficulties could emerge. Although this warning only applies to a small number of Pigs, those it does concern should heed these words well.

One other point the Pig needs to watch is that he should be careful not to over-commit himself and take on more than he can properly handle at any one time. Sometimes he can let his enthusiasm and good nature get the better of him and to prevent pressure and possibly disappointing others, the Pig does need to be realistic in his undertakings. If he bears this in mind, however, 1999 will be a truly successful year for him. By giving of his best, going after his aims and promoting his ideas the Pig can accomplish a great deal and for most of the year luck and good fortune will accompany him.

As far as the different types of Pig are concerned, 1999 will contain many interesting developments for the *Metal Pig*. He is blessed with some fine and admirable qualities, not least that he gets on well with others and uses his strengths and capabilities to their best advantage. These two traits will serve him well over the year, allowing him to progress and make a favourable impression in almost all he does. In his work, great opportunities await. Although in recent times the Metal Pig may not have been able to accomplish all that he would like, as the Rabbit year starts he should put past disappointments and reversals behind him and set his sights firmly on the present and immediate future. If he is dissatisfied with his current position or is seeking work then he should make every effort to follow up any openings that interest him. His persistence and drive, as well as his faith in his abilities, will be well rewarded and throughout the year, with any application he makes, he should make sure that he does not undersell himself. The Metal Pig does, after all, have a considerable amount to offer. The many Metal Pigs who do gain a new position or take on different duties over the year will be given every opportunity to show their true worth and impress, so much so that further advancement could take place within a comparatively short time. Any Metal Pigs who have a business venture or idea they are keen to develop would also do well to seek appropriate advice and test the initial reaction. The Metal Pig can make a fine entrepreneur, but to succeed he does need to pay attention to the groundwork and to those all-important initial stages which can so often mean the difference between success and failure. Also, with legal matters being a potentially troublesome area, the Metal Pig does need to make sure he obtains proper guidance with regard to any business venture or commitment he enters into; similarly, with any other transaction and agreement, he does need to pay careful attention to the fine print and make sure he is aware of any obligations he is placed under. The Metal Pig will, however, see a noticeable upturn in his financial situation over the year and while he will greatly enjoy this – and the Metal Pig does have a talent for savouring the finer things in life – he needs to maintain some control over his level of expenditure. Ideally he should plan his major purchases rather than give way to too much extravagance or too many spending sprees and would also do well to make some savings. In future years he could come to be grateful for a savings scheme started now or an investment made with a view to long-term growth. The Metal Pig's domestic life will bring him much joy, with the strong possibility of an addition to his family or another good cause for a personal and family celebration. Those around him will be supportive towards his endeavours and over the year he will be considerably bolstered and inspired by their encouragement and the obvious affection they have for him. They too share his faith that he can and will do well and when they offer him advice he should listen to their words carefully. As always, the Metal Pig will take a keen interest in the activities of those around him and will find that interests and projects he can share with family members will prove especially satisfying. For the unattached Metal Pig, 1999 could prove a significant year, with romance well aspected; indeed, many Metal Pigs will decide to get engaged or married. Overall, this will be a highly favourable year for the Metal Pig and he will be able to make significant progress in his work, while his personal life will be rich, rewarding and bring him considerable pleasure.

After some of the changes, pressures and aggravations that many *Water Pigs* will have experienced of late, the Rabbit year will come as a welcome relief. The Water Pig will now be able to spend time devcloping his ideas and activities in his own way rather than be so subject to events, many of which were outside his control. This will therefore be a satisfying year for the Water Pig, but in order to benefit from the favourable aspects, he would do well to decide what he would like to undertake over the next 12 months and plan his time accordingly. If not, there is a danger that the year could pass without him having accomplished as much as he otherwise might. For those Water Pigs born in 1983, this will prove an important and valuable year. In their education they will cover much important material and by setting about their studies in an organized and disciplined manner will make excellent headway. Some of what they learn over the year will prove of much relevance later, even having a possible bearing on their chosen career. It is therefore important that the young Water Pig gives of his best and learns well. In addition to the progress he will make in his education, the Water Pig's personal life will go well and over the year he will find himself much in demand with his many friends, with parties and other social events to attend and enjoy. He will also take satisfaction in spending time on his hobbies and interests and if he has aspirations in a certain sphere, whether technical, creative or in some other area, it really would be worth him furthering and developing his talent. Again, what he learns in 1999 could be of significance later and the time and effort that he puts into his interest now will be well worth his while. For those Water Pigs born in 1923, again their personal interests will bring them much satisfaction. Creative pursuits are especially well favoured and activities such as painting, writing, music, photography or something similar could all bring the Water Pig joy and fulfilment. However, if there is one particular interest or skill he wishes to develop or if there is an ambition he has long dreamt of, he should speak to others about this and see what can be arranged. As far as his ambitions and desires are concerned, the Water Pig does need to be forthcoming rather than keep them to himself. He will take much delight in following the activities of the members of his family over the year and can look forward to several pleasing family occasions and events. Those around him will also be most supportive and if at any time he has any matters concerning him, he should not hesitate to seek their opinions and advice. He will find that others will be able to do much to put his mind at ease. One area that could prove troublesome over the year concerns important forms and paperwork and if the Water Pig has any doubts over what is being asked of him he should seek further clarification and advice. If not, there is a danger that he could find himself embroiled in some additional and burdensome correspondence which he could well do without. More positively, however, travel is well favoured and all Water Pigs will enjoy any breaks and holidays that they take over the year. In addition, visits to places of local interest, particularly if arranged on the spur of the moment and as something of a treat, could turn out to be enjoyable and memorable occasions. In most aspects this will be a pleasant and fulfilling year for the Water Pig and by setting about his activities in an organized way and pursuing his interests he will be pleased with what he is able to accomplish. On a personal level, his family and many good friends will also be a source of considerable pleasure, making the year all the more gratifying for him.

This is the type of year that the *Wood Pig* will enjoy. After the rigours and pressures of the Tiger year he will at last be able to take stock of his position and be better able to plan his activities, rather than be subject to ever-changing situations or events outside his control. The year will therefore hold considerable promise for him and will contain many pleasing and satisfying occasions. The Wood Pig's family and social life is particularly well aspected and throughout the year he will find himself much in demand with those around him. As well as taking a full and active part in family activities, he can look forward to playing a central role in some family gatherings. At least twice during the year there will be excellent cause for celebration, such as the birth of a grandchild, a wedding or the success of a dear and close relation. As always the Wood Pig will take a caring interest in the activities of family members and while he may not wish to be viewed as interfering, any assistance and advice he feels able to pass on, particularly to a younger relation, will be much appreciated. He will also take considerable satisfaction in carrying out some projects he has had in mind for his accommodation and over the year will do much that will add to the decor and comfort of his home. Another well-aspected area concerns travel and any family holidays and breaks the Wood Pig is able to take will be among the happiest he has had for a long time, especially as his travels will allow him to visit places he has often wanted to see or to meet up with friends or relations living some distance away. The Wood Pig also places much store on his social life and this will certainly not disappoint in 1999. He can look forward to many pleasurable times with his friends and any Wood Pigs who move over the year will take great delight in building up a new and active social life. With his outgoing and friendly nature the Wood Pig will be quick to impress and will soon find himself forming new and good friendships. Also, for those Wood Pigs who may have had some adversity to contend with and be feeling low, the Rabbit year is one which offers hope and an improvement. Those around them will be most supportive and they would certainly be helped by discussing their feelings with others rather than keep them to themselves. They would also do well to involve themselves in activities that would help take their mind off their concerns and a new and perhaps more challenging interest could prove useful. Positive action on their part will be repaid and the Rabbit year will be supportive of what these Wood Pigs undertake. As far as financial matters are concerned, the Wood Pig should experience few problems, although he would do well to keep watch over his level of spending. With an active domestic and social life, plus various other items that he will want to buy, his expenditure could all too easily creep up and be far greater than he originally budgeted for. The Wood Pig should also check the terms and small print of any important form or transaction he enters into, as otherwise he could find himself involved in a complex matter which could take some time to sort out. Paperwork and matters of finance do need to be treated with care over the year. The Wood Pig will, however, get much satisfaction from his own interests, particularly those that take him out of doors or allow him to put his creative talents to good use. If he has been working on a project that can be displayed or viewed by others, perhaps by entering a competition, he should do so. He could receive some positive and encouraging feedback which will spur him on to do more. In almost all respects, the Wood Pig will enjoy the Rabbit year, particularly as he will get so much pleasure and fulfilment from his family and friends and from the various activities he undertakes.

This is a year which holds considerable potential for the *Fire Pig* and is one in which he will enjoy positive developments in many areas of his life. This will be all the more welcoming after some of the changes, challenges and pressures he has recently had to cope with. Particularly well aspected is his work and his experience and years of effort will be rewarded in quite a significant manner. For those Fire Pigs who are dissatisfied or frustrated in their present role, are seeking changes or looking for work, the Rabbit year will offer considerable opportunity and these Fire Pigs should redouble their efforts to attain a new position. Their determination will be rewarded, often in a surprising and fortuitous manner, perhaps arising from an advertisement seen by chance or an overheard remark. Also, if the Fire Pig has a business idea he wishes to promote, he should seek the advice of those able to give expert guidance. He does possess fine entrepreneurial skills, but before launching any venture he does need to prepare the groundwork properly and test the viability of his venture before committing himself too heavily. In 1999 the Fire Pig can do much to improve on his present situation and by setting about his activities in a determined way he will do well. The first quarter of the year in particular will contain some significant opportunities and developments. This will also be a good year for financial matters and the Fire Pig will enjoy a considerable improvement in his situation. However, he should not let this upturn tempt him into too many spending sprees. He will find it better, and more satisfying, to plan his purchases carefully than to succumb to too much impulse buying, and with his taste for fine living, he should also keep an eye on the amount he spends socializing. This can all too easily creep up and without a certain care and restraint the Fire Pig could find he has spent far more than he intended and – apart from the memories – has little to show for his outlay. Despite the financial upturn, some control over the purse strings this year would certainly not come amiss! As far as the Fire Pig's personal life is concerned, he will be in fine form. The Fire Pig always plays a central role in family affairs and his importance – and the love and affection family members have for him – will certainly be underlined over the year. In 1999 he will take an active and caring interest in the activities of those around him and will be justifiably proud of some of their achievements. Similarly, he too will benefit from the support, advice and encouragement he receives and if at any time he is in a dilemma over any-thing or has an important decision to make, he should not hesitate to seek the views of those around him. Over the year he will be considerably heartened by the care and interest shown in what he does and will gain much from the advice and input of family members. The Fire Pig's social life will also be more active than it has been in recent years, with parties, gatherings and other events to look forward to. At many of these the Fire Pig will find himself in sparkling form and will thoroughly enjoy himself. For those Fire Pigs who are keen to build up their social life and make new friends, the opportunities will certainly be there and, with his outgoing and friendly manner, the Fire Pig will quickly impress. However, while he will be kept fully occupied over the year, it is important he does not neglect his well-being and should make sure he gets sufficient exercise as well as eat a suitable and balanced diet. The Fire Pig does like to live life to the full and to do so it is important he takes proper care of himself. In most respects, though, this will be an excellent year for the Fire Pig. He will make good headway in his work and be given the chance to draw on his experience and promote his talents and ideas. His domestic and social life, too, will bring him much happiness. The one thing that he does need to watch is his level of spending. During 1999 he needs to keep control of those purse strings and, with so many temptations about, this may sometimes prove harder than he would like!

After all that the *Earth Pig* has learnt and accomplished in recent times, he is on course to make significant gains and progress in the Rabbit year. This will be an excellent time for him and give him the opportunity to develop his ideas as well as realize some of his aims and ambitions. His work is particularly well aspected. Over the last 12 months he will have much impressed others with his diligence and tenacity and in 1999 he will find his efforts rewarded with new responsibilities and promotion. For those Earth Pigs who are keen to move to another type of position, again what they have recently accomplished will stand them in good stead. These Earth Pigs should actively follow up any openings that they see and will find a bold, enterprising approach, together with a personable manner will, over the year, prove a winning and almost irresistible combination. Many of the Earth Pigs seeking work will also find their persistence rewarded, sometimes in an unusual and unexpected manner. In addition, they could find that one position they attain will develop in a most encouraging way, providing them with an excellent chance to use their talents to their best advantage, and this will inspire and motivate them even more. Once the Earth Pig is given the opportunity, he will truly impress. With the Rabbit year favouring cultural matters, it is also a good time for the Earth Pig to consider taking up a new interest or learning another skill, perhaps one he has been considering for some time. He will find this a stimulating challenge with some long-term benefits. The Earth Pig will also fare well in financial matters over the year. Not only will he enjoy a noticeable improvement in his income but he could also receive additional sums from other sources. This could be by putting an interest or hobby to profitable use, or through a gift or the fruition of an investment. While the Earth Pig will undoubtedly be pleased with this upturn, he should aim to put some of his money towards specific purposes, such as household items, equipment, transport and holidays, rather than go through the year without any sort of planning and control. In addition, if he feels able, he would do well to make some savings over the year; in the future he could come to be grateful for money saved at this time. The Earth Pig's personal life, meanwhile, will be busy and satisfying. He will greatly enjoy family activities over the year and several notable events will take place, at some of which he will play a significant part. He will also do

YOUR CHINESE HOROSCOPE 1999

much to assist others over the year and in particular some help and advice he is able to give a more senior relation will be of considerable benefit. Indeed, the Earth Pig may not realize just how much others value his judgement and considerate ways but in 1999 the affection and esteem in which he is held will certainly become evident and be something that will considerably gladden him. However, while there will be many pleasing times in the Earth Pig's domestic life, he will also face the usual household tasks and chores. Sometimes these may well appear to mount up and, at busy and demanding times, the Earth Pig would find it helpful to set himself priorities and avoid engaging in too many activities all at the same time. He will find that one job completed and well done is infinitely better than a lot started and left undone. In addition to the satisfaction his domestic life will bring, the Earth Pig can look forward to many pleasurable occasions in the company of his friends. Many Earth Pigs will extend their circle of friends and acquaintances over the year and, for the unattached Earth Pig, romance and a new friendship could figure prominently and bring him much happiness. Generally, the Rabbit year holds considerable potential for the Earth Pig. With his talents, enthusiasm and warm personable nature he has much in his favour and the Rabbit year will give him every chance to display his true worth and to progress.

FAMOUS PIGS

Russ Abbot, Bryan Adams, Woody Allen, Julie Andrews,
Fred Astaire, Sir Richard Attenborough, Lucille Ball,
Hector Berlioz, David Blunkett, Humphrey Bogart, James
Cagney, Maria Callas, Caprice, Dr George Carey, Richard
Chamberlain, Hillary Rodham Clinton, Glenn Close, David
Coultard, Sir Noël Coward, Oliver Cromwell, Billy
Crystal, the Dalai Lama, Bobby Davro, Phil Donahue,
Richard Dreyfuss, Sheena Easton, Ben Elton, Ralph Waldo
Emerson, David Essex, Henry Ford, Emmylou Harris,
William Randolph Hearst, Ernest Hemingway, Henry VIII,
Alfred Hitchcock, King Hussein of Jordan, Sir Elton John,
Tommy Lee Jones, C. G. Jung, Boris Karloff, Stephen King,
Nastassja Kinski, Henry Kissinger, Kevin Kline, Hugh
Laurie, David Letterman, Jerry Lee Lewis, Marcel Marceau,
Johnny Mathis, Dudley Moore, Patrick Moore, Morrissey,
John Mortimer, Wolfgang Amadeus Mozart, Michael
Parkinson, Luciano Pavarotti, Prince Rainier of Monaco,
Maurice Ravel, Ronald Reagan, Ginger Rogers, Nick Ross,
Arthur Rubenstein, Salman Rushdie, Baroness Sue Ryder
of Warsaw, Pete Sampras, Arantxa Sanchez, Carlos
Santana, Arnold Schwarzenegger, Steven Spielberg, Ann
Taylor, Emma Thompson, Tracey Ullman, Jules Verne,
Jacques Villeneuve, Michael Winner, the Duchess of York.

APPENDIX

---◆◆◆---

The relationship between the 12 animal signs – both on a personal level and business level – is an important aspect of Chinese horoscopes and in this appendix the compatibility between the signs is shown in the two tables that follow. Also included are the names of the signs ruling the hours of the day and from this it is possible to find your ascendant and discover yet another aspect of your personality.

PERSONAL RELATIONSHIPS

KEY

1   Excellent. Great rapport.
2   A successful relationship. Many interests in common.
3   Mutual respect and understanding. A good relationship.
4   Fair. Needs care and some willingness to compromise in order for the relationship to work.
5   Awkward. Possible difficulties in communication with few interests in common.
6   A clash of personalities. Very difficult.

	Rat	Ox	Tiger	Rabbit	Dragon	Snake	Horse	Goat	Monkey	Rooster	Dog	Pig
Rat	1											
Ox	1	3										
Tiger	4	6	5									
Rabbit	5	2	3	2								
Dragon	1	5	4	3	2							
Snake	3	1	6	2	1	5						
Horse	6	5	1	5	3	4	2					
Goat	5	5	3	1	4	3	2	2				
Monkey	1	3	6	3	1	3	5	3	1			
Rooster	5	1	5	6	2	1	2	5	5	5		
Dog	3	4	1	2	6	3	1	5	3	5	2	
Pig	2	3	2	2	2	6	3	2	2	3	1	2

BUSINESS RELATIONSHIPS

KEY
1 Excellent. Marvellous understanding and rapport.
2 Very good. Complement each other well.
3 A good working relationship and understanding can be developed.
4 Fair, but compromise and a common objective are often needed to make this relationship work.
5 Awkward. Unlikely to work, either through lack of trust, understanding or the competitiveness of the signs.
6 Mistrust. Difficult. To be avoided.

	Rat	Ox	Tiger	Rabbit	Dragon	Snake	Horse	Goat	Monkey	Rooster	Dog	Pig
Rat	2											
Ox	1	3										
Tiger	3	6	5									
Rabbit	4	3	3	3								
Dragon	1	4	3	3	3							
Snake	3	2	6	4	1	5						
Horse	6	5	1	5	3	4	4					
Goat	5	5	3	1	4	3	3	2				
Monkey	2	3	4	5	1	5	4	4	3			
Rooster	5	1	5	5	2	1	2	5	5	6		
Dog	4	5	2	3	6	4	2	5	3	5	4	
Pig	3	3	3	2	3	5	4	2	3	4	3	1

YOUR ASCENDANT

The ascendant has a very strong influence on your personality and, together with the information already given about your sign and the effects of the element on your sign, it will help you gain even greater insight into your true personality according to Chinese horoscopes.

The hours of the day are named after the 12 animal signs and the sign governing the time you were born is your ascendant. To find your ascendant, look up the time of your birth on the table below, bearing in mind any local time differences in the place you were born.

11 p.m.	to	1 a.m.	The hours of the Rat
1 a.m.	to	3 a.m.	The hours of the Ox
3 a.m.	to	5 a.m.	The hours of the Tiger
5 a.m.	to	7 a.m.	The hours of the Rabbit
7 a.m.	to	9 a.m.	The hours of the Dragon
9 a.m.	to	11 a.m.	The hours of the Snake
11 a.m.	to	1 p.m.	The hours of the Horse
1 p.m.	to	3 p.m.	The hours of the Goat
3 p.m.	to	5 p.m.	The hours of the Monkey
5 p.m.	to	7 p.m.	The hours of the Rooster
7 p.m.	to	9 p.m.	The hours of the Dog
9 p.m.	to	11 p.m.	The hours of the Pig

RAT: The influence of the Rat as ascendant is likely to make the sign more outgoing, more sociable and also more careful with money. A particularly beneficial influence for those born under the sign of the Rabbit, Horse, Monkey and Pig.

OX: The Ox as ascendant has a restraining, cautionary and steadying influence which many signs will benefit from. This ascendant also promotes self-confidence and will-power and is an especially good ascendant for those born under the signs of the Tiger, Rabbit and Goat.

TIGER: This ascendant is a dynamic and stirring influence which makes the sign more outgoing, more action-orientated and more impulsive. A generally favourable ascendant for the Ox, Tiger, Snake and Horse.

RABBIT: The Rabbit as ascendant has a moderating influence, making the sign more reflective, serene and discreet. A particularly beneficial influence for the Rat, Dragon, Monkey and Rooster.

DRAGON: The Dragon as ascendant gives strength, determination and an added ambition to the sign. A favourable influence for those born under the signs of the Rabbit, Goat, Monkey and Dog.

SNAKE: The Snake as ascendant can make the sign more reflective, more intuitive and more self-reliant. A good influence for the Tiger, Goat and Pig.

HORSE: The influence of the Horse will make the sign more adventurous, more daring and, on some occasions, more fickle. Generally a beneficial influence for the Rabbit, Snake, Dog and Pig.

GOAT: This ascendant will make the sign more tolerant, easy-going and receptive. The Goat could also impart some creative and artistic qualities to the sign. An especially good influence for the Ox, Dragon, Snake and Rooster.

MONKEY: The Monkey as ascendant is likely to impart a delicious sense of humour and fun to the sign. He will make the sign more enterprising and outgoing – a particularly good influence for the Rat, Ox, Snake and Goat.

ROOSTER: The Rooster as ascendant helps to give the sign a lively, outgoing and very methodical manner. Its influence will increase efficiency and is good for the Ox, Tiger, Rabbit and Horse.

DOG: The Dog as ascendant makes the sign more reasonable and fair-minded as well as giving an added sense of loyalty. A very good ascendant for the Tiger, Dragon and Goat.

PIG: The influence of the Pig can make the sign more sociable, content and self-indulgent. It is also a caring influence and one which can make the sign want to help others. A good ascendant for the Dragon and Monkey.

HOW TO GET THE BEST
FROM YOUR CHINESE SIGN
AND THE YEAR

To supplement the earlier chapters on the personality and horoscope of the signs, I have included in this appendix a guide on how you can get the best out of your sign and the year.

Each of the 12 Chinese signs possesses its own unique strengths and by identifying them you can use them to your advantage. Similarly, by becoming aware of possible weaknesses you can do much to rectify them and in this respect I hope the following sections will be useful. Also included are some tips on how you can get the best from the Year of the Rabbit. The areas covered are general prospects, career prospects, finance and relations with others.

THE RAT

The Rat is blessed with many fine talents but his undoubted strength lies in his ability to get on with others. He is sociable, charming and a good judge of character. He also possesses a shrewd mind and is good at spotting opportunities.

However, to make the most of himself and his abilities, the Rat does need to impose some discipline upon himself. He should resist the temptation (sometimes very great!) of getting involved in too many activities all at the same time and decide upon his priorities and objectives. By concentrating his energies on specific matters he will fare much better as a result. Also, given his personable manner, he should seek out positions where he can use his personal relations skills to good effect. For a career, sales and marketing could prove ideal.

The Rat is also astute in dealing with finance but, while often thrifty, he can sometimes give way to moments of indulgence. Although he deserves to enjoy the money he has so carefully earned, it may sometimes be in his interests to exercise more restraint when tempted to satisfy too many extravagant whims!

The Rat's family and friends are also most important to him and while he is loyal and protective towards them, he does tend to keep his worries and concerns to himself. He would be helped if he were more willing to discuss any anxieties he has. Those around the Rat think highly of him and are prepared to do much to help him, but for them to do this he does need to be less secretive and guarded.

With his sharp mind, keen imagination and sociable manner, the Rat does, however, have much in his favour. First, though, he should decide what he wants to achieve and then concentrate upon his chosen objectives. When he has commitment, the Rat can be irrepressible and, given his considerable charm, he can often be irresistible as well! Provided he channels his energies wisely he can make much of his life.

Advice for the Rat's Year Ahead

GENERAL PROSPECTS

Although the year will call for some care, especially where relations with others and spending are concerned, the Rat can gain much from 1999. He would do well to consider his objectives and future aspirations and direct his activities and energies accordingly. Purposeful and persistent effort will lead to constructive results, often culminating in considerable success in the year 2000. The Rat should also spend time on his hobbies and interests over the year; these will be fulfilling and bring him much pleasure.

CAREER PROSPECTS

What the Rat achieves in the Rabbit year often has far-reaching consequences. In 1999 he should set about his activities in his usual thorough and diligent way, re-maining ever mindful of developments taking place and being prepared to adapt to new situations and opportunities as they occur. The Rat's resourcefulness will serve him well, letting him make progress as well as sowing the seeds for further and future success.

FINANCE

In 1999 the Rat may sometimes find it hard to resist the many temptations he sees. To prevent problems he would do well to reflect carefully before making any major purchase or indulging in too many spending sprees. This is a year to keep a tight control over the purse strings.

RELATIONS WITH OTHERS

While the Rat can look forward to many enjoyable occasions with both family and friends, he does need to pay close attention to their views. This is not a year for him to be either too obtuse or unaccommodating in his attitude – especially if he wants to maintain the good relations he so values. Particular care is needed when dealing with colleagues. Fortunately the Rat's charm and skill will do much to avert problems, but tact and consideration could well be needed over the year.

THE OX

Strong-willed, determined and resolute, the Ox certainly has a mind of his own! He is also persistent and sets about achieving his objectives with a dogged determination. In addition, he is reliable and tenacious and is often a source of inspiration to others. The Ox is a doer and an achiever and in life he often accomplishes much. However, for him to really excel, he would do well to try and correct his weaknesses.

Being so resolute and having such a strong sense of purpose, the Ox can be inflexible and narrow-minded. He can be resistant to change and prefers to set about his activities in his own way rather than be too dependent on others. He should aim to be more outgoing and adventurous in his outlook. His dislike of change can sometimes be to his detriment and if he were prepared to be more adaptable he could find his progress both easier and smoother.

The Ox would also be helped if he were to broaden his range of interests and become more relaxed in his approach. At times he can be so preoccupied with his own activities that he is not always as mindful of others as he should be and his demeanour can sometimes be studious and serious. There are times when he would benefit from a lighter touch.

However, the Ox is true to his word and loyal to his family and friends. He is admired and respected by others and his tremendous will-power usually enables him to secure much in life.

Advice for the Ox's Year Ahead

GENERAL PROSPECTS

The Ox will thrive in the more settled and conducive atmosphere of the Rabbit year. By planning his activities and using his time effectively, he can obtain satisfying results in almost all areas of his life. A year in which to progress and one to enjoy!

CAREER PROSPECTS

Many Oxen will decide the time has come to make a concerted effort to improve upon their current situation. Accordingly they will set forth upon their objectives with vigour, determination and enterprise, and will see their efforts well rewarded. A new position, increased responsibilities and promotion are certainly within reach during the year.

FINANCE

There may be an improvement in the Ox's finances, but he should guard against going through the year without any sort of financial planning. He should set aside money for specific purposes and plan major purchases. By remaining alert, some good buys are possible, especially items for his accommodation and personal interests.

RELATIONS WITH OTHERS

A personally pleasing year with some enjoyable times spent with family and friends. Mutual interests and joint activities could go especially well. Many Oxen will also enjoy an appreciable upturn in their social life and those seeking new friends or romance will find it worth making the effort to join in more with group-oriented activities. They will be repaid with much happiness and some new and important friendships.

THE TIGER

Lively, innovative and enterprising, the Tiger is one who enjoys an active lifestyle. He has a wide range of interests, an alert mind and a genuine liking of others. He likes to live life to the full. However, despite his enthusiastic and well-meaning ways, he does not always make the most of his considerable potential.

By being so versatile, the Tiger does have a tendency to jump from one activity to another or dissipate his energies by trying to do too much at any one time. To make the most of himself he should try to exercise a certain amount of self-discipline. Ideally, he should decide how best he can use his abilities, give himself some objectives and stick with these. If he can overcome his restless tendencies and persist in what he does, he will find he will accomplish much more.

Also, in spite of his sociable manner, the Tiger likes to retain a certain independence in his actions and while few begrudge him this, he would sometimes find life easier if he were more prepared to work in conjunction with others. His reliance upon his own judgement does sometimes mean that he excludes the views and advice of those around him, and this can be to his detriment. The Tiger may possess an independent spirit, but he must not let his independence go too far!

The Tiger does, however, have much in his favour. He is bold, original and quick-witted. If he can keep his restless nature in check he can enjoy considerable success. In addition, his engaging personality makes him one who is much admired and well-liked.

Advice for the Tiger's Year Ahead

GENERAL PROSPECTS

A pleasing year, particularly as the Tiger will be able to spend time developing his ideas and extending his hobbies and personal interests. He would also do well to give some thought to his future and see if he can gain experience or skills that would help lead him to what he wants. This will be a very significant year as far as future planning and development are concerned and plans made, together with current achievements, will have an important bearing in years to come. Overall, a good and constructive year.

CAREER PROSPECTS

A year of positive progress. The Tiger should build on what he has already accomplished and seek to extend his experience. He should also actively follow up the opportunities that the year will bring as well as promote his ideas. Work matters are well aspected and several times the Tiger could benefit from unexpected developments or learn of opportunities by chance. The enterprising Tiger can achieve much in 1999 as well as enhance his future prospects.

FINANCE

Although an improvement is indicated, this should not lead the Tiger into complacency or tempt him to overspend. He should plan his major purchases and set sums aside for specific purposes. Care and financial planning will certainly not come amiss over the year.

RELATIONS WITH OTHERS

A splendid year with some happy and meaningful occasions with family and friends. Those around will be supportive and give much valuable advice – and the Tiger would do well to listen rather than leave so much to his own judgement. The spring and summer will be a particularly active time socially and for those seeking new friends and romance, some good times are in store! With his winning ways and outgoing nature the Tiger will find himself much in demand, as well as do much to impress.

THE RABBIT

The Rabbit is certainly one who appreciates the finer things in life. With his good taste, companionable nature and wide range of interests, he knows how to live well – and usually does!

However, for all his finesse and style, the Rabbit does possess traits he would do well to watch. His desire for a settled lifestyle makes him err on the side of caution. He dislikes change and as a consequence can miss out on opportunities. Also, there are many Rabbits who will go to great lengths to avoid difficult and fraught situations, and again, while few may relish these, sometimes in life it is necessary to take risks or stand your ground just to get on. At times it would certainly be in the Rabbit's interests to be bolder and more assertive in going after whatever he desires.

The Rabbit also attaches great importance to his relations with others and while he has a happy knack of getting on with most, he can be sensitive to criticism. In this, difficult though it may be, he should really try to develop a thicker skin. He should recognize that criticism, as well as some of the problems that occur in life (and which he strives so much to avoid), can be constructive and provide valuable learning opportunities.

The Rabbit, though, with his agreeable manner, keen intellect and shrewd judgement, does have much in his favour and invariably makes much of his life – and usually enjoys it too!

Advice for the Rabbit's Year Ahead

GENERAL PROSPECTS

An excellent year, containing many enjoyable times and some noteworthy successes. The only danger is that the Rabbit might go through the year without any plan or objectives in mind, thereby not making the most of himself, his talents or the superb opportunities that the year will bring. This is very much a year when he should go out wholeheartedly for his aims and aspirations and he will find positive, persistent action will be well rewarded.

CAREER PROSPECTS

A highly favourable year with many chances for the Rabbit to improve his position. Throughout 1999 he should actively follow up any opportunities he sees as well as promote his ideas. Those around will look well on his undertakings and provide much useful support and encouragement. A good year too for extending skills.

FINANCE

A positive year. By keeping alert the Rabbit will be able to spot some ideal purchases for his accommodation which will do much to add to both decor and comfort. A good year too for investing for the long term.

RELATIONS WITH OTHERS

The Rabbit will be in sparkling form with many good times with family and friends. There will be several pieces of pleasing personal and family news to look forward to, with the Rabbit benefiting from the advice and assurance of others. He will find it a fine year too for making friends and extending his social life, perhaps by joining a club. For the unattached, a great year for romance, with many getting engaged or married.

THE DRAGON

Enthusiastic, enterprising and honourable, the Dragon possesses many admirable qualities and his life is often full and varied. He is always one who gives of his best and even though not all his endeavours may meet with success, he is nonetheless resilient and hardy. As a person, he is much admired and respected.

However, for all his many qualities, the Dragon can be blunt and forthright and, through sheer strength of character, sometimes domineering. It would certainly be in his interests to listen more closely to others rather than be so self-reliant. Also, his enthusiasm can sometimes get the better of him and he can be impulsive. To make the most of his abilities, he should set himself priorities and set about his activities in a disciplined and systematic way. More tact and diplomacy might not come amiss either!

However, with his lively and outgoing manner, the Dragon is popular and well-liked. With good fortune on his side (and the Dragon is often lucky), his life is almost certain to be eventful and fulfilling. He has many talents and if he uses them wisely he will enjoy much success.

Advice for the Dragon's Year Ahead

GENERAL PROSPECTS

A pleasant year, while sometimes lacking the pace and activity that the Dragon so likes. However, he will be generally content with what he achieves. This is an ideal time for the Dragon to assess his current situation and give some thought to his future activities. Plans formulated now and ideas set in motion could become highly significant.

CAREER PROSPECTS

Although the Dragon may not be able to accomplish all he would like, by giving of his best and rising to the sometimes challenging tasks he is set, he will do much to impress as well as gain some valuable experience. This will stand him in good stead for the future.

FINANCE

A promising year. With enterprising thinking the Dragon could unlock an additional source of income by drawing on his skills or interests. He would also do well to try and make some savings over the year.

RELATIONS WITH OTHERS

Both his domestic and social life will bring the Dragon considerable pleasure and he should aim to involve those around him in his plans and activities. Over the year he will gain much from the encouragement, input and advice of others. His personal interests and any travel that he undertakes will also bring him much satisfaction.

THE SNAKE

The Snake is blessed with a keen intellect. He has wide interests, an enquiring mind and good judgement. He tends to be quiet and thoughtful and plans his activities with considerable care. With his fine abilities he often does well in life, but he does possess traits which can undermine his progress.

The Snake is often guarded in his actions and sometimes loses out to those who are more action-oriented and assertive. He can also be a loner and likes to retain a certain independence in his actions, and this too can hamper his progress. It would be in his interests to be more forthcoming and involve others more readily in his plans. The Snake has many talents and possesses a warm and rich personality but there is a danger that this can remain concealed behind his often quiet and reserved manner. It really would be in his interests to aim to be more outgoing and show others his true worth.

However, the Snake is very much his own master. He invariably knows what he wants in life and is often prepared to journey long and hard to achieve his objectives. He does, though, have it in his power to make that journey easier. Lose some of that reticence, Snake, be more open, be more assertive and do not be afraid of the occasional risk!

Advice for the Snake's Year Ahead

GENERAL PROSPECTS
A positive and fulfilling year, bringing some success and worthy achievements. The Snake should take full

advantage of the opportunities that occur and make a determined effort to go after some of his long-held ambitions. Purposeful action will lead to pleasing results. However, in all matters, the Snake should act in an honourable and ethical manner. If not, problems could ensue.

CAREER PROSPECTS

A splendid year. The Snake should set about his aims and aspirations with renewed determination. For the enterprising, considerable progress can be made. The Snake should actively promote his ideas, as these will be favourably received.

FINANCE

Skilful in money matters, the Snake will make some wise purchases and investments over the year. However, he should avoid tempting his luck too far.

RELATIONS WITH OTHERS

Some happy times ahead with family and friends and the Snake will find he can get much genuine pleasure by involving others more readily in his activities and interests. Sometimes he can be a little too reserved for his own good! A favourable year for romance; personal interests too will develop well over the year.

THE HORSE

Versatile, hard-working and sociable, the Horse makes his mark wherever he goes. He has an eloquent and engaging manner and makes friends with ease. He is quick-witted, has an alert mind and is certainly not averse to taking risks or experimenting with new ideas.

The Horse possesses a strong and likeable personality but he does also have his weaknesses. With his wide interests he does not always finish everything he starts and he would do well to be more persevering. He has it within him to achieve considerable success but when he has made his plans he should stick with them. To make the most of his talents he does need to overcome his restless tendencies.

The Horse loves company and values both his family and friends. However, there will have been many a time when he has spoken in haste and regretted his words or lost his temper. Throughout his life, the Horse needs to keep his temper in check and learn to be diplomatic in tense situations. If not, he could risk jeopardizing the respect and good relations he so much values by a thought-less remark or action.

The Horse, though, has a multitude of talents and a lively and outgoing personality. If he can overcome his restless and volatile nature, he can lead a rich and highly fulfilling life.

Advice for the Horse's Year Ahead

GENERAL PROSPECTS

A pleasant year in store but to profit from the favourable aspects the Horse needs to put his time and energy to efficient use. To dabble in a wide variety of activities or start projects only later to abandon them will lead to unsatisfactory results and missed opportunities. To benefit from the supportive trends that prevail the Horse should plan his activities and make the most of his ideas and considerable talents.

CAREER PROSPECTS

With his determined and enterprising approach the Horse will greatly impress over the year and many Horses will find their efforts rewarded with new responsibilities and promotion. The best results will come from the Horse concentrating on areas in which he has most expertise. He should also promote his ideas, as these will be well received, with some developing in an encouraging manner.

FINANCE

A good year, although the Horse should give careful thought to his purchases rather than succumb to too much impulse buying. He would also do well to set some money aside for travel and his longer term future.

RELATIONS WITH OTHERS

The Horse can look forward to some pleasant times with both family and friends and, by involving them in his activities, he will gain much from their input as well as be heartened by the interest shown in what he does. For the young and unattached Horse, romance and new friendships require care if they are to endure. Better to get to know each other well than rush into a hasty commitment.

THE GOAT

The Goat has a warm, friendly and understanding manner and gets on well with most. He is generally easy-going, has a fond appreciation of the finer things in life and possesses a rich imagination. He is often artistic and enjoys the creative arts and outdoor activities.

However, despite his engaging manner, there lurks beneath his skin a sometimes tense and pessimistic nature. The Goat can be a worrier and without the support and encouragement of others can feel insecure and be hesitant in his actions.

To make the most of himself and his abilities the Goat should aim to become more assertive and decisive as well as more at ease with himself. He has much in his favour, but he really does need to promote himself more and aim to be bolder in his actions. He would also be helped if he were to sort out his priorities and set about his activities in an organized and disciplined manner. There are some Goats who tend to be haphazard in the way they go about things and this can hamper their progress.

Although the Goat will always value the support and backing of others, it would also be in his interests to become more independent in his actions and not be so reticent about striking out on his own. He does, after all, possess many talents, as well as a sincere and likeable personality, and by always giving of his best, he can make his life rich, rewarding and enjoyable.

Advice for the Goat's Year Ahead

GENERAL PROSPECTS

A favourable year, but to benefit, the Goat should set about his activities with renewed resolve, determined to put past setbacks behind him, and go wholeheartedly after his aims and aspirations. Positive and determined action will lead to great results. For the Goat, the Rabbit year is one of the best!

CAREER PROSPECTS

Considerable progress is possible, but the Goat should not be reticent about promoting his skills or ideas or going after any openings that he sees. Much is possible and much can be attained, but the Goat must be the driving force behind the progress he makes. This is a year for positive action and, for the bold and enterprising, great results can be achieved.

FINANCE

A positive year, although the Goat would sometimes do better to wait and reflect on major purchases than act too hastily.

RELATIONS WITH OTHERS

A happy year with many meaningful times with those around him. Mutual interests and projects will bring much satisfaction. For the unattached, romance is splendidly aspected.

THE MONKEY

Lively, enterprising and innovative, the Monkey certainly knows how to impress. He has wide interests, a good sense of fun and relates well to others. He also possesses a shrewd mind and often has a happy knack of turning events and situations to his advantage.

However, despite his versatility and considerable gifts, the Monkey does have his weaknesses. He often lacks persistence, can get distracted easily and also places tremendous reliance upon his own judgement. While his belief in himself is a commendable asset, it would certainly be in his interests to be more mindful of the advice and views of others. Also, while he likes to keep tabs on all that is going on around him, he can be evasive and secretive with regard to his own feelings and activities, and again a more forthcoming attitude would be to his advantage.

The Monkey also possesses a most enterprising nature, although in his desire to succeed he can sometimes be tempted to cut corners or be crafty. He should recognize that such actions can rebound on him!

However, the Monkey is resourceful and his sheer strength of character will lead him to an interesting and varied life. If he can channel his considerable energies wisely and overcome his sometimes restless tendencies, his life can be crowned with success and achievement. Added to which, with his amiable personality, he will enjoy the friendship of many.

Advice for the Monkey's Year Ahead

GENERAL PROSPECTS

An active and progressive year, but to get most benefit from the prevailing aspects the Monkey should set about his activities in a disciplined, organized and purposeful manner. If not, chances could be missed and time wasted that could be put to better and more effective use.

CAREER PROSPECTS

Considerable advances are possible and, with his resourceful nature and wide-ranging skills, the Monkey is well placed to benefit from any opportunities. He should also actively promote his skills and ideas.

FINANCE

A good year, although the Monkey should avoid being in too great a hurry to spend his money. When making sizeable purchases he should take his time to consider the ranges on offer and how they best meet his requirements. He would also do well to keep proper financial records, as these could be needed later.

RELATIONS WITH OTHERS

The Monkey will be much in demand with family and friends, with his domestic and social life being active and bringing considerable pleasure. New friendships and romance too are well aspected. However, if he moves in 1999, or decides to carry out major practical projects, it is important the Monkey enlists the assistance and support of others rather than taking on too much himself.

APPENDIX
THE ROOSTER

With his considerable bearing and incisive and resolute manner, the Rooster makes an impressive figure. He has a sharp mind, keeps well-informed on many matters and expresses himself clearly and convincingly. He is meticulous and efficient in his undertakings and commands much respect. He also has a genuine and caring interest in others.

The Rooster has much in his favour but there are some aspects of his character that can tell against him. He can be candid in his views and sometimes over-zealous in his actions, and without forethought he can say or do things he later regrets. His high standards also make him fussy – even pedantic – and he can get diverted onto relatively minor matters when, in truth, he could be occupying his time more profitably. This is something all Roosters would do well to watch. Also, while the Rooster is a great planner, he can sometimes be unrealistic in his expectations. In making plans – indeed, with most of his activities – the Rooster would do well to consult with others rather than keep his thoughts to himself. By doing so, he will greatly benefit from their input.

The Rooster has considerable talents as well as a commendable drive and commitment, but to make the most of himself he does need to channel his energies wisely and watch his candid and sometimes volatile nature. With care, he can make a success of his life, and with his wide interests and outgoing personality will enjoy the friendship and respect of many.

Advice for the Rooster's Year Ahead

GENERAL PROSPECTS

A pleasant and satisfying year. The Rooster should, however, keep expectations within reach and avoid launching ambitious new ventures, particularly in areas where he has limited experience. Time spent with family and friends and in developing interests will lead to some rewarding occasions.

CAREER PROSPECTS

Although work matters may not always go as smoothly as the Rooster would like, they will present him with some interesting challenges which will usefully add to his skills and experience. His accomplishments will serve him well for the future and prepare him for the considerable success and progress that await in 2000.

FINANCE

Avoid risks and take great care when dealing with financial matters. Unless watched, money could all too easily be spent or lost.

RELATIONS WITH OTHERS

Some meaningful times with family and friends. Over the year the Rooster will find himself much in demand with many seeking his views and advice. He will also be heartened by the encouragement he receives for his own activities. New friends made over the year could become important and long lasting.

THE DOG

Loyal, dependable and with a good understanding of human nature, the Dog is well placed to win the respect and admiration of many. He is a no nonsense sort of person and hates any sort of hypocrisy and falsehood. With the Dog you know where you stand and, given his direct manner, where he stands on any issue. He also has a strong humanitarian nature and often champions good and just causes.

The Dog has many fine attributes, although there are certain traits that can prevent him from either enjoying or making the most of his life. He is a great worrier and can get anxious over all manner of things. Although it may not always be easy, the Dog should try to rid himself of the 'worry habit'. When tense or concerned, he should be more prepared to speak to others rather than shoulder his worries all by himself. In some cases, they could even be of his own making! Also, the Dog has a tendency to look on the pessimistic side of things and he would certainly be helped if he were to look more optimistically on his undertakings. He does, after all, possess many skills and should justifiably have faith in his abilities. Another weakness is his tendency to be stubborn over certain issues. If he is not careful, this stubbornness could at times undermine his position.

If the Dog can reduce the worrying and pessimistic side of his nature, then he will not only enjoy life more but also find he is achieving more as a result. He possesses a truly admirable character and his loyalty, reliability and sincerity are appreciated by all he meets. In his life he will do much good and befriend many – and he owes it to himself to enjoy life too. Sometimes it might help him to recall the words of another Dog, Winston Churchill: 'When I look back on all these worries I remember the story of the old man who said on his deathbed that he had had a lot of trouble in his life, most of which never happened.'

Advice for the Dog's Year Ahead

GENERAL PROSPECTS

Once the Dog has set his mind on something he will rarely let anything get in his way until he has reached his goal. The main thing is for him to decide what he wants to achieve in 1999 and then work purposefully towards this. The Rabbit year holds much promise for the Dog and by using his time and skills well he can accomplish much.

CAREER PROSPECTS

The year will give the Dog the opportunity to build on his skills and experience and make considerable headway. He should follow up any openings that become available as well as make the most of his ideas and the new situations that arise. With a determined and enterprising spirit the Dog can do much to improve on his present situation. Not only will he make gains in 1999 but his accomplishments could also have significant implications for the future.

FINANCE

A good year for financial matters, although the Dog should give careful thought to what he does with his money rather than succumb to too many spending sprees. Some carefully selected acquisitions for his home or projects undertaken could, though, bring much satisfaction. He should also try to ensure that he takes a proper holiday or break over the year as this will not only bring him much pleasure but prove most beneficial for him.

RELATIONS WITH OTHERS
The Dog can look forward to some agreeable and meaningful times with both his family and friends. As ever, he will play an important part in family activities, assisting and advising those around, and can look forward to several pleasing and noteworthy family events. A good year too for social matters, with new friends and romance well aspected.

THE PIG

Genial, sincere and trusting, the Pig gets on well with most. He has a kind and caring nature, a dislike of discord and often possesses a good sense of humour. In addition, he has a fondness for socializing and enjoying the good life!

The Pig also possesses a shrewd mind, is particularly adept in dealing with business and financial matters, and has a robust and resilient nature. Although not all his plans in life may work out as he would like, he is tenacious and will often rise up and succeed after experiencing setbacks and difficulties. In his often active and varied life he can accomplish much, although there are certain aspects of his character that can tell against him. If he can modify or keep these areas in check then his life will certainly be easier and possibly even more successful.

In his activities the Pig can sometimes overcommit himself and while he does not want to disappoint, he would certainly be helped if he were to set about his activities in an organized and systematic manner and give himself priorities at busy times. He should also not allow others to take advantage of his good nature and it would be in his interests if he were sometimes more discerning. There will have been times when he has been gullible and naïve; fortunately, though, the Pig quickly learns from his mistakes. He also possesses a stubborn streak and if new situations do not fit in with his line of thinking, he can be inflexible. Such an attitude may not always be to his advantage.

The Pig is a great pleasure-seeker and while he should deservedly enjoy the fruits of his labours, he can sometimes be indulgent and extravagant. This is again something he would do well to watch.

However, though the Pig may possess some faults, those who come into contact with him are invariably impressed by his integrity, amiable manner and intelligence. If he uses his talents wisely, his life can be crowned with considerable achievement and the good-hearted Pig will also be loved and respected by many.

Advice for the Pig's Year Ahead

GENERAL PROSPECTS

A favourable year and the Pig should set about his activities with renewed purpose, determined to make the most of himself and his abilities. When the Pig sets himself on a task, he will let little stand in his way and, by deciding upon and going after his objectives, he will obtain some good results. A year when tenacity and enterprise will be well rewarded.

CAREER PROSPECTS

A year of considerable progress. All Pigs should take advantage of the positive and progressive aspects that prevail and aim to improve on their present position. If the Pig is seeking work, wanting to change his present duties or would like promotion, he should follow up the opportunities that become available, or see if he can create some himself. For those keen to develop business ideas, this would be a good year in which to take their idea further, seeking appropriate advice and assessing initial reaction.

FINANCE

The Pig will enjoy an upturn in his financial position over the year and many will decide to take advantage of this by moving or carrying out alterations on their accommodation. However, despite this upturn, the Pig should not be tempted to take undue risks with his money or embark on too much impulse buying.

RELATIONS WITH OTHERS

The Pig can look forward to some happy and meaningful times with his family and friends and will be heartened by the support he is given and affection shown. With his love of life and amiable nature he will find himself much in demand. There will also be opportunities to make some new friends and for many Pigs there will be good cause for some personal celebration. This is a year the Pig will greatly enjoy.